Christmas 2015

The Architecture of Historic Rockbridge

The Architecture of
Historic Rockbridge

J. DANIEL PEZZONI

Published by Historic Lexington Foundation

Distributed by the University of Virginia Press

Daniel Pezzoni

© 2015 Historic Lexington Foundation

P.O. Box 901

Lexington, Virginia 24450-0901

www.historiclexington.org

Photo captions credit key

> Rockbridge Historical Society — credited RHS.

> Special Collections and Archives, James G. Leyburn Library, Washington and Lee University — credited SC, WLU.

> Virginia Department of Historic Resources — credited DHR.

Design and production by Robert S. Keefe

Printed in Hong Kong

ISBN 978-0-9777220-4-4

First edition, first printing

Front endsheet: Fairfield. Photo (ca. 1900) courtesy RHS/SC, WLU

Back endsheet: A Lexington garden photographed in 1883. The Washington and Lee Colonnade extends along the ridge, in front of it Lee Chapel and below and slightly to the right of the chapel the Blue Hotel. Courtesy of H. E. Ravenhorst

Frontispiece: Dog's-head stair railing at Stono. Photo by Sally Mann

Title-page spread: The James River and Kanawha Canal near the mouth of the Maury River as portrayed by Edward Beyer in his *Album of Virginia* (1858). The residence shown in the far distance may represent the Salling House in Glasgow. Courtesy of the Library of Virginia

Tribute

THE ARCHITECTURE OF HISTORIC ROCKBRIDGE, which is a companion to *The Architecture of Historic Lexington* by Royster Lyle and Pamela Simpson, is offered as a tribute to those two pioneering authors and preservationists.

Lyle and Simpson, who are memorialized by monuments on either side of Lexington's Hopkins Green, led the way in a wide variety of civic and preservation endeavors in Lexington and Rockbridge County. With great imagination and energy, they worked together on many activities that have added to the attractiveness and livability of this area. And their disciples have continued to carry forward their work.

Many of their community efforts were channeled through Historic Lexington Foundation (HLF). Lyle was not only a founder but also a leading planner for HLF at a crucial period in Lexington's history. Simpson served as HLF's energetic president for several terms. Under her leadership the Roberson-Phalen House, one of Lexington's oldest residences, was literally lifted out of the mud and revitalized.

With an alert grasp of the national preservation movement, Lyle, as a member of Lexington's Planning Commission, spearheaded the creation in 1971 of the city's downtown historic district which has

Royster Lyle (right) and Pam Simpson (center) sign copies of *The Architecture of Historic Lexington* along with Sally Mann (left) in a 1999 event at the Campbell House headquarters of the Rockbridge Historical Society in Lexington. Joining them (behind) are former HLF director Cynthia Coleman and former HLF president Chuck Phillips. Courtesy RHS/SC, WLU

profoundly influenced the appearance of the city. He prepared a plan which organized HLF's initial preservation work in the North Main Street area. He was in the thick of HLF's effort to save both the Alexander-Withrow House and the McCampbell Inn, which have become adornments to the city and are now, while retaining their earlier names, operated as inns under the name "The Georges."

Simpson, in her architecture history classes at Washington and Lee, assigned her students to do research papers on many of the city's older buildings, thus developing an archive that has been very helpful to researchers and to owners applying for rehabilitation tax credits.

Many significant individual buildings stand as monuments to the preservation skills of Lyle and Simpson. In the early days of HLF, Lyle was in the forefront of its successful push to save the Barclay House (later known as Beaumont) and thus preserve the integrity of a block on Lee Avenue that is one of the city's most beautiful residential groupings. Simpson's persuasion was a key factor in saving the Lyric Building. This not only maintained the integrity of Lexington's cityscape, but also helped launch Lexington's downtown residential revival. Her efforts were critical in saving the Haden and Rebecca Holmes House, one of the oldest in Lexington built by African Americans. Indeed, this was one of her last major preservation projects.

It was not a difficult transition for her to go from leading HLF to being the effective president of the venerable Rockbridge Historical Society.

But Lyle and Simpson's interests were far broader than preservation and involved major civic commitments. Lyle brought the Rockbridge area its first walking trails. He initiated a study that resulted in Lexington's popular Woods Creek Park trail. When the flood of 1969 washed out the rail line to Lexington, he was largely responsible for bringing in the Nature Conservancy to convert the railroad right-of-way between Lexington and Buena Vista into the Chessie Nature Trail.

Another popular Lexington civic asset, Hopkins Green, was made possible by Lyle's creative thinking. The most visible of his accomplishments was his leadership in bringing the beloved landmark House Mountain into the public domain. For his conservation efforts the Rockbridge Area Conservation Council named a new public shelter in Goshen Pass the Royster Lyle Jr. Shelter.

Lyle and Simpson's book on Lexington's architecture was widely praised. The work is richly illustrated by handsome photographs, which were primarily the work of nationally noted photographer Sally Mann. Both Simpson and Lyle had their names on additional books and articles resulting from extensive research. Simpson was author of *Cheap, Quick & Easy: Imitative Architectural Materials, 1870–1930* (1999), and also, in a light-hearted vein, *Corn Palaces and Butter Queens: The History of Crop Art and Dairy Sculpture* (2012), and Lyle was co-author with Barbara Crawford of the ground-breaking study *Rockbridge County Artists and Artisans* (1995). Lyle also explored the history and architecture of the Hotel Buena Vista, home of Southern Virginia University, and the now-vanished hotels in Glasgow and Goshen in his *Virginia Cavalcade* article, "Rockbridge County's Boom Hotels" (1971).

Lyle took pride in the fact that he was editor of Volume VI of the *Proceedings of the Rockbridge Historical Society*, the first volume to be indexed. The index included all the articles in the first six volumes of the *Proceedings*. Simpson was a leading force in regional and national organizations such as the Vernacular Architecture Forum and the Southeast Chapter of the Society of Architectural Historians.

As is not unusual with such energetic persons, both Simpson and Lyle were pursuing significant careers while engaged in these public contributions. Simpson, professor of art history at W&L, was the first female tenure track professor at the university, the first female assistant dean of the college of arts and sciences, the first female professor to receive an endowed chair and the first female professor to be honored with an endowed professorship in her name, the Pamela H. Simpson Professorship.

In the mid-1980s she was chairwoman of W&L's co-education steering committee, helping the college to create a smooth transition to co-education. In the wider community she was president of Project Horizon, which provides help to battered women and their families, and also headed the local branch of the National Organization for Women (NOW).

Lyle was affiliated with the George C. Marshall Research Foundation for 31 years, holding various leadership posts including museum curator and associate director.

In addition to their keen minds and boundless energy, both Simpson and Lyle had superb skills at inspiring and involving people. How fortunate this locality was to have had them in its midst.

MATTHEW W. PAXTON JR.

Contributors

Historic Lexington Foundation gratefully recognizes those whose gifts have helped make the publication of *The Architecture of Historic Rockbridge* a reality.

UNDERWRITER

The Estate of James A. Hight Jr.

BENEFACTORS

Mr. and Mrs. H. E. Ravenhorst

*In Memory of Henry L. Ravenhorst, architect
and John W. Ravenhorst, archaeologist*

Washington and Lee University

FRIENDS

Arthur and Margoth Bartenstein

Ugo Benincasa

Stephanie Bond

Allan and Marian Carlsson

Philip and Ava Clayton

Ben and Elizabeth Cline

Mr. and Mrs. H. E. Derrick Jr.

Nancy Epley
In Honor of Maury Hanson

Mary Stuart Gilliam

Mr. and Mrs. Thomas L. Goad
In Memory of Pamela Simpson

Josephine and Grant Griswold

David Grizzle

Will and Janie Harris
In Memory of Bill and Louise Harris

Donald Hasfurther
In Honor of Edlow Morrison

Gary Hayes and Dee Joyce-Hayes

Charles and Constance Horner

Mr. and Mrs. Farris Pierson Hotchkiss
In Honor of Beverly Tucker

Mr. and Mrs. William Loughridge

Bruce and Sunny Macdonald

G. Otis Mead III
In Memory of Royster Lyle Jr. and Pam Simpson
In Honor of Sally Mann

Mr. and Mrs. Matthew W. Paxton Jr.

George and Pree Ray

Suzanne Read

Suzanne Barksdale Rice
In Memory of Mary Marshall Dupuy Taylor
and Jean and Flournoy H. Barksdale

Merrily E. Taylor
In Memory of Barbara J. Brown

The Rev. George J. Tompkins

Dan and Kathleen Vance

Mr. and Mrs. Charles Watson

Lyn and Carol Wheeler
In Memory of Winifred and Fred Hadsel

Alec and Linda Wilder

Mr. and Mrs. David W. Zwart

Contents

Above: The kitchen at Buffalo Forge. Photo by H. E. Ravenhorst

Preface

ROCKBRIDGE COUNTY is defined by mountains. When the Virginia legislature created Rockbridge out of Augusta and Botetourt counties in 1778, it chose the Blue Ridge as the new county's eastern border. A later adjustment established the western border as the parallel ridges of North Mountain and Mill Mountain. Rockbridge County's human history, beginning with the first Native Americans ten or more millennia ago and followed by settlers of European and African descent within the past three hundred years, has unfolded against this mountain backdrop.[1]

Between the county's mountain walls lies a fertile limestone valley, a section of the celebrated Valley of Virginia, watered by the James River and a main tributary, the Maury River, formerly known as the North River, as well as numerous creeks and runs. Near the center of the county's 607-square-mile land area rise the twin peaks of Big House Mountain and Little House Mountain, flat-topped landforms that reminded early settlers of houses in profile. Even more distinctive in appearance is the geological curiosity that gave Rockbridge its name, the Natural Bridge of Virginia.

Landscape shaped the county's history and architecture. The Blue Ridge separated the county from Piedmont and Tidewater Virginia, and though the mountain range was a permeable barrier, it channeled most settlement from the north, from the demographic "hearth" of southeast Pennsylvania, rather than from the east. The first European Americans to arrive in appreciable numbers were Scots-Irish

Above: Little House Mountain with Tuckaway (Willson House) in the near distance. The south end of Big House Mountain is visible beyond. Collectively the two mountains are known as House Mountain.
Photo by Don Hasfurther

xiii

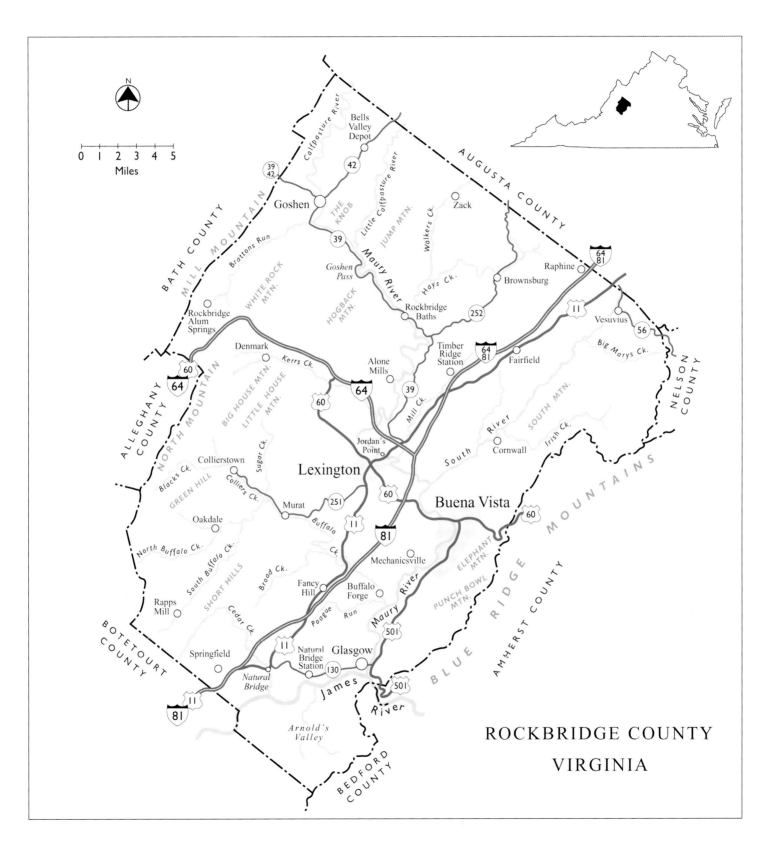

ROCKBRIDGE COUNTY
VIRGINIA

Presbyterians during the middle decades of the eighteenth century, joined by others of English- and German-speaking stock. (The Scots-Irish are known by other names including Scotch-Irish and Ulster Scots.) African Americans were present from the first decades of settlement, though a general dearth of archival evidence makes it difficult to trace their early history. A notable exception is Edward Tarr, a free black blacksmith who in the 1750s owned land in the Timber Ridge area of the settlement known as Borden's Grant. Tarr's remarkable story is told by historian Turk McCleskey in *The Road to Black Ned's Forge* (2014).[2]

Rockbridge County's early settlers erected buildings that resembled in many ways those built farther north in the Valley of Virginia, marked by a greater reliance on log and stone construction than prevailed in Tidewater Virginia. Frame construction may also have been common, as suggested by the 1778 specifications for the county's first courthouse, which was to be "well-framed, and weatherboarded with feather-edged plank." The more affluent settlers eventually replaced their first-generation buildings with the large brick houses that are today a familiar sight in the county landscape. Towns formed, beginning with the county seat of Lexington in 1778, followed by Brownsburg and

Facing page: Map by
Michael Southern

Right: The Buffalo Creek-area
William Davidson House
is built into a bank so that its
first and second stories are
accessible from ground level.
Photo by Arthur Bartenstein

Georgian paneling in Marlbrook.
Photo by Leslie Giles, courtesy DHR

Fairfield and a host of smaller communities centered on mills and crossroads. Railroads prompted a wave of urbanization around 1890, giving rise to the communities of Buena Vista, Glasgow, and Goshen in the local version of the Southern-wide economic miracle known as the Boom. Urbanization introduced a host of new and specialized building types, a trend that intensified in the twentieth century. Through it all, building technology and style underwent a constant evolution.[3]

The county's architectural development from the eighteenth century on is the story told by *The Architecture of Historic Rockbridge*, a book that has been nearly forty years in the making. The book's sponsor, Historic Lexington Foundation (HLF), intended to publish an account of the county's historic architecture soon after the publication of *The Architecture of Historic Lexington* (1977) by Royster Lyle Jr. and Pamela Hemenway Simpson with photographs by Sally Mann. The "Lexington book" proved to be a landmark in Virginia architectural studies and an indispensable resource for understanding and preserving the architectural legacy of Lexington and its two institutions of higher learning, Virginia Military Institute and Washington and Lee University. No sooner had the ink dried on the pages when Royster and Pam began to gather and analyze information on the buildings of the rural areas that surround Lexington, but HLF's other preservation initiatives intervened and the county book project was placed on hold.

The situation changed in the fall of 2012 through the initiative of Professor Delos Hughes. He served on the Washington and Lee University faculty when Pam Simpson joined the university in the 1970s and after her death in 2011 thought that a county architectural history should be undertaken, in part, as a tribute to her. HLF, an organization with which Simpson had a long association, decided to explore the idea, and in the fall of 2013 a committee consisting of HLF Executive Director Donald Hasfurther, HLF board member Maury Hanson, architectural historian J. Daniel Pezzoni, and Pam Simpson's son, restoration carpenter Peter Simpson, met to formulate an approach which was submitted to the HLF board and approved. The effort was assisted during the period by preservationists Eric Wilson and Kurt Russ.

In 2014 HLF contracted with Pezzoni to research and write the manuscript. Pezzoni was assisted by a book committee composed of Hasfurther, HLF President H. E. "Skip" Ravenhorst, and HLF board members Alison Bell and Suzanne Barksdale Rice. The book was seen to completion during Beverly Tucker's term as HLF president beginning in 2015. The design and other aspects of book production were provided by Robert S. Keefe who brought his considerable professional expertise in bookmaking to bear. Matthew W. Paxton Jr., HLF President during the formative period of *The Architecture of Historic Lexington*, drew upon his many years of friendship with Royster and Pam to write the tribute that begins the book. The manuscript was edited for content by architectural historian Michael Pulice and copyedited by Clara Belle Weatherman. The dust jacket was designed by Anne Drake McClung and Arthur M. Lipscomb.

Halfway House with its Georgian dentil cornice.
Photo by Arthur Bartenstein

Early on, the book committee made decisions that would shape the content and character of the book. The committee adopted a mission statement with five main objectives. First, the book would further HLF's mission to "interpret and present the historical heritage and fabric of Rockbridge County." Second, the book would be both scholarly and engaging, presenting architectural analysis in a manner accessible to a general readership. Third, the book would be of quality design and production. Fourth, as befits the visual nature of the subject matter, the book would be richly illustrated. And lastly, extensive duplication with *The Architecture of Historic Lexington* would be avoided, though aspects of Lexington's architectural development that were not addressed in the earlier book would receive coverage. The subject of the book was another consideration. The City of Lexington is separate from the county in a jurisdictional sense, as is the other city within the county's boundaries, Buena Vista, but the two cities and the county's smaller communities and rural areas form a single community, the *Rockbridge* of the book's title, and the book committee decided that all jurisdictions and areas within the county's boundaries should be included.

The Architecture of Historic Rockbridge shares many similarities with *The Architecture of Historic Lexington*, though it also differs in important

The Federal style house known as Tuckaway or the Willson House.
Photo by Dan Pezzoni

Spring Meadow Farm with its belvedere and Greek Revival portico.
Photo by Michael Pulice, courtesy DHR

respects. The Lexington book was part overview, part inventory of individual buildings, and part photo essay. The Rockbridge book is more purely an overview, an extended essay rather than an inventory, amply illustrated with photos and other images. Individual buildings, both standing and no longer extant, appear inasmuch as they relate to the architectural and historical themes that constitute the book's chapters. The book does not attempt to include every significant building in the county but is a sampling. Chapters may be thematically specific (churches, schools, resorts) or broad (building practices, styles), and some are synthetic in character, for example the chapter entitled "Cities" which discusses the interplay of urbanization, industrialization, and architecture at the end of the nineteenth century.

The chapter sequence is generally chronological. Evidence for early building practices is treated mostly in the first chapter, entitled "Approaching Buildings," whereas architectural developments from the era of urbanization to the present are covered in the final chapters. So too the organization within chapters is generally, though not rigidly, chronological. The chapter on churches, for example, follows the story of the county's religious buildings from their earliest occurrence in the mid-eighteenth century to the advent of architectural modernism in the mid-twentieth century, but begins by highlighting an 1870s church which is representative of earlier church building forms. Certain themes, such as decorative interior painting, span chronological periods or building types and are discussed where deemed appropriate. Some themes are split chronologically between chapters. The industries chapter, for example, ends the discussion for most industrial building types in the 1880s but leads into the next chapter, "Cities," which discusses later industrial buildings.

The Architecture of Historic Rockbridge reflects a development in architectural scholarship that was in its infancy when the Lexington book was written, which is the recognition of "vernacular" architecture. Pam Simpson was a leader in the field of vernacular architecture studies. In her book *Cheap, Quick, & Easy: Imitative Architectural Materials, 1870–1930* (1999) she noted that the traditional art historical approach to the study of architecture, which treated buildings as art objects on pedestals, was inadequate to explain the majority of the buildings in a given area. Instead, a scholar should seek to relate buildings to their social, cultural, economic, and technological contexts. In this way all buildings have potential to provide insights on the historical conditions that led to their construction. The vernacular approach can also lead to a fuller understanding of "high-style" buildings. "Whereas traditional architectural histories had relied on biography, description, formal analysis, and style as the primary factors for study" of high-style buildings, Simpson wrote, "the vernacular approach probed deeper." Vernacular has other meanings with connotations of folk, ordinary, or everyday: common buildings.[4]

The vernacular approach broadens our understanding of and appreciation for historic buildings, but the traditional stylistic approach remains an important tool and is used throughout the book. The author and book committee are aware that stylistic and architectural terminology can perplex non-specialists; therefore terms are typically defined in context or in the glossary. To help readers further, the following quick primer summarizes the major themes.

Rockbridge County's early non-native settlement occurred in the 1700s during a long stylistic period known as Georgian, so named after the British monarchs George I, II, and III whose reigns covered

A Greek Revival mantel in the Margaret E. Poague House *(right)* and marbling and graining in the house *(above)*.
Photos by Dan Pezzoni

most of the century and, like the style itself, overlapped into the 1800s. The Georgian style belonged to the classical architectural tradition rooted in ancient Greece and Rome, revived during the Renaissance, and firmly established in Restoration Britain from which it was transmitted to the American colonies. The classical tradition was characterized by symmetry in the composition of building facades and floor plans; use of the Greek orders, the systems of form and ornament known as the Doric, Ionic, and Corinthian orders; and use of specific structural and decorative elements and treatments like columns, pediments (triangular roof ends), dentil moldings (tooth-like ornament), and fluting (concave gouges on column surfaces). The county's oldest documented houses typically show the influence of the Georgian style. The oldest building to survive in the county has been a matter of discussion over the years, although current scholarship points to Timber Ridge Presbyterian Church, built 1755–56. Though other buildings of this vintage seem unlikely, it is not inconceivable that future research may turn up surprises.

The Federal style followed the Georgian style in the early 1800s and was in turn superseded in the 1830s and 1840s by the Greek Revival style, which remained popular in Rockbridge County until the Civil War. These are approximate timeframes; the influence of all three styles lingered after their peak popularity. Like the Georgian style, the Federal and Greek Revival styles were inspired by classical architecture, especially the Greek Revival style which emulated, often very closely, ancient Greek architecture. The interest in architectural classicism reflects in part the broader influence of classical culture and politics in the young American republic. Among the county's classically inspired houses are the locally famous Seven Hills of Rockbridge, a group of finely detailed brick houses which have (or formerly had) the word "hill" in their name (though not all early houses with hill names are considered a part of the group). These houses are discussed throughout the text.

Readers will note a particular emphasis on fireplace mantel form and detail in the discussion of the Georgian, Federal, and Greek Revival styles. This is because the style of a given house was usually most evident, even epitomized, by its mantels, the visual focal points of the interior. A mantel is a sort of litmus test for the period of construction of a house and can point to affinities with other houses and, occasionally, the identity of builders and finish carpenters. Georgian mantels

Gothic Revival miniatures: the barroom and post office/store at Rockbridge Alum Springs.
Courtesy DHR

are characterized by robust moldings, frame motifs, and paneling. Federal mantels are lighter in character, with delicate ornamentation like reeding and repetitive gouged and applied detail, and are often marked by tripartite (three-part) symmetry. Greek Revival mantels typically feature a frieze (a horizontal element spanning the fireplace opening) which is visually supported by pilasters in tribute to the post-and-lintel or column-and-entablature architecture of a Greek temple.

The late antebellum period saw the first local challenge to classicism, illustrated by the Lexington Presbyterian Manse (1848) and other buildings which referenced the non-classical Gothic architecture of the Middle Ages. Gothic Revival architecture abandoned the Greek orders in favor of visual motifs like the pointed lancet arch, and architects working in the style were more inclined toward asymmetrical compositions; for example, Lexington's R. E. Lee Memorial Episcopal Church (1870s–80s) with its off-center bell tower. The Gothic Revival style mirrored an intellectual current of the era, the Romantic movement that also transformed literature and music. Virginia Military Institute is a prominent local example of the Gothic Revival style which has lent an appropriately military air to the institution since the construction of the Barracks in 1851.

Along with two other locally occurring period styles, the Italianate and Second Empire styles, the Gothic Revival style set the stage for

The Second Empire style mansard roof of the Buena Vista Company Building in Buena Vista.
Photo by Dan Pezzoni

Queen Anne architecture at the end of the nineteenth century, the richly embellished "Victorian" architecture built in the boom towns of Buena Vista, Glasgow, and Goshen and new neighborhoods in Lexington. The architecture of this period is sometimes described as *technomorphic*, meaning form as the expression of the technology that created it, for instance the intricate scrolling patterns made possible by mechanized saws. The pendulum swing of fashion brought classicism back into vogue around 1900. The type of classicism known as the Colonial Revival style, which was in a sense a revival of a revival (the classically inspired Georgian and Federal styles), dominated local construction for much of the twentieth century and remains popular today, as the ubiquitous "Colonials" of suburbia prove.

The twentieth century was also the period of exotic revivals like the Mission and Tudor Revival styles and of the Craftsman style epitomized by the compact bungalow house form built locally from the 1910s through the 1930s. The Craftsman style marked a sea change

Buena Vista's Arcade Building has milled ornament from the city's boom era.
Photo by Dan Pezzoni

Preface

The Buena Vista Post Office combines Classical Revival and Colonial Revival features.
Photo by Dan Pezzoni

in American domestic architecture: it was the first nationally popular style to mostly eschew historic reference, and it paved the way for the local adoption of architectural modernism after World War II. Historicist styles remained popular, however, and the tension between historicism and modernism continues as a defining theme in contemporary architectural debate, locally and nationally.

The Architecture of Historic Rockbridge follows the story of the county's architectural development into the early post-World War II period, then traces one strand to the present: the local development of historic preservation. Since its establishment in 1966, Historic Lexington Foundation has been at the forefront of preservation awareness, promoting "brick and mortar" preservation of historic properties through such instruments as a revolving fund for the purchase and rehabilitation of buildings and a façade easement program for the protection in perpetuity of Lexington's streetscapes. HLF has also supported heritage education and tourism initiatives, not least through the publication of the 1977 architectural history and this book.

In its work on *The Architecture of Historic Rockbridge*, HLF has received support from a number of individuals and organizations. Historian Charles Bodie, author of *Remarkable Rockbridge: The Story of Rockbridge County, Virginia* (2011), a county history sponsored by the Rockbridge Historical Society (RHS), offered his insights on the county's history and reviewed the manuscript. RHS provided indirect assistance through its series *Proceedings of the Rockbridge Historical Society* (1941 on), which presents scholarly articles on a wide range of local historical topics. So too the RHS photograph collection housed at Washington and Lee University proved helpful. Researchers who advised on individual chapters and other portions of the text included Arthur Bartenstein (Resorts) and Taylor Sanders (Churches). The Special Collections and Archives at Washington and Lee University's James G. Leyburn Library opened its sizable collection of local history materials to the project. Tom Camden, Head of Special Collections and Archives, and Byron Faidley, Seth McCormick-Goodhart, and Lisa McCown at the collections assisted the project in many ways. Other individuals who offered their time and expertise to the project include Stewart Bennington, Susan Brady, Arthur Cusick, Beth Cusick, Joseph D'Aurora, Ted DeLaney, Jean Dunbar, Donald Gaylord, Keith Gibson, Leslie Giles, Maury Hanson, Patrick Hinely, Quatro Hubbard, Diane Jacob, John Jacobs, Randall B. Jones, Fred Kirchner, Margaret Kirkby, Lauren Leake, Karen Lyle, Michael Lynn, Bruce Macdonald, Kent McMichael, Louise Mikell, Chris Novelli, Dana Puga, Alyson Ross, Lorna Smith, and Andy Wolfe.

Washington and Lee's Special Collections provided the majority of the archival images used in the book. Also important in this regard was the survey collection at the Virginia Department of Historic Resources (DHR) in Richmond. As Virginia's State Historic Preservation Office, DHR is the repository of photographs and other information on buildings generated by state-assisted architectural survey

The Rustic style
Cave Mountain Lake
picnic pavilion.
Photo by Dan Pezzoni

and historic registration programs. DHR's predecessor agency (the Virginia Historic Landmarks Commission) supported Pam Simpson's survey efforts in the 1970s and 1980s, the principal source of architectural information on historic county buildings along with other survey files at DHR. An earlier survey effort, the New Deal-era Virginia Historical Inventory, provided information for James McClung's *Historical Significance of Rockbridge County* (1939). The Virginia Historical Inventory information for Rockbridge County is available at the Library of Virginia in Richmond and online at the library's website. (This and other websites are listed in the bibliography.) Substantial or important contributions of photographs were also made to the project by various individuals, among them Jeremy Leadbetter, Sally Mann, Anne Drake McClung, Michael Pulice, and by the author, book committee members, and others.

This book uses an abbreviated citation method in the endnotes which provides the last name of the author, the title or abbreviated title, and page number(s) for cited information. Full citations appear in the bibliography. Photograph credits are also shortened in some instances. Most historic images were provided by the Washington and Lee Special Collections, which is credited in the captions as *SC, WLU*. A number of these historic images came from the holdings of the Rockbridge Historical Society which is abbreviated *RHS*. Another common abbreviation is ca., which stands for *circa*, a Latin word

Boxerwood, perhaps the county's earliest modernist house, shows the influence of architect Frank Lloyd Wright's Usonian house designs. Photo by Dan Pezzoni

meaning "about" used for dates that are approximate or inferred. A circa date may in some instances be close to the actual date (to the extent that can be determined) or it may differ from it by decades, especially in the case of vernacular buildings which belong to traditions that changed little over time, providing few architectural clues for more exact dating. Some exact dates and other information in the text may be incorrect. History is an evolving process, with new and more accurate information always coming to light, and it is hoped future research will correct any inaccuracies that may be in the book. Addresses are given for most town and city buildings but not for rural buildings. Readers interested in seeking out properties profiled here should, of course, respect private property rights.

The Architecture of Historic Rockbridge, despite its title, is "a" history of the architecture of the county rather than "the" history. It is a sampling of the wealth of information available on the subject that necessarily omits much that may be of interest. Rockbridge County is particularly blessed with architectural information, in large part due to Royster Lyle and Pam Simpson's research and Simpson's course in local architectural documentation at Washington and Lee University, which resulted in numerous student papers on buildings in and around Lexington. Historians Francis Lynn and Lynda Miller have published information on historic buildings in Buena Vista and Glasgow, respectively; the late Douglas E. "Pat" Brady Jr. researched smaller communities and rural areas; and a number of researchers have written detailed accounts of selected county buildings and historic districts for listings in the Virginia Landmarks Register and the National Register of Historic Places, information available online at the Virginia Department of Historic Resources website. Another useful source is the volunteer architectural survey conducted under the aegis of the Ruth Anderson McCulloch Branch of the Association for the Preservation of Virginia Antiquities beginning in the 1990s.

These initiatives focused on existing buildings, though some of the buildings that were surveyed are now gone. Architecture from the first generation or two of non-native settlement has almost completely vanished — with the notable exception of Timber Ridge Presbyterian Church (1755–56), possibly the oldest surviving Virginia building of any kind west of the Blue Ridge and south of the Shenandoah Valley. Late eighteenth and early to mid-nineteenth century buildings are skewed toward the elite end of the socioeconomic spectrum, the houses of the rich and powerful. For a more representative sense of construction from the early period, several sources proved helpful. The records of the Mutual Assurance Society of Virginia, an insurance company most active locally in the first two decades of the nineteenth century, provide many insights. The society's agents described and sketched over a hundred county buildings ranging from grand plantation houses to industrial buildings like gristmills, sawmills, and blacksmith shops, to barns and domestic outbuildings. (The Mutual Assurance Society coverage applications generally do not note the locations of rural buildings although this is sometimes known from other sources.) More limited geographically but richer in detail are papers related to legal proceedings that pitted Buffalo Forge ironmaster William Weaver against the iron manufacturing firm of Jordan, Davis and Company. The papers contain descriptions of industrial buildings and worker housing associated with a forge and furnace near Goshen in the 1820s and 1830s including information on now locally extinct vernacular building technologies such as board roofing and wooden chimneys. Remarkably, the depositions in *Weaver v. Jordan, Davis & Company* preserve the words of the people who lived and worked in these long-lost buildings, a conversation about architecture in the Rockbridge dialect of nearly two centuries ago.

If the premises of this book could be distilled to a single idea, it would be that architecture and history are intertwined. Both relate to each other and to geography, technology, society, and other areas of human endeavor and study. But historic architecture transcends most other forms of historical information in that it is tangible. A twenty-first century Rockbridge County resident can experience a historic house interior in much the same way the original occupants did, and an ornately carved mantel is as much a thing of beauty now as it was when it was created.

Buildings hint at their meaning through their construction, form, and detail, a theme of the "Approaching Buildings" chapter that begins the book proper. Add various forms of archival and oral information to the physical evidence of the buildings and the story becomes all the richer. Generations of researchers have contributed to our understanding of Rockbridge architectural history yet, despite their efforts, concrete information on original owners, builders, and building dates remains elusive for many of the county's historic sites. Intensive physical documentation, National Register-level research using land and census records, and more complete reviews of existing building histories have the potential to yield this information. May future researchers avail themselves of these and other sources to enhance our understanding of Rockbridge County's irreplaceable architectural heritage.

ONE

Approaching Buildings

"WE HAD A PROBLEM," wrote Pam Simpson. After publication of *The Architecture of Historic Lexington* in 1977, Simpson and co-author Royster Lyle turned their attention toward the county, but they soon realized the vernacular architecture they found did not fit neatly, or fit at all, into the stylistic categories that had served them so well in Lexington. When they encountered simple rural log and frame houses, Simpson confessed that "we did not know what to do."[1]

To understand what they were seeing, Simpson and Lyle tapped the emerging field of material culture studies. Anthropologists, cultural geographers, and folklorists regarded buildings as material expressions of a society's culture. Buildings encoded information about ethnicity, socioeconomic status, intellectual culture, and other aspects of human endeavor. The material culture approach was a key for unlocking the complexities of otherwise plain-looking buildings, and it is why Simpson sub-titled her 1980 article on the county's architecture in the *Proceedings of the Rockbridge Historical Society* with the question: "How does a house mean?" Or, in the phrasing of the title of this chapter, how does a researcher approach a building to understand the historical and cultural meanings encoded in it?

As Simpson's title indicates, she focused her research on houses, specifically floor plans. Plan types are relative constants in historic domestic architecture, traceable over generations and detectable in

An East Lexington log house
depicted by Lexington photographer
William Hoyt, probably in the 1930s.
Hoyt's mother, artist Margaret Hoyt,
used the photograph for her
painting *The Wash Line*.
Photo courtesy SC, WLU

various materials and stylistic guises. In Rockbridge three plans were most common: the one-room plan, the hall-parlor plan, and the center-passage plan. The first is easy to visualize: a single, undivided, rectangular room. The hall-parlor plan, also rectangular, has an interior subdivided into a larger hall, an all-purpose room with exterior entries and a fireplace, and the smaller parlor, usually unheated. The center-passage plan features a center passage or hallway between equal-sized rooms. Like subatomic particles, the plans constitute the building blocks of the county's traditional vernacular housing. They are its underlying grammar.[2]

The plans relate to social interactions, function, and aesthetics as well. In the one-room and hall-parlor plans a visitor entered directly

Approaching Buildings

into the family living space (the hall in the case of the hall-parlor house). But with the center-passage plan, a late arrival on the local scene, "there was a way station" as Simpson put it, "a separation from visitor and visited, a new privacy." Simpson and other architectural historians equated the new arrangement with social change. "When society reached a point where most of the members of a community no longer intimately knew each other" there was a reason to exclude strangers from the "heart of the house" (strangers but also those perceived as social inferiors). The center-passage plan was typically the form of the larger and more stylish houses.[3]

A symmetrical façade was another consequence or concomitant of the center-passage plan. Renaissance architects resurrected classical symmetry as a defining feature of palaces and great houses, and the British landed gentry and the American elites who emulated them adopted the new regularity as indicators of their cultural refinement and social superiority. As Simpson put it, the center passage and the symmetry it imposed "intellectualized" the house. One-room or hall-parlor houses might have balanced three-bay (window/door/window) fronts but nothing about their plans led naturally to symmetry, and in fact the hall-parlor plan with its unequal interior division was often expressed in an asymmetrical two-bay exterior. But a center-passage house usually had an entry on axis with the center hallway and a window centered on each flanking room — or two windows per room, the five-bay arrangement associated with the county's finest Federal style houses.

The center passage generated modular possibilities for the form and enlargement of houses. By extending the passage to the

The Wallace-Wilson House (early 1800s) near Natural Bridge has a symmetrical three-bay elevation.
Photo by H. E. Ravenhorst

Cedar Hill (early 1800s) is representative of the five-bay house form.
Photo by H. E. Ravenhorst

rear, the flanking rooms could be duplicated to create what is known as the double-pile (two-room-deep) center-passage plan. In its two-story manifestation the two-room-deep variant resulted in eight large rooms, space enough for entertaining on the first floor and privacy on the second. An ambitious but cash-strapped homebuilder might initially build only the front half of a planned two-room-deep house. Or two-thirds of it, the passage and a single or double pile of rooms to one side, with the intention of adding the other room or rooms on the other side of the passage as finances allowed. The two-thirds approach was apparently the strategy of Matthew Houston who built the original part of the house known as Forest Oaks (ca. 1806), although the arrangement may also have reflected Houston's reported use of the first floor as a dry goods store and the floor above as a dwelling.[4]

The center passage had additional advantages. With doors open at both ends it promoted cross ventilation. In this respect the passage functioned as a genteel version of a dogtrot, the breezeway that separated the two pens of certain double-pen log Southern houses. A true dogtrot-form house has apparently not been identified in Rockbridge County but the "Old Paxton Place," which formerly stood on or near the James River near Glasgow, came close. The log house, reputed to date to 1747 and possibly once the home of Alexander Paxton, featured a roofed breezeway which separated two side-by-side log pens or units, one one-story in height and the other a story with a garret. This may have been the same dwelling as the Paxton House at Balcony Falls, described in an 1874 Lexington newspaper account that claimed it was used as a blockhouse, an impromptu fort for protection against Indian attack during the frontier era.[5]

The "Old Paxton Place." Courtesy RHS/SC, WLU

In two-story versions of the center-passage plan it made sense to put the stair in the passage. This concentrated circulation, the movement of people around the house, in one space, a benefit to the convenience and privacy of occupants. In one-room and hall-parlor houses with upper stories the connection was typically made by an enclosed or "boxed" winder stair: cramped, poorly lit, and hence inconvenient and even dangerous. A center-passage stair with its handsome newels, balusters, and tread brackets was not merely functional; it made an architectural statement. The center-passage plan also encouraged the symmetrical arrangement of chimneys. In one-room-deep versions of the plan these were typically two in number, placed at the two ends of the house. In two-room-deep houses the chimneys were often placed between the front and back rooms with back-to-back fireplaces, an economical use of bricks. The center passage plan appeared locally in the 1700s and continued in use into the twentieth century.

Simpson noted one other early plan type: the three-room plan, a generally enlarged version of the hall-parlor plan with the parlor subdivided into two rooms. The plan is sometimes known as the "Quaker plan" but it was also used in non-Quaker contexts by English and Scots-Irish settlers alike. A center-passage version of the three-room plan was popular in parts of the Valley of Virginia, and there are a number of examples of it in Rockbridge County. One is (or was before it was modified) the late eighteenth century stone house known as Vineyard Hill which has a single fireplace on one end of its first floor serving a single large room and, at the other end, a single chimney mass with two fireplaces separated by a beaded board partition that appears to have formed two rooms of a three-room plan. The two fireplaces are not back to back, probably to allow for the flue of a large cooking fireplace in the working basement below. Vineyard Hill, like many other early houses, is built into a bank permitting ground-level entry to the basement on one side and the main level on the other.[6]

Wood (log and frame), stone, and brick were the materials of choice for traditional house construction, and of the various options

Vineyard Hill.
Photo by Dan Pezzoni

log construction was the easiest and least expensive. During the settlement period log building served dual purposes; cutting timber to clear the land for crops generated logs for construction. Log buildings could be crude and impermanent. In 1839 just such a bottom-end log structure was described by a witness in *Weaver v. Jordan, Davis & Company*. The witness, Bath Iron Works furnace tender James Lowe, was questioned about a coal house, a structure for storing the charcoal used in ironmaking. "Was it not a very small one built of small sap pine logs with the bark on," Lowe was asked, "set down under the bank on the ground . . . and was it possible in the nature of things for it to last long?" Lowe answered, "It was about 30 feet square I reckon, which be a small coal house: the logs were small pine, but I think one side knocked off a little with a falling [felling] axe . . . it could not last many years." The coal house was "just built for present use" Lowe added.[7]

Likewise, the joining of the logs at the corners, known as corner notching, could be rough and slapdash or done with a degree of precision approaching furniture joinery. The scooped-out saddle notch is an example of the crude technique whereas v-notching and half- and full-dovetail notching were the better sorts. Some scholars consider log construction to be a heritage of the Germans, picked up by the Scots-Irish and other ethnic groups who passed through the area of heavy German settlement in southeastern Pennsylvania on their way into western Virginia; however, more recently cultural geographers Terry Jordan and Matti Kaups have restated the earlier view that the core American log building tradition has a Finnish-Scandinavian origin and was transmitted to the backcountry via the New Sweden settlement established on the lower Delaware River in the mid-1600s. Whatever its origins, log building was common in Rockbridge County during the historical period, so much so that some four hundred log structures were documented by the Ruth Anderson McCulloch Branch of the Association for the Preservation of Virginia Antiquities in its survey of the county beginning in the 1990s. Vernacular log buildings (as opposed to Rustic style revivals) were built into the twentieth century in the county.[8]

Half-dovetail corner notching on the Hamilton Schoolhouse (1823).
Photo by Michael Pulice, courtesy DHR

Stone was another abundant local material and there is evidence of early use as the 1755–56 stone Timber Ridge Presbyterian Church attests. This building and its Scots-Irish affinities notwithstanding, Lyle and Simpson detected a German flavor in local stone construction. "The presence of a large German settlement in Rockingham and other counties to the north seems to have contributed to the use of this material in the Rockbridge area."[9]

The Long-Leech House, an early stone dwelling.
Photo by Michael Pulice, courtesy DHR

Representative of the finer early stone houses is the William Mackey House near Timber Ridge, definitively dated to 1796 by a date stone which also bears William Mackey's initials. (Surviving building receipts also confirm completion in 1796.) The walls of the two-story house are laid up with irregularly coursed limestone rubble reinforced at the corners by larger stones. The walls are capped by an original cornice described by architectural historian Calder Loth, who wrote the National Register nomination for the house, as "an elegant composition of crown molding, fascia, scrolled modillions, dentils and bed moldings." Inside is one of the county's more intact Georgian style interiors with architrave mantels (molded frames around the fireplace) and a stair with turned newels and balusters. The original Mackey House at the location, apparently built ca. 1756, is said to have been a log dwelling. Stone

William Mackey House.
Courtesy DHR

was also popular for outbuildings including the cottage-like stone dependency behind the antebellum Leyburn House, also known as Elmwood or Elmcroft. Most stone buildings were constructed with the bluish-gray limestone that underlies much of the county, but the so-called Elder House near Lake Robertson, believed to date to the late 1700s, is built from variegated brownish stone, probably predominantly sandstone, with courses on the front elevation punctuated by small dark stones as though the stonemason meant to evoke Flemish bond brickwork.[10]

Brick entered the local building repertoire later than stone despite the fact it was a popular material for elite architecture in the eastern part of the state by the time of Rockbridge County's settlement. This is probably because brick making was an exacting, time-consuming, labor-intensive activity, and time and labor were resources in short supply among hard-pressed settlers. When brick did come into common use at the end of the eighteenth century it was for high-profile or elite structures such as the county's 1786–87 courthouse and the 1780s Alexander-Withrow Building in Lexington (also known as the Alexander-Withrow House). With time, brick use passed down through society, coming to replace stone for foundations and chimneys and serving more often for buildings in their entirety. Brick construction was more resistant to fire than wooden construction, which probably explains why the Alexander-Withrow Building survived Lexington's "Great Fire" of April 11, 1796, which decimated the early wooden building stock. (The Castle, a two-story stone house on Randolph Street dated to ca. 1790, also survived the fire.) Many Lexington merchants and householders eventually rebuilt in brick, as indicated by period insurance policies and early photographs. Others crossed their fingers and stuck to wooden construction.[11]

Brick was frequently fired in an updraft kiln known as a clamp, often in a single batch at the construction site. Something is known about the process locally from the discovery of a brick clamp at Liberty Hall, the location from 1782 to 1803 of the academy that grew into Washington and Lee University. In the 1970s Washington and Lee archaeologists excavated a "multi-channeled clamp kiln" near the remains of the academy's 1799 Rector's House, a two-story brick dwelling. The kiln remains consisted of rows of bricks representing the bottom courses of the stacks of bricks that were subsequently used to build the adjacent house. The gaps between the rows were the channels or *eyes* through which hot air moved during firing. Fires were lit at the mouth of each eye and the rectangular mass of bricks was sealed with mud, sand, or other non-combustible materials to hold in the heat. Architectural historian Michael Pulice has documented the vast amount of wood needed to fire a clamp for the construction of a good-sized brick house and found that it is equivalent to over 300,000 board feet of lumber, enough to build several large modern houses. "This equation effectively illustrates the level of wealth that was once necessary to build a large brick house," Pulice writes, "and the extent to which a brick house must have marked the high status of its owner."[12]

Bricks were laid in various patterns known as bonds. The bond favored in the 1700s was Flemish bond, which alternates the long (stretcher) and short (header) sides of the bricks. Flemish bond dominated until the late antebellum period when it gave way to common bond,

William Mackey House mantel.
Courtesy DHR

Elder House.

Below: Flemish bond brickwork on the McCown House (early 1800s).
Below right: The builder of the John McKemy House used glazed header bricks to write the date 1829 on the façade.

consisting of multiple rows of stretcher courses separated by single rows of header courses. There were other bonds as well, popular during various periods—stretcher bond (all stretchers), English bond, and Flemish variant bond—each imparting a distinctive look. Firing of bricks often resulted in vitrification or glazing, a glossy gray or bluish surface, which could be put to decorative effect either by alternating glazed headers with non-glazed stretchers to create a checkerboard effect in Flemish bond or to create the diamond pattern known as diapering in the Alexander-Withrow Building, a tour de force of early Rockbridge brickwork. The various traditional brick bonds were employed for solid load-bearing construction; in later eras brick veneer construction, brick as a cladding material for frame buildings, became prevalent.[13]

Remains of the brick clamp
at Liberty Hall.
Photo (ca. 1977) courtesy of the
Laboratory of Anthropology,
Washington and Lee University

Because clay is a plastic material, bricks could also be molded with curved ends in various profiles. The county's antebellum brick houses are noted for their decorative cornices constructed of molded bricks with curved ends. According to Pam Simpson, over forty percent of the antebellum brick residences she documented in her Rockbridge County survey had molded brick cornices. The houses date chiefly from the mid-1810s to the 1840s and many are associated with the Lexington-based construction firm of John Jordan and Samuel Darst.[14]

Another demanding building technique of the era was frame construction. Framing was generally more labor-intensive and skill-dependent than log building, though as with log notching there were different grades of refinement. During depositions for *Weaver v. Jordan, Davis & Company*, house carpenter Jacob Clyce was asked, "Are there not two classes of carpenters throughout the county of Rockbridge, to wit, one that [does] the higher order of work, the other that [does] the rough and inferior work?" Clyce replied, "It matters not how work is done whether rough or smooth, if it is done right and in a workman-like manner. There are carpenters who do rough jobs which the higher carpenters do not like to do if they can get finer jobs."[15]

Whether frame construction was crude or fine, the sills, corner posts, studs, joists, plates, rafters, and other structural members had

A molded brick cornice on the springhouse at Glen Maury (ca. 1831) in Buena Vista. Photo by Michael Pulice, courtesy DHR

to be fashioned and joined with some precision. The members might be hewn with an adze or axe, the cruder shaping technique, or they might be expensively pit-sawn. Pit-sawing involved two sawyers stationed above and below a log resting on trestles or spanning a saw pit. Water-powered sawmills were another sawing option, their reciprocating sash saws essentially mechanized versions of manual whipsaws. Joinery involved the cutting of slot-like mortises and the tongue-like tenons that fit in them, the whole assembly pinned with wooden pegs. Nails were used in frame construction to varying degrees; they simplified joinery but were expensive and were not suited for the joining of large timbers. In fact, Valley of Virginia barn builders favored mortise-and-tenon construction for their heavy-timbered structures well into the twentieth century.

Frame buildings were usually sided with clapboards or weatherboards. In the finer early houses, up to about the Civil War era, the weatherboards were planed and beaded, that is, smoothed with a plane and cut with a beading plane to give them a rounded edge. Well-preserved beaded weatherboards with traces of white paint survive on a gable end of the original section of the Buffalo Forge mansion, known as Mount Pleasant, where the formerly exterior wall was

Offset Flemish bond creates a striped appearance on the front of Roundview. Photo by H. E. Ravenhorst

encapsulated by a ca. 1830s addition. Later in the antebellum period, board-and-batten siding came into vogue, especially for Gothic Revival architecture where the vertical boards and the battens that covered the gaps between them created a suitably vertical Gothic effect. An occasional feature of Rockbridge frame construction is nogging, the filling of the wall cavities between framing members with bricks and brickbats (brick fragments), either for insulation, rodent control, or both. The original ca. 1790 section of Mulberry Grove near Brownsburg is nogged.[16]

As the nineteenth century progressed, frame construction was transformed by improvements in sawmilling and nail manufacture. The sawmilling revolution was based on two innovations: steam power and the circular saw. Steam-powered sawmills were probably rare in the county before the Civil War but common after. The advantage of steam power was portability; the mill went to the timber, not the other way around. The circular saw, a toothed disc that allowed continuous high-speed sawing, improved the efficiency of sawmills. Early evidence of circular sawing is found in an 1854 advertisement for the Rockbridge Foundry Works at Irish Creek which offered mill-owners "Circular Saws fitted up in the neatest style."[17]

Traditionally, nails were individually hand-forged and hence relatively expensive. The aforementioned beaded weatherboards at Buffalo Forge are attached by nails with hand-forged or wrought heads. In the early nineteenth century inventors perfected ways to mass produce nails by cutting them from sheets of iron. These "cut nails" were more affordable and they replaced the older wrought or "rose-headed" nails (for the characteristic petalled or faceted look of the hand-forged heads) fairly rapidly in the early nineteenth century. Wrought nails might continue in use for certain applications and larger nails and spikes were typically hand-forged. A further development occurred in the 1880s when nails cut from lengths of wire began to flood the market. "Wire nails" were even cheaper than cut nails and generally replaced them although cut nails continued in limited use. Nail chronology serves as a rough index for dating buildings. The presence of wrought nails suggests construction before about 1810

A rafter couple photographed at the ruins of Searson Mill, Steeles Tavern vicinity. The photo shows features of traditional framing such as a pegged mortise-and-tenon joint and the chiseled Roman numerals the carpenter used to match rafter to rafter. Regular up-and-down saw cuts are also visible, suggesting the rafters were sawn in a sawmill. Photo (1974) by Edward Chappell, courtesy DHR

This mill, which may have stood in Rockbridge County, has an attached water-powered sawmill.
Courtesy SC, WLU

and cut nails generally indicate construction between ca. 1810 and the end of the nineteenth century.

Important documentary evidence for the county's early architecture is found in the declarations or coverage applications of the Mutual Assurance Society. The society, essentially a fire insurance company, was incorporated by the General Assembly in 1794 and included a substantial number of Rockbridge buildings among the thousands of properties it insured. The company's agents recorded such pertinent information as building use, dimensions, distance from other structures, story height, construction material, roof covering material, and appraisal value. They also drew sketch plans which sometimes portray details of building form. The company was most active in rural Rockbridge from 1800 to about 1820. In 1822 the Mutual Assurance Society's "country branch" was discontinued owing to heavy fire losses among rural properties and the company concentrated on coverage for in-town buildings, writing policies for buildings in Lexington, Brownsburg, and Fairfield into the mid-nineteenth century.[18]

Rockbridge County's rural houses were a varied lot according to the Mutual Assurance Society declarations. Many were wood, some stone, and a few, the cream of the crop, prestigious brick. When one considers the declarations are skewed toward the more valuable properties it seems likely most dwellings of the period were constructed of wood, either frame or log (the declarations do not distinguish). Among the largest insured residences was that of Joseph Walker, appraised at $3,400 in 1805 and described as "3 storys one of stone and two of Brick." In 1803 the same house was described as three stories of brick construction. The discrepancy may be explained if what appears to have been a stone basement story was counted in 1803 but its construction material ignored. A little house in Brownsburg appraised for Henry B. Jones in 1838 had a partially stuccoed exterior. Roofs were generally covered in wood, meaning they were wood-shingled, although barns were occasionally thatched.[19]

Ordinarily, insured dwellings were portrayed in the elevation sketches as simple rectangles with roofs, chimneys, and foundations, but these features are more on the order of graphic conventions than true depictions. Occasionally more information was provided. In 1803 the two-story wooden house of Christopher Clyce (also spelled Clice or Kleis) featured a one-story wing containing a workshop connected to the dwelling by a small "lumber" room, a storage room that probably contained the stacks of wood Clyce used in his trade as a wagon maker (among other occupations). Clyce's house also had a porch, fashionably described as a "piazaa" in reference to an Italian piazza, an open-air gathering place. The same arrangement appears in subsequent declarations in 1805 and 1816. In 1816 the piazza is termed a "shade 10 feet wide"

Joseph Walker's Mount Pleasant Farm, documented by a Mutual Assurance Society Agent in 1803, included a three-story brick house with four chimneys (upper left), a barn, a storehouse, and two secondary dwellings. Mount Pleasant was a common place name of the era with at least two occurrences in the county.
Courtesy DHR

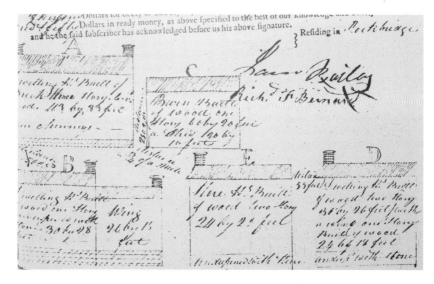

and the workshop an "addition." The lumber room had become a "loging" (presumably lodging) room and the end of the front porch/piazza/shade was enclosed as a second "loging" room. Similar porch rooms are known elsewhere in the South as "pizer" or piazza rooms, small unheated spaces separated from family living areas. Pizer rooms served as sick rooms or to put up travelers or the minister when he came to call.[20]

The Mutual Assurance Society records are weighted toward the county's costlier buildings, those that owners might wish to insure. A glimpse of building practices at the other end of the socioeconomic spectrum is provided in the aforementioned Bath Iron Works case, a collection of inventories and depositions contained in a petition brought to the Virginia Court of Appeals in *Weaver v. Jordan, Davis & Company* and published in 1842. Weaver was William Weaver, the largest slaveholder in Rockbridge County and owner of furnaces and forges scattered through the county and beyond. Jordan was Samuel F. Jordan, the son of builder and ironmaster John Jordan who was Weaver's chief competitor in the region's iron industry, and Davis was an ironmaster in business with Jordan. Weaver operated Bath Furnace and an associated forge on the Maury River just upstream from Goshen Pass, collectively known as Bath Iron Works, which Jordan and Davis managed beginning in 1830, an arrangement that proved unsatisfactory to the parties and led to litigation in the late 1830s. The story in all its legal intricacy is told by historian Charles Dew in *Bond of Iron* (1994), the acclaimed study of master-slave relations at Weaver's iron plantations.[21]

What is remarkable about the case from the perspective of architectural history is the detailed information it contains on now mostly vanished vernacular building practices. Ironworks employees and contractors from managers, millwrights, and carpenters to ore miners and furnace stokers were deposed on behalf of the litigants. An important witness for the plaintiff was fifty-three-year-old Michael Ham, who when asked his profession stated, "I follow ore digging [which] has been the principal business of my life." He worked as an "under hand" for three years at the ore banks in the mountains near the ironworks before graduating to "head man," his duties involving the management of a portion of an ironworks work force that included, in 1830, over fifty slaves. Ham was likely illiterate; he signed his deposition with "his mark."[22]

Ham was questioned about the simple log houses of the miners at the ore banks. They were three in number, he reported, although one was "taken away" at some point. Ham's wording suggests the house was moved. This may have been done on skids or rollers, a common practice for small wooden structures which might be moved around towns and farms as need dictated, or since it was log the house may have been dismantled and re-erected. Of the two remaining houses "the upper one I think the logs were notched," Ham recalled, suggesting its companion was not notched. What Ham meant by this is unclear. Perhaps he did not consider saddle-notching to be a form of notching, or the logs of the house were laid one on the other without being notched together.[23]

Ham described the upper house as having "a clapboard roof, it had a floor in it above and below." The other ore bank houses were "built in pretty much the same manner, they are what I should call cabins

William Weaver's Buffalo Forge plantation in a ca. 1860 image. This remarkable view shows Weaver's house, Mount Pleasant, at the top, the stone Buffalo Forge mill to the left, and Buffalo Creek toward the bottom. Courtesy SC, WLU

Brick and log houses at Jordan's Point photographed by William Hoyt in the 1930s. The four-bay, window/door/door/window form of the log dwelling suggests it may have housed workers at the Point's industries. Courtesy SC, WLU

[and] they all had wooden chimneys." A chimney built of wood might seem a recipe for disaster, but with an insulating layer of mud inside and perhaps a stone hearth floor and backing a wooden chimney was considered a serviceable expedient for low-cost buildings at the time, less expensive to build than a rock or brick chimney.[24]

Nevertheless, wooden chimneys were potential fire hazards and town authorities frowned on their use in towns. The de facto building ordinances contained in the acts of establishment for Lexington (1778) and Brownsburg (1793) stipulated that houses be built with "a brick or stone chimney." In 1800, not long after fire devastated Lexington, the legislature passed an act to the effect "that if any fire or combustible shall be put in any house [or] wooden chimney [in Lexington] so as to endanger the loss of property," the property owner would be required to remove the hazard.[25]

The clapboard roof described by Ham is also of note. Most buildings at Bath Iron Works had wood shingle roofs, the normative period roofing material, with shingles nailed to an underlayment of boards (called "sheeting" in the building inventories published with the case) to create a snug, watertight roof system. But wood shingle roofs consumed a great number of nails, and although an ironworks would have been the ideal place to find nails, they were still an expense. Alternative wood roofing technologies like lapped clapboards used fewer nails and the boards could even be pegged to the rafters, a laborious chore but sometimes necessary in the early days of settlement when nails were scarce.

Ham also described a log house on the ironworks farm which had a "plank" roof. "Plank" suggests something thicker and longer than a clapboard and may point to a more primitive board roof system in which weight poles held long boards or planks in place. Known as a ridgepole-and-purlin roof, the system was associated with traditional log buildings and relied for its structure on log purlins that spanned from gable to gable, rather than rafters that spanned from eaves to ridge. The Hinkle House, built in 1820 on the flanks of House Mountain and now in ruinous condition, had a ridgepole-and-purlin roof documented by Lexington photographer Michael Miley in the 1890s. Although clapboard and plank roofs were not as weather-tight as shingle roofs, the boards tending to warp from sun and rain, it is clear that management at the Bath Iron Works considered them sufficient for worker housing.[26]

Ham estimated the length of the upper ore bank dwelling as twenty feet. Other ironworks dwellings were smaller, some so small that they were described as "not larger than a common size chicken coop."

The Hinkle House with its ridgepole-and-purlin roof. Shown here are former occupants Carolina and Preston Hinkle (seated) and visiting members of the Knick family on a picnicking and squirrel-hunting excursion.
Michael Miley photo courtesy of the Virginia Historical Society and Anne Drake McClung; information from Stewart Bennington

A log slave house at Buffalo Forge photographed in 1935 shortly before it burned down. Courtesy SC, WLU

Several ore bank house windows had sashes, suggesting at least the intention of glazing (Ham was unable to recall whether the glass was intact or missing). Unglazed shutter windows are suggested for some ironworks buildings and some floors consisted of rough, unplaned boards that were apparently loosely laid down, not nailed or "jointed." Loose floorboards were a cut above no floors at all, the case for some dwellings, and a "sort of a kitchen" described by Ham "had no floor, nor roof except just over the fire-place."[27]

Mudsill construction, the wooden structure resting directly on the ground without a foundation, is another vernacular building expedient described in the depositions. James Dixon, William Weaver's agent, was asked about worker houses built at the ironworks in the late 1820s. "Had they not been built in a cheap and temporary manner with the foundation logs resting on the earth?" Dixon confirmed they were built that way, in other words with mudsills rather than true foundations. Of the many worker houses at and around the ironworks, a proportion would have been occupied by slaves given the number of slaves who are known to have worked there, but there are few instances of dwellings specifically described as slave houses. A building contract included in the case papers called for the construction of a "good tight and substantial negro cabin" but the dwelling was not apparently built.[28]

Antebellum Rockbridge would have had many slave houses. According to the 1860 census, on the eve of the Civil War nearly 4,000 slaves lived and worked in the county, twenty-three percent of the total population of over 17,000. William Weaver owned 66 individuals in 1860 although the number fluctuated considerably from census to census: 39 slaves in 1830, 102 in 1840, and 74 in 1850 (of whom five resided at Bath Iron Works). Something is known about slave living arrangements at Weaver's core plantation at Buffalo Forge from the historical record and surviving houses. Slave houses stood at three locations on the Buffalo Forge plantation: in a "quarters" near the main house and kitchen; downhill from the main house across the road (present-day Forge Road); and in small rows and groupings at peripheral locations

Two brick brick slave houses stand near Mount Pleasant, the ironmaster's house at Buffalo Forge.
Photo by H. E. Ravenhorst

up and down Buffalo Creek. The surviving slave houses consist of two stuccoed brick dwellings built ca. 1858. Both were constructed of bricks hauled to the site by Weaver's slaves. A stone dwelling across Buffalo Creek is also believed to have been occupied by slaves. In the 1930s photographer William Hoyt photographed what is identified as one of the Buffalo Forge slave houses, which stood on the road between the carriage house and icehouse across from the main house. The one-story log house featured a garret and brick end chimney.[29]

Many slave quarters had a characteristic two-room plan with a center chimney and back to back fireplaces serving the two rooms. The type is illustrated by a v-notched log dwelling at Fruit Hill in the lower Buffalo Creek area traditionally identified as a slave house, one of many that formerly stood on the plantation. Archaeological investigation by current owner Kurt Russ suggests a date of construction of around 1840. Slave houses remained in use after the Civil War as dwellings for freed blacks but are now rare. Like so many other small vernacular Rockbridge County houses from before the Civil War, time has thinned their ranks.[30]

A log slave house at Fruit Hill.
Photo by Dan Pezzoni

TWO

Styles

THE BROWNSBURG-AREA HOUSE known as Mulberry Grove preserves one of the county's more remarkable examples of eighteenth century folk art: a decorative cast iron fireback attributed to South River ironmasters Halbert and Moses McCluer. The fireback portrays a winged and trumpeting angel who proclaims "Peace & Unity" to a cloud of thirteen stars representing the original thirteen United States. The stars provide a clue to the fireback's date; the casting presumably dates to before 1791 when Vermont, the nation's fourteenth state, joined the Union.[1]

In one interpretation the angel represents Fame, a stock figure in artistic representation of the era, but additional content is hinted at by what appears to be a crest of hair that extends from the forehead to the neck of the figure's otherwise shaved head. In other words, a Mohawk, for the angel also appears to represent an Indian. Indians were often depicted as stand-ins for America and Americans in political cartoons and other politically-charged material culture of the Revolutionary era. The 1783 cartoon "Proclamation of Peace," one of many to make the identification, depicts an exultant Indian waving his tomahawk at the personified European powers and crying, "I have got my Liberty and the Devil Scalp you all!" The Boston Tea Party is another example, the Indian disguises of the participants a form of Revolutionary performance art.[2]

Facing page: The Italianate-style Rockbridge Alum Springs spring pavilion. Photo (ca. 1900) courtesy RHS/SC, WLU

Above: Rare representational painting on an antebellum mantel from an unidentified Buffalo Forge Station house. Photo by Dan Pezzoni

The patriotic fireback at Mulberry Grove. Courtesy DHR

But in matters of architectural taste the citizens of the young United States, Rockbridge County included, were decidedly less bellicose toward their mother country and its culture. In fact, American elites eagerly copied British architectural fashion. At the end of the eighteenth century that meant the delicate version of classicism known as the Adam style after its foremost practitioners, the Scottish architect-brothers Robert and James Adam. Robert Adam, like many affluent, cultured Britons of his day, traveled to Italy to study Roman ruins and claimed as his artistic mission a desire to revive "the beautiful spirit of antiquity [and] transfuse it, with novelty and variety."[3]

The Adam brothers were sought-after society architects, trend setters for the British aristocracy, which is why there is a certain irony to the name by which their architecture is known in America: the Federal style. In a broader sense the style is another phase of the classical revival that began during the Renaissance. Architectural historians Virginia and Lee McAlester consider it a "development and refinement of the preceding Georgian style," and given that there are instances of transitional or hybrid Georgian/Federal houses in Rockbridge, the characterization is apt.[4]

The Georgian Style owes its name to the three Hanoverian Georges who ruled the American colonies, beginning with George I in 1714 and ending with George III in 1776, though Georgian stylistic influence in America continued well after the Revolution (just as George III's reign continued into the 1800s in Britain). In Rockbridge the style is characterized by robust classical forms and a penchant for paneling, a room finish treatment with a long history in British domestic architecture. Marlbrook, a ca. 1790s brick house near Natural Bridge, has extensive Georgian paneling on one fireplace wall as well as a dentil cornice and an overmantel with fluted pilasters. Historically known as Cherry Hill, the house was likely built for David Greenlee, the son of Mary Elizabeth McDowell Greenlee, said to be the first non-native woman to settle in the early Borden Grant area (in 1737) and a tavern keeper described by historian Oren Morton as having a "striking personality" and a "caustic tongue." The best, though idiosyncratic, local example of the style is the remarkable house known as Thorn

Hill, built ca. 1793 for John Bowyer, a county militia colonel and an original trustee of Liberty Hall Academy. The Flemish-bond brick house occupies a lofty ridge-top site southwest of Lexington and has the symmetrical five-bay elevations that marked it as the home of a man of consequence. An early entry porch on the west façade has such refinements as a modillion and dentil cornice, scalloped fascia boards, and porch posts in the form of slender colonnettes.[5]

Georgian influence is strong in Thorn Hill's interior, expressed in heavy ceiling cornices, paneled wainscots, door surrounds with broken pediments, and a center-passage stair with a paneled spandrel, turned balusters, and lattice carving in the tread brackets. The rooms are dominated by their fireplace treatments which combine mantels and overmantels in impressive floor-to-ceiling compositions. One downstairs mantel, broad and squat, features fluted pilasters and a wedge-shaped fluted keyblock over the fireplace. Its overmantel has a molded segmental arch with turned finials at the ends and a fluted keyblock at the apex. Similar arches and finials crown niches to either side. The overmantel is framed by fluted pilasters, as is the overmantel panel of the mantel in the main upstairs bedroom. That mantel, narrower than the one downstairs, has a frieze with triglyph-like fluting and incised, concave-sided diamond motifs. Its overmantel panel is crowned by a floating broken pediment with a center fanfold plume.[6]

As the above description suggests, Thorn Hill exhibits a full range of classical treatments. Architectural historians Dell Upton and Margaret Peters, the authors of the National Register nomination

Marlbrook exterior and interior.
Photos by Leslie Giles, courtesy DHR

Thorn Hill: early west elevation porch, *above,* and mantel with overmantel, *right.* Photos by Dan Pezzoni

for the property, credit the interior detail to an "uneducated but highly skilled joiner" whose "sense of proportion and detailing give it a fantastic quality." Upton and Peters consider Thorn Hill eccentric and even entertaining in its interpretation of classical forms, but nevertheless note the "exceptional architectural interest" of the house.[7]

Simpler but otherwise similar mantels appear in the Zachariah Johnston House (1797; also known as Stone House) located just south of Lexington. One mantel has narrow fluted pilaster strips and a center frieze tablet with a chevron of shallow flute-like gouges, features that in combination have a three-part organization that seems to anticipate the Federal style with its tripartite symmetries. Zachariah Johnston, like Thorn Hill's Bowyer, was active in civic affairs. As a member of the House of Delegates representing Augusta County and later Rockbridge County, he chaired the standing committee on religion during the 1780s and successfully pushed for passage of the bill that established freedom of religion in the Commonwealth. Another beautifully detailed Lexington area house, Mulberry Hill, a brick dwelling dated to the first decade of the nineteenth century, also contains fluted mantels of tripartite design that seem transitional between the Georgian and Federal styles. Mulberry Hill was the home of Andrew Reid, first clerk of the Rockbridge County Court and one of the county's wealthiest citizens in the early 1800s. There is some evidence to suggest the house may incorporate earlier fabric. Georgian detail such as a paneled closed-stringer stair survives in the ruins of the once-impressive Moore House located west of Lexington. The house known as Halfway House, located in the Poplar Hill vicinity, has a dentil cornice and other features suggestive of Georgian influence.[8]

The Georgian style ended not with a bang but a whimper, grading almost imperceptibly into the

The Kessler House in Fairfield
features a Georgian overmantel.
Photos by James C. Foreman,
courtesy SC, WLU

The main parlor mantel at Fruit Hill. Photo by Dan Pezzoni

Federal style, as some of the above examples attest. Full-blown Federal is in many ways epitomized by the lower Buffalo Creek-area house known as Fruit Hill (1822) which Pam Simpson in her survey form for the property admired for the "excellence of its detailing." The two-story brick house features Flemish bond brick construction and a symmetrical five-bay façade indicative of the center-passage plan within. The detail admired by Simpson is most evident in the north parlor mantel which celebrates the technical virtuosity of its carver. The mantel pulsates with visual complexity, encrusted and incised with gougework and reeding; stack moldings, pearl moldings, and linenfold moldings; and a center fanfold ellipse and flanking fanfold paterae. But minus the visual fireworks the basic form is simple and representative of the Federal style: a tripartite composition with a center frieze tablet, the blank rectangle onto which the ellipse is carved, and subsidiary tablets at the two ends of the frieze which crown the pilasters below. Some of the carving, such as the pearl moldings and a pattern of alternating vertical and plus-sign gouges, continues around the room in a chair rail, the top element of a wainscot ornamented with rectangular panels with scalloped corners. Fruit Hill was built for Joseph Grigsby but in the late 1700s the farm was the home of "Soldier John" Grigsby who as a young man participated in an expedition against the Spanish in the Caribbean city of Cartagena and whose epithet suggests long service in the military.[9]

The artisan who carved Fruit Hill's mantel may have worked on other Rockbridge houses, and stylistic clues may someday lead to his identity. The Federal style Brownsburg area brick house known as Level Loop, built for farmer William Houston about 1819–22, has a principal mantel with an elliptical frieze tablet and a deeply incised linenfold band similar to details on the Fruit Hill mantel. The frieze of the Level Loop mantel has columns of tiny "thumbnail" gouges, like fingernail impressions in dough, which also appear on mantels in the nearby McChesney House (Briarwood). Distinctive features of the Level Loop mantel, not seen in the other houses, are pilasters formed by paired colonnettes and, in the end frieze tablets, carved fylfots, a pinwheel form generally associated with Pennsylvania German material culture.[10]

The Level Loop mantel illustrates a phenomenon that first became common in the county during the Federal period: the reliance on pattern books as a source of inspiration. Pattern books were architectural how-to manuals, richly illustrated with examples of the classical orders and designs for elements like mantels, stair railings, and entry surrounds. Level Loop's carver used *The Young Carpenter's Assistant* (1805) by Philadelphia architect Owen Biddle, but as Calder Loth writes in the National Register nomination for the house, "Although the woodwork is based on academic prototypes, it is freely adapted with the gusto of folk interpretation." Biddle cautioned builders "not to overload the work" with excessive ornamentation, but as Loth notes, this advice was ignored at Level Loop. Conceivably, the carving at Level Loop was the work of multiple craftsmen, a "school" of folk carvers at work in the county who swapped designs and techniques. Such would explain similarities between houses without attributing them to single craftsmen.[11]

The tripartite symmetry of Federal mantels is also expressed in the overall composition of houses. The house known as Stono, built above Jordan's Point by building contractor and industrialist John Jordan in 1818 (the house is also known as the Turman House), and a similar house south of Lexington known as Little Stono (ca. 1816) illustrate the form: a two-story center block flanked by one-story wings. In both houses the center block extends as a portico on monumental two-story columns supporting a pedimented gable roof, evocations of the temple

Level Loop mantel detail.
Photo courtesy DHR

Stono. Courtesy RHS/SC, WLU

front that is a prototype of classical revival architecture. Lyle and Simpson noted that the classicism at Little Stono was solidly in the Federal camp whereas Stono is more Roman in character. They considered Stono to be more closely allied with the brand of classicism championed by Thomas Jefferson and revealed in his masterworks, Monticello and the University of Virginia. This is not surprising since John Jordan worked on the construction of Monticello. Tripartite composition probably debuted in the Rockbridge community during the Georgian stylistic period with the design of the second county courthouse (built in 1786–87 but planned in 1779), which featured a center courtroom of 30 by 25 feet flanked by 12 feet square jury rooms. Holly Hill, a brick house insured by Alexander Trimble in 1812, had a two-story center block of 32 by 22 feet flanked by one-story wings measuring 16 feet to a side. In the schematic plan that appears in Holly Hill's Mutual Assurance Society declaration, a rounded form is shown at the center of the front elevation, perhaps a semicircular entry porch. The Trimble house, now known as Springdale, was probably built ca. 1812 and had its flanking wings raised to two stories in 1914. Three-part symmetry guided the trustees of Washington College in their long-term planning and construction of the Colonnade, the row of column-fronted buildings that developed as the core of the Washington and Lee campus during the first half of the nineteenth century.[12]

The county's Federal mantels might be likened to snowflakes, with seemingly infinite visual variety superposed on simple underlying forms. Some are reserved in treatment. The tripartite parlor mantel at Cedar Hill near Mechanicsville, which may date to the 1810s or 1820s, has an uncommonly small center tablet superficially incised with a gridwork of dots and dashes. Shallow gougework dashes also ornament the end tablets and dashes and tiny crosses run in a band under the shelf. In contrast to the ethereal delicacy of the Cedar Hill ornament, mantels in the Brownsburg-area

A reeded mantel in the John Moore House.
Photo by Leslie Giles, courtesy DHR

Turned mantel ornament
at Chapel Hill.
Photo by Dan Pezzoni

James McChesney House have a muscular dimensionality. One features bowed pilasters, like squashed Greek columns, with fluted shafts and capped by thick, fluted, console brackets. Heavy stack moldings project in a cornice over the brackets and over the wide center tablet, which is adorned by a fanfold ellipse with a center button. Between the center tablet and the end brackets are rectangular frieze panels carved with fanfold paterae set into incised wells and framed by lenticular perforations. The two-story brick McChesney house is traditionally dated to 1819–22 although its mantels may be later. They may relate to a tradition of robust mantel carving seen in the Shenandoah Valley and epitomized by the dramatic three-dimensional Federal mantel in Augusta County's Seawright House.

Rockbridge carvers were fond of reeding, fine parallel ridges and grooves, which they occasionally used to create visually exciting corrugated effects. The ca. 1831 John Moore House, a two-story Federal style brick house near Denmark, has a mantel with a wide reeded band under the shelf and a reeded frame around the fireplace opening. Ornament akin to reeding appears in the early nineteenth century brick house at Mount Pleasant Farm in the Plank Road area. A mantel in the house has a band of what looks like bullet cartridges under the cornice as well as quarter sunbursts or fanfolds at the top of the pilasters. A mantel at Level Loop has pilasters striped with diagonal slashlike ornament that also recalls reeding.[13]

Another Moore House mantel has unusual vase-form turned pilasters and the room in which the mantel stands has a wainscot divided into panels by knobby turned half-spindles. Lathes for turned work were common equipage in period carpentry shops but the furniture-like turning of the Moore House mantel and wainscot is rarely seen in period architectural work outside of stair detailing since local carpenters preferred to emulate the classical aesthetic which rarely featured decorative turning.

Another rare example of turned mantel detail appears at Chapel Hill, the ca. 1842 house of Henry and Sarah Amole in the Mechanicsville area of the county. Henry Amole was a manufacturer of farm machinery known as wheat or winnowing fans. A parlor mantel in the house has circular and elliptical figures created with bowling pin-like turned elements sawn in half lengthwise and applied to the frieze (the effect is reminiscent of 1960s pop-art flowers). An upstairs mantel at Chapel Hill consists of contrasting panels of vertical and horizontal molding strips, like gratings in appearance. The unusual character of the Chapel Hill mantels may indicate the involvement of a craftsman who was skilled as a woodworker but whose design sensibility lay outside normative architectural finishwork of the era. Perhaps he was an employee in Amole's wheat fan factory or was Amole himself. Architectural detail that bears the stamp of the tools or machinery that produced it, and relies on that technological signature for its visual impact, is termed *technomorphic*. With the introduction of advanced woodworking machinery after the Civil War, technomorphic milled ornament became a defining feature of the county's domestic architecture.[14]

The Federal style passed out of favor locally in the 1840s. Like the transition from Georgian to Federal, the later phase of Federal style hybridized with the succeeding Greek Revival style, but unlike the situation earlier in the century the new style did not have the field to itself. A very different architectural aesthetic — the Gothic Revival style — vied for the attention of builders and their clients. The Gothic Revival style grew out of interest in the so-called Gothic architecture that preceded the Renaissance. Medieval castles and churches with their characteristically pointed lancet arches inspired aesthetically adventurous English aristocrats of the 1700s to ornament their country estates with "Gothick" follies, architectural sculptures that provided focal points for hilltops and vistas. Wealthy eccentrics like Horace Walpole and William Beckford, who also happened to be the authors of some of the first Gothic novels, decided they were not content merely to gaze upon their Gothic follies, they also wanted to live in them, and from country villas the style jumped to churches, a natural fit considering most Britons associated Gothic with ecclesiastical architecture. It was a church, St. Mary's Seminary Chapel (1806–08) in Baltimore, that introduced full-fledged Gothic Revival to America, and the style arrived in Rockbridge in the 1840s and 1850s with such seminal buildings as the Lexington Presbyterian Manse (1848) and the VMI Barracks (1851) roughly when the first true Greek Revival buildings appeared in the county. Though the merits of the two styles were hotly debated nationally during the period — the so-called Battle of the Styles waged by architects and pattern book authors — on the local scene Greek and Gothic appear to have achieved an amicable coexistence.

Of the two styles, the Greek Revival had a clear advantage among the county's antebellum plantation owners and wealthy merchants,

Maple Hall.
Photo by Michael Pulice,
courtesy DHR

in part because classicism was so entrenched in elite culture, but also because the style resonated with a still-young republic that looked to the classical philosophers and statesmen to invent its democracy. Rockbridge County's adopted favorite son Robert E. Lee lived for a time in one of the nation's earliest Greek Revival houses: Arlington House (1818), with its monumental portico overlooking Washington across the Potomac.

Maple Hall (1855) is a prominent local example of the Greek Revival style for its scale and refinement but also because of its visibility from the Interstate 81/US Route 11 interchange at Timber Ridge. Built for John B. Gibson, the owner of milling and distillery operations and several farms, and owned by the Lyle and McCorkle families in the twentieth century, the large two-room-deep brick house has a three bay façade indicative of the center passage plan within. The front is graced by a two-story portico with monumental columns modeled on the Doric order (the simplest of the three Greek architectural orders) and a gable roof defined by projecting cornices that create a pediment, the triangular gable of a Greek temple. The columns rise from a high masonry base that exaggerates their apparent height, and they support a balcony for a second-story entry with cruciform railing panels ornamented with lozenges and four-pointed stars.[15]

Maple Hall's interior is literally by the book, its trim and mantels taken from plates in Asher Benjamin's *The Practical House Carpenter* (1830). Benjamin was a New England house builder who published his first builder's guide in 1806. Through *The Practical House Carpenter* and other later works he popularized the Greek Revival style in western Virginia perhaps more than any other individual. A copy of *The Practical House Carpenter* is reported to have been discovered in the house during 1980s rehabilitations. The mantels at Maple Hall that are direct copies of Benjamin designs feature as their main visual motif a fretwork pattern known as the Greek key. In one the Greek key runs as a continuous frieze across a lintel supported by fluted Doric columns. In another the key appears singly at each end to cap fluted pilasters. The Greek key motif is a direct borrowing from Greek architecture but the mantels also express the Grecian spirit through their emphasis on basic geometric forms and planar surfaces, a reaction against the fussiness of the Federal style.[16]

Interestingly, though, the mantel with the Greek key pilaster caps has an essentially Federal tripartite, center frieze tablet form, another example of the melding of the Federal and Greek styles. Hickory Hill, the 1823–24 home of Reuben Grigsby in the lower Buffalo Creek area, also appears to be a fusion. Its main parlor mantel is unmistakably Federal in feel, with a tripartite form and the popular Federal elliptical motif in its center and end frieze tablets, but its planar simplicity, the definition provided by moldings rather than gougework and reeding and other tricks of the Federal finish carpenter's trade, as well as the

An Asher Benjamin-inspired mantel in the Margaret E. Poague House.
Photo by Dan Pezzoni

Hickory Hill parlor and stair. Parlor photo by Bruce Hasfurther, courtesy DHR; stair photo by H. E. Ravenhorst

smooth Doric columns that serve as pilasters, suggest either early Greek Revival influence or the possibility the mantel is later than the house.[17]

Hickory Hill's original owner Reuben Grigsby served his community in military and civic capacities as a militia captain, sheriff, member of the House of Delegates, trustee of the Ann Smith Academy and Washington College, and treasurer of his church, Falling Spring Presbyterian. He knew most prominent local citizens of his day, including the prolific builders John Jordan and Samuel Darst, the latter to whom Grigsby was related by marriage through a daughter. Though no evidence has come to light linking Hickory Hall to Jordan or Darst, Grigsby would have been familiar with their work. His ties to the community grew stronger through the marriage of his daughters to various leading families including the McCormicks whose members included Cyrus McCormick of mechanical reaper fame. The Grigsbys and their close relations were something of a community unto themselves; the refined local houses known as the Seven Hills of Rockbridge are all connected to the Grigsby family or the related Welch and Greenlee families.[18]

Stair and mantel details at Liberty Hill.
Photos (1981) by Pam Simpson,
courtesy DHR

Federal/Greek Revival blending is seen in a series of exquisitely carved mantels in the Natural Bridge-area house Liberty Hill (1836), a two-story brick residence built for Thomas Welch III and his wife, Eliza Grigsby Welch. Three of these are tripartite in composition and are also richly carved, but the carving is more Grecian in character than Federal and hence Greek Revival. The most ornate of the three features a center ellipse in the form of an eight-lobed rosette with petals inspired by acanthus leaves, the curling serrated leaves of the Mediterranean *Acanthus* plant which are depicted in the capitals of the Corinthian order, one of the three Greek orders. The mantel's pilasters are treated as columns with the cushionlike volutes of the Ionic order, another specific reference to Greek architecture. The rosette motif also appears as an ornament in the elliptical fanlight over the front entry, and it and the console brackets and grating-like frieze panels of various mantels are reminiscent of mantel ornamentation in the aforementioned house Chapel Hill (1842), suggesting Liberty Hill may have served as a source of inspiration for the later house.

Greek Revival mantels often explicitly evoke the trabeated or post-and-lintel construction of ancient Greek architecture. The frieze, the horizontal lintel element that spans the fireplace, is treated as though it is actually supported by the vertical pilasters, which consequently are given the form of Greek (or Roman) columns. The parlor mantel in the Margaret E. Poague House (ca. 1847; pictured in the preface)

Church Hill.
Photo by Sally Mann

near Natural Bridge illustrates the treatment. It is modeled on the "chimney piece" in Plate 51 of Benjamin's *The Practical House Carpenter* (1830) and has a Greek key frieze which is visually supported by fluted Doric pilasters with narrow incised necking bands and plain plinths. The proportions of the pilasters are less robust than in Benjamin's design, and they are engaged rather than full round as in the book, but otherwise the detail and the underlying trabeated form are the same. Church Hill (ca. 1848), a two-story side-passage-plan house built for Horatio Thompson next door to Timber Ridge Presbyterian Church where Thompson served as minister, has a Benjamin Asher-inspired mantel but with plain (unfluted) Doric pilasters and an unadorned frieze.[19]

Church Hill illustrates two other aspects of the Greek Revival style in Rockbridge: façade pilasters and a temple-form porch. The two front corners of the house project and are stuccoed and painted white to contrast with the red brickwork. These pilasters (also called piers or *antae*) were meant to evoke Greek columns. Façade pilasters are a defining feature of the classical revival architecture at Washington and Lee and they are seen on Presbyterian churches from the era such as New Providence, Collierstown, and Oxford, though in those buildings they are treated as part of the wall fabric (unpainted brick or painted with a red wash) rather than stuccoed and painted white to masquerade as marble columns.

By the antebellum period porches had long been an important functional and decorative element in the county's domestic architecture. Church Hill's Greek Revival entry porch features four smooth Doric columns and a clearly defined pediment. Pointed motifs like printer's ornaments of the period decorate the frieze. Similar in form to the Church Hill porch is the entry porch on the brick house at 312 South Main Street in Lexington, a part of the former public library. Though the porch is only one story, its pediment and heavy Doric columns, in this case fluted, give it a gravitas that seems out of proportion to the diminutive house. Tradition ascribes a date of 1824 to the house; if correct the porch is probably later. The Natural Bridge-area house Pleasant View, which has a transitional Federal-Greek Revival mantel and other features that may indicate construction in the 1830s, has an entry porch with vase-form turned posts on high plinths and, halved, as pilasters against the house wall. The double-tier porch at Hickory Hill (1823–24) is a fine example from the Federal period, its unfluted Doric columns an early occurrence of the literalism that became more prevalent in the Greek Revival period. An arresting feature of the porch is the elliptical medallion in the tympanum of the pediment, carved with a cornucopia and foliage. Monumental columns were sometimes added to earlier houses during the antebellum period, such as the house known as Tuscan Villa located in the South River vicinity.[20]

Monumental porticoes made grand architectural statements. An interesting mix of forms and materials distinguishes the portico at Whiteside, a two-story antebellum brick house in Vesuvius. Its two-tier portico has square brick columns in the lower tier and beautifully crafted fluted wooden Doric columns in the upper tier, the latter suggestive of Asher Benjamin influence (several mantels inside are verbatim Benjamin copies). The handrails on both tiers have graceful cast iron supports with curlicues and anthemion designs based on a Benjamin prototype. Iron presented a number of advantages for porches, among them strength,

Cornucopia carving on the portico pediment at Hickory Hill.
Photo by Dan Pezzoni

Cedar Hill porch.
Courtesy DHR

Glen Maury.
Photo by H. E. Ravenhorst

Entry fanlight in the James
McChesney House. Photo (1979)
by J. Manuel, courtesy DHR

weather- and decay-resistance, and aesthetic expressiveness, though porch supports and railings made entirely of cast iron such as seen in Richmond, New Orleans, and other Southern cities were rare in Rockbridge. Among the few surviving examples are the porch of the James Gardner Paxton House (1867) at 3 Lewis Street in Lexington and the one on Cedar Hill, a Mechanicsville-area Federal style house that appears to have received its cast iron porch several decades after original construction. The porches of each house have florid open-work supports and frieze bands; the Paxton House also features a cast iron balcony railing on the roof.[21]

Fanlights, half-round or elliptical transom windows placed over entryways, were common features of the county's larger antebellum residences. Glen Maury (ca. 1831; also known as the Paxton House) in Buena Vista, the home of plantation owner Elisha Paxton who shipped his products on the Maury River just down the hill from his house, is distinguished by its monumental Greek Revival portico but also by its multiple fanlights. Fanlights appear over its two front entries, which open onto the two tiers of the portico, and over other entries and as windows in the gables and portico pediment. The motif is repeated in the elliptical stucco panels over the large front windows on the first story. Glen Maury, now home to the Paxton House Historical Society, belonged to the last generation of county houses to typically have fanlight-form transoms—during the height of the Greek Revival period most transoms were rectangular—but elliptical fanlights were revived during the Classical Revival style around the turn of the twentieth century.[22]

The Greek and Gothic revival styles share an interesting connection in Lexington. Prominent early examples of both styles were built for a single client, the town's Presbyterian congregation. The congregation completed its Doric-columned Greek Revival church on Main Street in 1845; two years later it was planning the construction of a Gothic Revival manse. There is no indication of an aesthetic schism in the congregation, though there is evidence the building committee for the manse was aware of the novelty of the Gothic style. In 1847 committee member and early VMI booster J. T. L. Preston announced, "we hope that the architectural design, under the Gothic order, will enable us to present quite a model for imitation to other churches in the Valley."[23]

The Lexington Presbyterian Manse, completed in 1848 at 6 White Street in Lexington, is a sophisticated expression of the Gothic Revival style as applied to domestic architecture. The steep side-gable roof has an equally steep-pitched front gable, the steepness intended to reinforce the verticality to which the style aspired. Sawn vergeboards have a tendril-like sinuous form in the front gable and a scalloped pattern with trefoil pendants in the side gables. Bay windows with diamond-pane sashes, inspired by medieval oriel windows, flank

Lexington Presbyterian Manse.
Photo by Sally Mann

A Gothic Revival mantel at Roundview.
Photo by Pam Simpson

Falling Spring Presbyterian Manse.
Photo by H. E. Ravenhorst

the center entry. The porch stands on hexagonal posts, modern reconstructions of posts shown in nineteenth-century photos, and the south gable has a quatrefoil window with lancet lobes.[24]

The Gothic theme carries through to the interior; a mantel features pilasters of clustered colonnette form that imitates the nave piers of Gothic churches. The colonnettes are capped with small semi-hexagonal capitals. Not only were the exterior and interior of the manse Gothic, there is a hint that the original furnishings were style-appropriate. In 1847 the minister was told to refrain from purchasing furniture unless absolutely necessary, since "it was the design of the congregation to put into [the house] the heavier and more standard articles of household furniture." The suggestion is of ponderous pieces more in keeping with the style than the relatively lightly constructed furniture of local manufacture.[25]

As Preston's comments indicate, Lexington Presbyterians saw their new manse as a model for other congregations to emulate. It is fitting, then, that their manse was itself the product of emulation. In Rockbridge and nationwide, Gothic Revival "cottages" were inspired by the publications of Andrew Jackson Downing, a New York-based landscape architect and architectural popularizer who considered the Gothic style especially suited for rural residences. Downing promoted the style through his magazine, *The Horticulturalist, Journal of Rural Art and Taste*, and through books such as *Cottage Residences* (1842) and *The Architecture of Country Houses* (1850), the latter two publications in the collection of Lexington's contemporaneous Franklin Society library. The story of these and other architectural titles and their influence on Lexington-area homeowners and builders is related by Royster Lyle and Pam Simpson in an appendix to *The Architecture of Historic Lexington*.[26]

The Lexington Presbyterian Manse closely resembles a Gothic Revival house pictured in the July 1846 issue of *The Horticulturalist*, down to such details as the pattern of its front gable vergeboard

VMI has one of Virginia's most important collections of Gothic Revival architecture. Architect Alexander Jackson Davis prepared these studies for faculty residences in the early 1850s.
Courtesy of VMI Archives

Graining on a door at Bellevue and on a pew at Oxford Presbyterian Church. Door photo (1979) by J. Manuel, courtesy DHR; pew photo by Dan Pezzoni

and the diamond-pane bay windows. Other Gothic Revival houses in the Downing vein, or inspired by the designs of architects he published such as his friend and fellow New Yorker Alexander Jackson Davis, sprang up in Lexington in later years, houses such as the Gables (1850; 303 South Jefferson Street), Apple Cottage (1868; 6 Jordan Street), and the Pendleton-Coles House (1868; 309 Letcher Avenue). The Gables, like the Presbyterian manse, is brick, whereas Apple Cottage and the Pendleton-Coles House use a cladding material often associated with the Gothic Revival style: board-and-batten. The vertical boards and the battens that covered the gaps between them reinforced the upward-pointing verticality of steep gables, pointy finials, and lancet-arched window heads. So distinctive was the Gothic lancet arch that homebuilders could cost-effectively evoke the style by adding a single lancet window or door opening to the front of a house, and there are examples of that very strategy in Goshen and East Lexington (represented in the latter community by the house occupied by The Jefferson Florist and Garden).[27]

Hopes that the Lexington manse would inspire other Presbyterian congregations to build in the Gothic mode bore fruit in 1856–57 with the construction of the Falling Spring Presbyterian Manse in the Buffalo Forge vicinity. The story-and-a-half brick house of Gothic Revival design features a decorative front gable with a lancet-arched door that formerly opened onto a second porch tier. Inside the house, an arch-like motif with a turned pendant and brackets separates the back of the center passage, which contains the stair, from the front. In November 1856 the Lexington paper reported on construction of the manse by builders John B. and William F. Poague with John G. Pole of Lexington as "the skillful and efficient contractor for the carpenter's work." A. J. Downing's publications are considered an inspiration for the house although a specific model has not been identified. The manse has many interesting details including a Taylor's patent (1860) bronze door bell and crank. The original occupant of the manse was Rev. William F. Junkin, the son of George F. Junkin, who was president of Washington College during the Civil War, and the brother of poet Margaret Junkin Preston.[28]

Rockbridge houses of all styles and status were generally painted on the interior. Log houses with exposed logs on the interior were typically whitewashed, that is, their walls and ceilings were coated with a milky white substance consisting of lime and other ingredients.

Whitewash brightened dark rooms and gave them a cleaner, more
finished look, a deep-rooted preference also expressed in whitewash-
ing exterior siding or painting siding with white lead. Some householders applied interior whitewash annually or every few years to
cover the soot from smoky fires, candles, and lamps. Ocher, a locally
abundant iron oxide pigment, was added to whitewash to give it a
pleasing tan or yellowish color. Edward Beyer's paintings of towns
in western Virginia show buildings of the 1850s, especially outbuildings, with a yellow color suggestive of ocher-tinted whitewash. Red
ocher was used to color the hewn logs of the famous Red House,
the Borden Grant home of early settler John McDowell said to have
been built in 1737. Other coloring agents could be added to create
calcimine or "milk paint."[29]

Rockbridge County adjoins a region with a vibrant decorative painting tradition. Architectural historian Ann McCleary has documented
the tradition in Augusta County and attributes it largely to Germanic
artistic sensibilities of the kind also seen in painted chests and *Fraktur*
calligraphy, though she notes that the style spread to other ethnic
groups. German settlement in Rockbridge was lighter than in the
counties to the north and presumably played a smaller role in the
development of the county's decoative traditions.[30]

In Rockbridge, as elsewhere, painters varied in style and skill level.
Some were local artisans, others were itinerants who traveled from
county to county, even state to state, plying their trade. Most painters were able to do graining, the painting of false wood grain used
to make commonplace wood look more costly or visually interesting.

Marbled stair risers at Liberty Hill *(top)* and Church Hill *(bottom).* Liberty Hill photo by Don Hasfurther; Church Hill photo by Dell Upton, courtesy DHR

Close inspection of areas where painted historic wooden trim has chipped will often reveal evidence of earlier graining, sometimes multiple layers in different colors and patterns, for graining enjoyed a long popularity from the 1700s into the twentieth century. Most of the painters are now unknown, though the spirited graining in the John McKemy House (1829), located between Lexington and Rockbridge Baths, is inscribed with McKemy's name and the date 1839. The name and date appear to have been written into the paint while it was still wet, but it is unclear whether McKemy did the graining or whether he put his stamp on the work of another.[31]

Pam Simpson documented many examples of graining in her county survey. The early nineteenth century Brownsburg-area house known as Bellevue, which has Georgian and Federal interior features, has doors and at least one mantel that are grained, the door with a squiggle pattern created by dragging a comb through wet brown paint overlaid on a lighter base coat. The effect is not very convincing as wood grain, but then the point was to add visual interest as much as it was to suggest wood. The painter who grained the pews in Oxford Presbyterian Church (1867–69) aimed for greater fidelity. The wood he mimicked was oak, and some pew ends are patterned with flowing chains of knots that extend from the base to the scrolled top. Though the church dates to the 1860s the graining may be later, suggested both by its style and what may be an earlier white paint scheme showing through where the graining has chipped (although the white may be an underlayment for the graining).

Marbling, also known as marbleizing, was another popular form of imitative painting. Where it survives it is generally found on mantels, baseboards, and stair risers, architectural elements that in more palatial residences might plausibly have been made of marble. When photographed by Pam Simpson in 1981, the stair risers and some of the richly carved Federal-Greek Revival mantels at Liberty Hill (1836) were marbled with muted veining on a lighter ground, a convincing effect. Miranda, an antebellum Greek Revival brick house in the southwest part of the county, long associated with the Shaner family, has soft marbling like that at Liberty Hill on its baseboards but two Asher Benjamin-inspired mantels are vibrantly painted with light speckles on a darker ground, a granitic effect possibly related to graniteware cookware, which became popular in the second half of the nineteenth century.

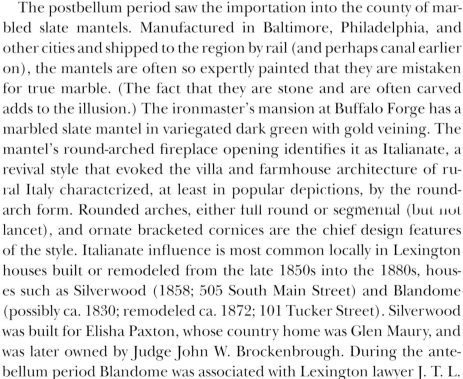

Stone blocking on the porch wall at Mount Pleasant, the ironmaster's house at Buffalo Forge, and a marbled slate mantel inside. Blocking photo by Michael Pulice, courtesy DHR; mantel photo by Dan Pezzoni

The postbellum period saw the importation into the county of marbled slate mantels. Manufactured in Baltimore, Philadelphia, and other cities and shipped to the region by rail (and perhaps canal earlier on), the mantels are often so expertly painted that they are mistaken for true marble. (The fact that they are stone and are often carved adds to the illusion.) The ironmaster's mansion at Buffalo Forge has a marbled slate mantel in variegated dark green with gold veining. The mantel's round-arched fireplace opening identifies it as Italianate, a revival style that evoked the villa and farmhouse architecture of rural Italy characterized, at least in popular depictions, by the round-arch form. Rounded arches, either full round or segmental (but not lancet), and ornate bracketed cornices are the chief design features of the style. Italianate influence is most common locally in Lexington houses built or remodeled from the late 1850s into the 1880s, houses such as Silverwood (1858; 505 South Main Street) and Blandome (possibly ca. 1830; remodeled ca. 1872; 101 Tucker Street). Silverwood was built for Elisha Paxton, whose country home was Glen Maury, and was later owned by Judge John W. Brockenbrough. During the antebellum period Blandome was associated with Lexington lawyer J. T. L.

Stone blocking in the VMI Mess Hall. Cadet quarters in the Barracks were also block painted.
Courtesy of VMI Archives

Preston, known as "Lexington's Demosthenes" for his oratorical skills, and was later owned by Jacob Fuller and occupied by politician John Randolph Tucker and his wife, Laura H. Tucker. The Italianate Buffalo Forge mantel was likely purchased and installed after the Civil War by then-owner Daniel C. E. Brady who made other upgrades to the mansion during the period.[32]

Marbled slate mantels also appear in non-domestic contexts such as Washington and Lee's Newcomb Hall, built in 1882. True marble mantels and other uses of marble were rare in the county before the period of urbanization in the late 1800s. An exception is seen in a construction detail of the ca. 1870s Hileman-Hamric Tombstone Workshop in Lexington. The simple two-story brick building, located across from the Stonewall Jackson Memorial Cemetery at 319 South Main Street, has window sills made of white marble, a material that the original owner used in his tombstone business.

Mount Pleasant at Buffalo Forge illustrates a form of exterior decorative wall painting akin to marbling known as stone blocking.

Plasterers and/or painters lightly scored fresh stucco to create an appearance of regular ashlar masonry. The scored vertical and horizontal lines were then penciled (painted with ruled lines) in white or black that contrasted with the buff color of the stucco. Pencilling was also a common brickwork finish, the mortar joints painted with white lines to make them look more regular.

The stone blocking at Buffalo Forge may be another Brady-era upgrade, and it was altered at least once when the black joint lines were overpainted in white under the front porch. Decorative painters also executed stone blocking on a wing of the 1880s house known as New Alsace, which stood on Brushy Hill near Lexington, and on Lexington Presbyterian Church (1843–45). The church was block-painted at least twice as shown in sequential late nineteenth century photographs. A photograph believed to have been taken in the 1880s and reproduced in Lyle and Simpson's book depicts a dramatic scheme of blocks painted in at least four different shades, the lightest with rippling diagonal slashes for veining. Perhaps the effect was too garish, for another, slightly later photograph shows undifferentiated blocks defined by light-colored penciling. The VMI Barracks and Mess Hall had similar multi-tone blocking on interior walls, as revealed in photos from around 1900, though the finish is likely earlier. Lee Chapel (1867) at Washington and Lee also had an early interior blocking scheme. A photograph of Robert E. Lee's body lying in state in the chapel in 1870 shows blocking with light-colored penciled joints done in such a way as to suggest arches with voussoirs over the building's round-headed Italianate windows.[33]

Marbling and graining exist side by side in the Margaret E. Poague House (ca. 1847; see photo in preface) near Natural Bridge. In one second-floor room the mantel and baseboards are painted in imitation of gold-veined black marble. To either side of the mantel are closet doors and door trim with rich maple graining in orange, red, and brown. The trim is darker and redder than the doors and the door panels are lighter than the rails and stiles. This spectacular painting was preserved by the owner, architectural historian Delos Hughes, in his recent rehabilitation of the house. Church Hill (ca. 1848) at Timber Ridge also combines graining and marbling, the graining on the center-passage doors in imitation of mahogany, the marbling on the center-passage stair risers done in light gray with divisions meant to evoke joints between blocks of stone.[34]

Painted and carved inscriptions on bricks at Cherry Hill and Liberty Hill. Photos by Michael Pulice, courtesy DHR

Painting apart from imitative treatments like marbling and graining could be either reserved or vibrant. A rehung six-panel door in the attic of Mount Pleasant at Buffalo Forge has rails and stiles in a medium shade of brown and panels in a lighter shade. Ghost impressions of HL hinges over the brown suggest the scheme is early (the house core appears to date to the early nineteenth century), and the paint is less faded where the hinges protected it. At the more festive end of the spectrum is evidence for the historic palette in the John Moore House (ca. 1831) near Denmark. The parlor trim was apparently painted yellow and cranberry red and the mantel pilasters were once marbled in gray and white. Another room had "decoratively feathered dark green and peach paint colors," according to the National Register nomination by Everett Martin and Leslie Giles.[35]

Rarest of all was figural or scene painting. A Greek Revival mantel originally from a house near Buffalo Forge Station (pictured at the front of the chapter) has an elliptical frieze panel painted with a design of leafy twigs, flowers, and fruit in shades of green, yellow, red, pink, and orange. A butterfly flutters toward a flower and a ribbon tied to a twig reads "farewell." The sentimental tableau may have been painted by an occupant of the unidentified house, rather than a professional painter.

Proud homeowners and artisans occasionally carved or painted initials and construction dates on houses, a practice that spanned the historic period. The 1797 Zachariah Johnston House is an early example of the phenomenon. A gable end date stone bears the owner's name (spelled Zechariah) and the name of the presumed stonemason, John Spear, along with asterisk and floral ornaments. Marlbrook (ca. 1790s and later; formerly known as Cherry Hill) has a brick addition with a row of bricks on which is painted "1804 / TH 12 / June / D G." The D and G, standing for owner David Greenlee, are followed by what may be fleurs de lis. Liberty Hill, built by Thomas Welch III in 1836, incorporates a brick inscribed LHEHB with a border of delicate twining leaves. Perhaps the B identified LH and EH as the builders or brickmakers, just as period tombstones were sometimes inscribed with the carver's name and the word *fecit*, Latin for "made by." S. Lyle left his name carved into a brick at Little Stono. Raphine Hall near Raphine, associated with sewing machine innovator James Edward Allen Gibbs, is also noted for its many inscribed bricks.[36]

The main part of Tuckaway (also known as the Willson House), located west of Lexington, is datable in part by "1812" painted on bricks to either side of the front entry. Dates and initials are also doodled on the house's mortar joints. People, both residents and guests, routinely wrote their names and other information on the mortar joints of masonry houses, a traditional practice that continued well into the twentieth century. The finely crafted, golden-hued prism mortar joints of the Buffalo Forge area stone house known as Vineyard Hill, which dates to the late eighteenth century, have written and inscribed initials and dates, the earliest identified dating to 1800. Though such graffiti are minor details, best studied with a magnifying glass, they tie historic houses to past generations and enrich our appreciation for Rockbridge County's architectural heritage.[37]

THREE

Town and Country

A WALK THROUGH THE HEART of Lexington, or through downtown Buena Vista or the village centers of Brownsburg and Fairfield, is likely to produce any number of impressions, but one will be a sense of underlying order. The buildings form regular rows, masses separated by the voids of the streets which are also regular. A modern resident takes this regularity for granted but it is not accidental. The spatial order that characterizes the county's historic communities is the product of urban design traditions that reach back over two thousand years.

The county's principal communities were born on paper, in carefully ruled grid plans that governed all that followed. Grid planning was a legacy of the Greeks perfected by Roman military engineers who used it to lay out everything from field camps to cities to farm landscapes. The Roman word for camp, *castra* (pl.), survives in English place names like Chester, Chichester, and Colchester, towns with roughly orthogonal street and block layouts derived from the Roman camps from which they grew. Grid planning reemerged in the Middle Ages and became the norm in the Renaissance with that era's emphasis on rationalism. When colonial Virginians established towns they based them on grids, a practice that carried over into the early national period when Rockbridge County's first planned communities were founded.[1]

The act to establish Rockbridge County out of Augusta and Botetourt counties, passed on January 12, 1778, designated a county seat

Facing page: Lexington's Main Street in an 1860s view.
Courtesy of VMI Archives

Above: Barn, Denmark vicinity.
Photo by Dan Pezzoni

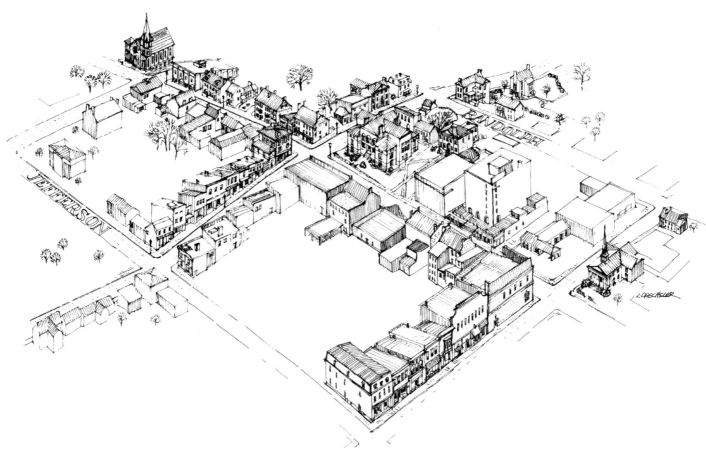

Downtown Lexington.
Drawing by Larry Drechsler from
The Architecture of Historic Lexington

"to be called Lexington" in honor of the 1775 Battle of Lexington. The town act also specified Lexington's shape and size, 900 by 1,300 feet, which suggests some idea of the town's plan existed in the minds of promoters when the act was drafted. Interestingly, the act did not determine Lexington's location. Timber Ridge was in contention, but the justices charged with the task of locating the new county seat chose a sloping ridgeline approximately a mile south of the modern East Lexington Bridge. The bridge marks the spot where the Maury (formerly North) River was crossed by the Great Road, a migration route that linked western Virginia and the Upland South with the major ports of Philadelphia and Baltimore. A narrow stream valley led travelers from the crossing straight to the new town site. At that site surveyor James McDowell fitted into the predetermined rectangle a grid of thirty-six half-acre lots so that the center axis, Main Street, followed the southwest-to-northeast trending ridgeline, the probable course of the Great Road.[2]

The Rockbridge County Courthouse (1896–97 building; to right) and other buildings on Main Street in Lexington.
Photo by Dan Pezzoni

The new town was defined on the east or Randolph Street side by Town Branch, a focus of water-intensive early industries like tanneries and potteries. Tanneries, also known as tanyards, were where tanners converted hides into leather and were well represented in the region's early towns. Lexington may have a rare vestige of the activity: the John Parry House (105 North Main Street) at the foot of the Main Street hill, an early nineteenth century brick house that belonged to tanner John Parry in the 1820s and which backs up to Town Branch where Parry's tanyard was located. Lexington's sloping Main Street and the streets that branch from it would have facilitated drainage, important for rain and snowmelt runoff and also for ridding the town of the leavings of horses and livestock.[3]

Courthouse town plans often featured specially designated public squares at central locations, set off from the common lots and usually in axial relationship to the main street. Lexington did not; the two lots chosen for the courthouse and jail were indistinguishable from other lots in size and shape, although they were located at the corner of Main and Washington streets near the center of the town. As it happened, the first courthouse, a frame building measuring 16 by 20 feet, was not built on this provisional public square but at another location. Lyle and Simpson speculate that this kept the designated site open for construction of a finer building, which ultimately occurred

Fairfield. Photos by
H. E. Ravenhorst
and Dan Pezzoni

with the building of the first brick courthouse in 1786–87. The original courthouse, adaptable in form, was subsequently auctioned off for another use. Successive county courthouses occupied the Main and Washington location, the last being the 1896–97 courthouse at 2 South Main Street. The impressive Classical Revival brick building was vacated when the present Rockbridge County Courthouse was completed on East Nelson Street in 2009 and the older building subsequently rehabilitated for offices by Washington and Lee University.[4]

Lexington's early residents typically built flush to the street, as was the practice in the towns of England and other European source regions of settlers. In aggregate this resulted in aligned building fronts that neatly defined the edges of streets and blocks and gave Lexington an orderly appearance. Order was good, a sign of economic and social stability that attracted prospective residents, merchants, and tradesmen. With the gradual replacement of small wooden buildings by large brick ones over the course of the nineteenth century, downtown Lexington presented a prosperous urban demeanor, the realization of the hopes of the town's original promoters and a character-defining aspect of the town today.

If, as it appears, Lexington was sanctioned by the legislature before details of its plan were worked out, its establishment was unusual. The county's other principal early towns — Brownsburg, founded in 1793, and Fairfield, founded in 1800 — were already laid off into lots and streets at the time of their legislative establishment. All three communities specified minimum dimensions for the buildings lot purchasers were required to build, a standard town act provision intended to discourage speculation and set the minimum amount of investment for compliance. Lexington's town trustees required lot purchasers to erect a house at least 16 by 20 feet in dimension within three years of purchase. Brownsburg required "a dwelling house sixteen feet square at the least." Fairfield, however, gave lot purchasers more latitude. The legislature empowered Fairfield's trustees "to make such rules and regulations for the regular building of houses in the said town, as to them shall seem best." Lyle and Simpson suggest the wording of Lexington's building requirements anticipated the initial construction of log dwellings, which is what happened; an account of the town in 1790 noted "about fifty houses, most of which are built of logs and boards." The reference to boards may indicate weatherboard-sided frame construction, the other standard wooden construction form of the period, or to board roofing. Lexington and Brownsburg's regulations required lot purchasers to build brick or stone chimneys, by implication ruling out the cheaper option: the wooden chimneys deemed unsafe in the close confines of towns.[5]

High Bridge Presbyterian Church. The early 1800s building shown here and the present church at the site were associated with the village of Springfield. Courtesy SC, WLU

Not all towns of the era were as successful as Lexington or the thriving market villages of Brownsburg and Fairfield. About 1797, Revolutionary War veteran John McConkey established the village of Springfield near High Bridge Presbyterian Church at the south end of the county. Springfield got off to a good start, in part the consequence of its sensible plan: forty lots along a single street (Main Street), the lots formed into blocks separated by the stubs of cross streets that could be used to extend the grid if warranted. Early businesses included a tailor shop, a hatter's shop, a wagon and rope shop, a blacksmithy, and a tavern. Jacob Siler, of German ancestry, operated a gun shop and is supposed to have made a gun stock for Daniel Boone. But according to tax records from the 1820s, the first decade during which buildings were valued separately from land in Virginia, few Springfield buildings were appraised at more than $100. The tax record evidence suggests a stock of mostly small log dwellings and workshops, relatively modest investment after a generation of development that may indicate a lack of faith in the town's long-term prospects. Springfield appeared on John Carmichael's 1883 county map but it faded in the twentieth century and was finally obliterated by the construction of Interstate 81. Springfield is Rockbridge County's closest approximation to a ghost town, although there were many smaller and more informal communities that have now vanished.[6]

Lexington, on the other hand, prospered from the advantages of the county court and two institutions of higher learning for young men, Washington College and VMI, and the Ann Smith Academy for females. The elegant female academy was built in 1808–09 on an elevated site outside the town grid, and it inspired Lexington's first suburb, the large brick houses that line the north side of Lee Avenue from Nelson to Preston streets. Several of these houses were built by the contracting firm of Jordan and Darst. The Pines (111 Lee Avenue), built in 1819 and enlarged in 1885, was the first of the Lee Avenue villas, followed by a spate of construction in the early 1820s resulting in the Barclay House (Beaumont; 109 Lee Avenue), the Rectory (Charles P. Dorman House; 107 Lee Avenue), and the Reid-White-Philbin House (105 Lee Avenue, more recently 208 West Nelson Street). The Ruffner House at 110 Preston Street also belongs to the group. Watercolor-tinted section and elevation drawings of the Reid-White-Philbin House survive, drawn by the original owner and architect of the house, Samuel McDowell Reid. To the rear of the

Reid-White-Philbin House extends a stone kitchen wing, a preexisting house dating to the second half of the eighteenth century.[7]

Houses in towns and villages, and in rural areas as well, were typically accompanied by one or more domestic outbuildings that augmented the activities of the household. Cooking often occurred in a detached kitchen which removed the mess and smell of cooking from the dwelling and also its heat. "If you don't like the heat, get out of the kitchen," as Harry Truman famously said, although more often than not the solution was to get the kitchen out of the house. Perhaps the most compelling reason for separating kitchen from house was the danger from fire. An out-of-control cooking fire might burn down a detached kitchen but spare the main house.

Of the various kitchen arrangements indicated in Mutual Assurance Society declarations from the first two decades of the nineteenth century, detached is the most common. The way detached kitchens appear in the sketch plans offers an inadvertent commentary on their construction. They are often shown small, without dimensions, and labeled simply "wooden kitchen." Whereas the house and other buildings were carefully (if schematically) drawn by the insurance agent using a straight edge, the kitchen was often sketched in freehand. Pictorial hierarchy reflected architectural hierarchy: detached kitchens were often cheaply built, expendable buildings, an inconvenience if they burned but not a calamity. At least not for the property owner though potentially calamitous for others; antebellum kitchens often doubled as residences for slave cooks and their families.[8]

The county's larger houses, especially those with working basements, sometimes had two kitchens: a detached "summer kitchen" for hot weather use and a basement "winter kitchen," the heat from which added to the comfort of the living quarters above. Some early houses contain kitchens in side wings. Such is the case at the Brownsburg-area house Mulberry Grove (ca. 1790) to which a brick kitchen wing was added, probably in the late 1820s. The lack of a direct connection to the rest of the house and the wing's brick construction reduced the threat of fire and mitigated the other negatives associated with kitchens. Front and rear porches, each with heavy chamfered porch posts, facilitated passage between the kitchen and the main house and probably functioned as adjuncts to the kitchen, open-air work areas for food preparation.[9]

Other houses with early side kitchens include the Lexington-area Tuckaway (also known as the Willson House), a two-story brick dwelling with a brick kitchen wing that retains evidence for a large cooking fireplace. Mount Pleasant and Montillico also have kitchens with cooking fireplaces. As the nineteenth century progressed kitchen wings moved from the side to the rear where they were often paired with the dining room. An early example of rear kitchen placement is seen in the Mutual Assurance Society declaration for Mount Pleasant, the three-story stone house of John McConly, which in 1803 had what is depicted as an attached, one-story, rear kitchen wing of wooden construction.[10]

Other domestic outbuildings served for food storage and processing, and of these smokehouses were among the most common. A smokehouse served for the curing and storage of hams, bacon, and the like. Preservation was often achieved by curing the meat with smoke from a fire or coals on the floor, either on the dirt or in a hearth or brazier, and because smoke rises and an even distribution was required, smokehouses typically have relatively tall and narrow forms with the meat hung from beams and hooks. Another consideration was security; smokehouses were typically constructed using materials and methods that would deter theft of the meat, and they lacked windows. Among domestic outbuilding groupings, smokehouses often stood closest to the house for convenience, to help guard the contents, or both.

Log was a common early smokehouse construction material. The smokehouse at the Buena Vista-area house Cedar Hill illustrates the type: a squarish building of close-fitting half-dovetailed hewn logs, most likely built in the first half of the nineteenth century, covered by a wood-shingled pyramidal roof. The pyramidal roof form was common and may have been more able than a gable roof to carry the load of the heavy meat suspended from its structure; or may have aided distribution of the smoke; or may have been an aesthetic decision made possible by the square form of the building underneath. Mulberry Grove also has a log smokehouse though the corners are v-notched and the roof is gabled. Wooden smokehouses, log or frame, often show a distinctive bleaching and furring of wooden structural members that have come into prolonged contact with salt, a substance used in the curing process. Salt troughs made from boards or hollowed-out logs occasionally survive in the region's smokehouses.

The fanciest smokehouses are brick, a material that added fire resistance and durability to the form and which might harmonize with stylish brick residences. Brick smokehouses often have vents in the form of holes made by omitting bricks. A small brick building with a molded brick cornice, located behind the Federal style house Raphine Hall near Raphine, probably functioned as a smokehouse as suggested by

Smokehouse, Mulberry Grove.
Photo by Pam Simpson, courtesy DHR

Smokehouse, Herring Hall.
Photo by H. E. Ravenhorst

The office and icehouse at Stono.
Photos by Michael Pulice,
courtesy DHR

the tiers of hole-vents on its front gable end. Herring Hall (early 19th c.; earlier known as Clover Hill) near Natural Bridge has a hexagonal brick smokehouse that was clearly intended to complement the handsome late Federal style main house and is probably contemporaneous with it. The Herring Hall smokehouse vents are in the form of hexagonal clusters of holes, an aesthetic decision that referenced the building's hexagonal form.

A convenient and dependable water supply was an important consideration in the siting of houses and farms. Natural springs were dug out and lined with rock, or springhouses were built near or over them. Early springhouses, used to keep dairy products and other foods cool, were often built of stone, and their simple gabled forms in blue-gray local limestone are a common sight on farms in the main Rockbridge valley. Another outbuilding type designed for cooling was the icehouse, used to store ice cut on a river or pond so that it could be used when needed in the warm months. A stone icehouse of round form with a corbeled brick cornice and a conical roof stands on the grounds of Stono (1818) at Jordan's Point.[11]

Homeowners often arranged their domestic outbuildings in rows or loose orthogonal groupings behind the dwelling. Orthogonal arrangement reflected the same desire for orderliness seen in town design, and backyard placement expressed hierarchy. The house with its often stylish front, not mundane outbuildings, was what the owner wished to present to the community. Rockbridge farms expressed an additional layer of hierarchy, the distinction between domestic and agricultural. Beyond the residence and its domestic outbuildings were the buildings where the work of the farm took place.

The Mutual Assurance Society records are the most detailed archival source for the character of Rockbridge County's early farm buildings. Some barns of the first two decades of the nineteenth century were large. Hugh Weir's Mount Hill Farm had a two-story wooden barn that measured 66 by 20 feet. Joseph Gilmore's two-story barn at View Mont Farm was comparable in size — 60 by 29 feet — with a stone

The function of this Timber Ridge area log dependency, recorded for the Historic American Buildings Survey, is unknown, though it is similar to certain 19th-century loom houses. Courtesy of the Library of Congress

The former bank barn at Chapel Hill.
Courtesy of Lorna A. Smith

first story and a wooden upper story. The elongated forms of the Weir barn and others suggest they were constructed with center drive-through threshing floors into which wagons could be driven to offload hay into the mows on the sides and where grain could be threshed to remove the chaff. The fact that some barns were described as two stories with stone lower stories suggests they were bank barns, a type of barn built into a bank so that both the upper and lower levels could be accessed from ground level. The bank barn form was ultimately German or Swiss in origin and in fact was referred to as a "swisher barn" on at least one occasion in the county. Some barns had sheds on one or more sides to serve as work areas or to shelter livestock and farm equipment. An 1860 Lexington newspaper advertisement for the Rock Castle Farm touted its "large *Shedded Barn* [with] stable room for 9 or 10 horses."[12]

Two wooden barns, one belonging to John McKee and the other to John McClure, were "covered with straw" when they were recorded for the Mutual Assurance Society: in other words, they had

A Fairfield vicinity bank barn
with a cantilevered forebay.
Photo by Dan Pezzoni

thatched roofs. The thatching seems likely to have been a survival of the common old-world British roofing technique. Around the turn of the twentieth century an anonymous photographer snapped a picture of a barn somewhere in the county with what appears to be a thatched "loafing shed" or cattle shelter extending from its side. The structure, which was supported by log posts, was similar in form to the brush arbors of the era (impermanent brush-roofed structures favored for outdoor preaching), and the thatch appears to have been held in place with poles similar to the weight poles of some forms of board roofing. The McKee and McClure barns are also interesting for their long dimensions, respectively 60 by 22 feet and 63 by 22 feet. The McKee barn was notable for having an L-shaped form with a wood-shingled wing longer than the thatched wing, and the barn also appears in a second declaration dated 1817 in which the wings are portrayed as almost abutting separate buildings.[13]

Among the county's largest early farm buildings are the barns at Hickory Hill and Buffalo Forge. The Hickory Hill barn is a superb example of heavy timber frame construction. A double row of massive hewn posts extends the length of the interior, each post rising to a complicated mortise-and-tenon joint at the equally massive cross beams. Joints are pinned with stout wooden spikes. In the haymow

The lower level of the Hickory Hill barn.
Photo by Dan Pezzoni

above, angled struts of sawn, cut-nailed wood spring from the hewn structure to support the roof. The sawn structure may be a nineteenth-century replacement of the original roof members, or it may be that lighter nailed construction was considered adequate to carry roof loads without the need for the heavy hewn framing used below. The barn has a cornerstone with the crudely pecked inscription "Wilson 1800" followed by what may be the initials WRS. Although it is possible the barn dates to such an early date, reuse of the cornerstone from another structure, perhaps an earlier barn on the farm, seems more likely, and construction of the Hickory Hill barn contemporaneous with the house (1823–24) seems plausible, although detailed examination of tax records might turn up an increase that could be interpreted as construction of the barn at another time.[14]

The barn at Buffalo Forge is unusual in that it has a brick lower level and a frame upper haymow level that projects to create a wraparound

Horse barn, Buffalo Forge.
Photo by H. E. Ravenhorst

The center drive-through is readily apparent in this view of a barn off Robinson Lane west of Lexington. Photo by Dan Pezzoni

sheltered work area on two sides. These characteristics may relate to the building's apparent use as a horse barn. The projection is supported by an assortment of posts, including one heavy chamfered upright, but the original supports, which are mortise-and-tenoned to the plates that span above them, are round log sections with tapered lower ends. The haymow shares with the Hickory Hill barn angled roof supports but in a different configuration, and whereas many of the long beams of the Hickory Hill barn are continuous members, the long hewn beams of the Buffalo Forge barn are shorter sections joined by pegged scarf joints. The barn's doors are hung on strap hinges with spade-form ends; these and other hardware items were presumably made at the farm's renowned forge.

At the opposite end of the size spectrum are the county's numerous small frame and log barns. Many early settlers favored log construction for farm buildings for the same reasons they built their dwellings from logs: ease and cheapness of construction. Unchinked log construction had the added advantage of providing ample ventilation for hay storage. Log "crib" barns were well suited for expansion into the form known as the double-crib barn: two log cribs separated by a center drive-through or threshing floor, the whole contained under a single roof.

Mountain View Farm, the Davidson-Hotinger Farm at the foot of Hogback Mountain, has a double-crib barn of v-notched log construction that may date to the ca. 1854 period of the present farmhouse or

Corncrib, Fruit Hill.
Photo by Dan Pezzoni

may be up to a half century older. Some of the logs extend to tie into the structure of surrounding cowsheds, a feature that in combination with the mortise-and-tenon frame construction of the sheds suggests they also date to before the Civil War. The Brownsburg-area Mulberry Grove farm has a v-notched double-crib log barn that may date to the first half of the nineteenth century. It too has surrounding sheds as well as half-lapped and pegged rafters. Other local double-crib log barns are pictured by Anne Drake McClung and Ellen M. Martin in their study, *Rockbridge County Log Structures* (2008).[15]

Corn was a staple of county agriculture and corncribs for its storage are still a common sight on local farms. Many up to the end of the nineteenth century (and perhaps later in mountain hollows) were constructed of logs. The gaps between the logs encouraged air flow through the piled corn. Some corncribs featured a partition that divided the interior into a small anteroom and a larger storage space behind. Details of the (probably) nineteenth century log corncrib at Fruit Hill provide clues to the function of the front space, which in this example is formed by a log partition v-notched into the outer logs. Boards with angled slots once attached to the jambs of the opening between the two spaces; the slots held boards that could be removed or added as the pile of corncobs grew and shrank with the seasons. The anteroom apparently served as a sheltered work area where the corn could be husked or shelled.

Granaries for storing wheat and other grains were also common. Their function was similar to that of corncribs, and in fact it is sometimes unclear whether early text references are to granaries or corncribs. The Mutual Assurance Society field agents recorded "corn houses" on local farms, using an adjective that may have meant corn (maize) or grain. In 1803 farmer William S. Bailey insured his wooden corn house which measured 16 by 20 feet. Since many log corncribs were built narrow to maximize the corn's exposure to air, the relatively large dimensions of the Bailey corn house may indicate it was a granary, though he may have owned a large corncrib that he valued highly enough to insure. Complicating the picture is evidence for the storage of corn and grain in the same building. The Rock Castle Farm, advertised for sale in the Lexington paper in 1860, boasted a "large double *Corn Crib* with Garners." Garners are grain bins and their presence in the Rock Castle Farm corncrib suggests the building also served a granary function.[16]

Farmers followed common-sense practice in grouping their farm buildings together for functional expediency. The most affluent farmers, those most likely to build showcase brick houses, might locate their farm buildings behind their residences for aesthetic reasons. This was the approach at Col Alto, the historic core of the present Hampton Inn in Lexington. James McDowell, governor of Virginia from 1843 to 1846, had the house built in 1827 on an eminence overlooking the town, hence the Italian name, "high hill." A main group of farm buildings, consisting of a cow barn, stables, carriage house, and corncrib, stood behind and to the east of the house; another barn and the property's extant log cabin stood behind to the south. The cabin is known to have served as a dwelling for servants; whether it dates to before the end of the Civil War and was used as a slave house is unknown, according to the National Register nomination for the property. Because of the topography of the site, these buildings (some probably built by the Tucker family, a later owner) would have been partially hidden when the house was viewed from the front. Also, Col Alto's farm buildings were downwind (given the area's predominantly westerly winds), and this placement plus the breezy hilltop setting would have reduced objectionable odors.[17]

Rockbridge farmers were always on the lookout for ways to increase yields and profits. John Alexander, the antebellum owner of the Clifton farm in East Lexington, took special care of his land, as recalled by Lexingtonian William H. Ruffner, first state superintendent of public schools. "His [Alexander's] 'Clifton' farm was one of the best and my impression is that he was considered one of the best farmers in the county. He raised big crops, and kept his land improving. His watchword was 'clover.' The contents of the barnyard went to the poor spots, and he kept the land turning under the plow." Clover was promoted by agricultural reformers of the era as a "green manure" that returned nitrogen to soils and made them more fertile. Doubtless it was Alexander's slaves who did most of the physical labor of soil amendment described by Ruffner. Agricultural lime for soil amendment was a product of the Rockbridge Lime Works developed ca. 1905 on Lexington's western edge, now the site of Lime Kiln Theater. Limestone was burned in the stone kilns of the lime works. Associated with the works were a reservoir, a stave and barrel factory, a company store, and a row of worker houses on Lime Kiln Road. At Clifton, a later owner was William Preston Johnston, a Washington

Cream separators on exhibit at the Rockbridge County Fair in the early 1900s. Courtesy RHS/SC, WLU

and Lee English professor and an early excavator of the Hays (or Hayes) Creek Mound, a prehistoric Native American burial mound in the county.[18]

"Scientific" farmers in the Alexander mold organized the Rockbridge Agricultural Society in 1827 to make "careful and diligent investigation of the many subjects with which the progress, prosperity, and operations of good husbandry and domestic manufacture are connected." Rockbridge was particularly blessed with agricultural innovators, among them Cyrus McCormick whose mechanical reaper propelled him to fame and fortune, and these men (and some women) were eager to share ideas and show off the products of their farms and gardens and their workshops as well. In 1834 the society held its first fair on Lexington's courthouse square and in 1859, reorganized as the Rockbridge Agricultural and Mechanical Society, it acquired a fairgrounds site on the southern outskirts of Lexington.[19]

"The first foot of lumber was placed upon the fair grounds on the 28th of October," remarked the *Lexington Gazette* in December 1859, and yet within a matter of weeks the fairground was ready for the four to five thousand fair-goers who descended upon it. Halls for the exhibiting of livestock, poultry, and other farm animals, as well as tents, stalls, foot walks, carriage ways, and a judging stand numbered among the facilities. By opening day the following year the organizers had set out a new track "for the exhibition of horses, which is an exact circle," with a building for the display of "articles of domestic manufacture" at the center of the track. The fair in 1860 concluded with a tournament and the awarding of silver cups to the winning "knights." Tournaments with medieval trappings were featured attractions of county springs resorts before and after the Civil War.[20]

The Lexington fairgrounds were pressed into service as a Confederate enrollment station and hospital during the war and temporary buildings erected. At the close of the war, refugee freedmen camped on the grounds. Historian David Coffey writes that the squatters were "presumably searching for work, assistance, or family members separated from them during years of bondage." The Rockbridge Agricultural and Mechanical Society was not pleased by the occupation and had the squatters evicted, the temporary wartime buildings demolished, and in 1866 held its fair, said to be the first in the South after Appomattox. New buildings were erected in 1883 and again, after the fair had lapsed for a number of years, in the 1920s. The 1920s construction included a new grandstand seating five hundred spectators with space for girls' and boys' clubs underneath, and, in 1923, permanent exhibit halls which presumably replaced tents or some other makeshift arrangement. "Show your neighbors what you have contributed toward raising the standard of farm products," the fair advertised in 1924. "Exchange ideas and contribute constructive suggestions. Study the exhibits and profit by what the other fellow has accomplished." Among the marvels on display at the 1923 fair was a green pig which, the Lexington paper noted, was "viewed with varying degrees of satisfaction."[21]

Nineteenth century Rockbridge farmers, gardeners, and orchardists consulted horticultural publications and selected from the offerings of seed suppliers. Thomas J. "Stonewall" Jackson was an avid gardener at his property on Washington Street in Lexington, purchased in 1858. According to his wife, Mary Anna Jackson, his "garden was a source of very great pleasure to him: he worked in it a great deal with his own hands, and cultivated it in quite a scientific way." Jackson relied on Robert Buist's *Family Kitchen Gardener* (1847; 1858 edition) and a garden "calendar," probably a tome like Bernard McMahon's 600-plus page *American Gardener's Calendar* (1806 and later). Jackson knew of and perhaps patronized New York City seed dealer James Thorburn, and in an April 1859 letter he mentioned eating lettuce from his "hot-bed," a special bed for keeping plants warm when there was a threat of frost. Before he was called upon to repulse Northern armies, Jackson built a fence to keep marauding chickens out of his Lexington garden. The green thumb aspect of Jackson's personality is evoked by the recreated kitchen garden behind the Stonewall Jackson House, an 1801 brick house that was Jackson's residence at the outbreak of the Civil War and is now operated as a house museum.[22]

William Hoyt photographed this county fair scene in the 1920s.
Courtesy SC, WLU

The large brick barn at Balcony Downs near Glasgow, which appears to have achieved its final form in the early 1900s, was a sophisticated farm building for its day. The remains of interior silos occupy two inside corners. Photo by Michael Pulice, courtesy DHR

After the Civil War and into the twentieth century, farm building practices from the earlier era persisted, such as the construction of small, functionally specialized buildings, but new forms and construction techniques also appeared. Mountain View Farm illustrates the mix of old and new characteristic of the period, and the story of its development is representative in many ways. The farm's earliest buildings appear to date to the Davidson family's ownership, which began in 1816. By the late antebellum period the farm produced large crops of wheat and corn on 1,400 acres of which half were improved, probably mostly cultivated, hayfields, or pasture, and the other half unimproved, likely forested mountain land. The farm workers, which census returns suggest included slave and free hands, harvested a prodigious eighty tons of hay, much of it to feed the farm's herd of eighty-five cattle. The cattle would also have foraged in surrounding woods.

The practice of free range, permitting cattle, hogs, and other livestock to wander at will through uncultivated lands, continued after the Civil War in Virginia. Some of the farm's meat went to nearby Rockbridge Alum Springs, most likely delivered to the resort on the hoof.[23]

Abraham Hotinger purchased Mountain View Farm in 1895. Trained as a blacksmith, Hotinger had served in a Confederate infantry unit until he was detailed to California Furnace (located near Rockbridge Alum) due to what his obituary described as "an urgent need for his services as a smith." After the war Hotinger made farming his main livelihood, aided by his sons. One son, Rice Hotinger, gained ownership of the farm after Abraham's death in 1903, and he continued the farm's traditional emphasis on cattle raising, herding his cattle to higher elevations in Bath County for summer grazing. Rice established a sideline weighing livestock for neighboring farmers in the farm's surviving scales house, and his interest in agricultural affairs prompted his appointment to a county Agriculture Advisory Committee and, in 1921, a stint as president of the Rockbridge County Fair.[24]

One indication of Rice Hotinger's progressive interests is his construction of an unusual interior silo in a livestock and hay barn he built in 1915. Ensilage, the partial fermentation of green fodder to preserve it for future use, was a relatively new concept in the area. The interior placement of Hotinger's tubby cylindrical silo, which is constructed of tongue-and-grooved pine staves held in place by steel hoops, protected the wood from the elements and the silage from freeze-thaw action which might reduce its quality. In later years Hotinger served as a county supervisor and it is in that capacity that he met his future daughter-in-law, Sara Lantz Hotinger, whom he and his fellow supervisors hired as the county's first Superintendent of Public Welfare in 1935. Sara Hotinger, who lived at Mountain View Farm after her marriage to Rice Hotinger's son Leonard, joined the board of the Stonewall Jackson Memorial Hospital in Lexington in 1944 and was instrumental in fundraising for a new hospital facility and in the acceptance of black physicians to the staff. Sara Hotinger was remembered as "an active champion of the rights of everybody."[25]

The barn at Mountain View Farm.
Photo by Dan Pezzoni

Boiling sorghum on the Welsh Farm. Photo (1937) by William Hoyt, courtesy SC, WLU

Mountain View Farm includes other specialized buildings such as a blacksmith shop, a corncrib/wagon shelter, and a two-story granary. Such functional diversity also characterized other period farms. The Kennedy-Lunsford Farm near Raphine, owned by the Kennedy family in the 1790s (the possible date of the house on the farm) and by the Lunsford family in the twentieth century, has a syrup house, a simple frame building where sorghum (presumably) was made into syrup for molasses. It was a hot process, which explains provisions for ventilation such as the building's roof monitor and wall vents. Collierstown had a cress packing shed adjacent to a spring-fed pool where watercress was grown. The shed housed supplies used in the enterprise, which entailed cutting the edible salad plant, tying it in bundles, and packing it with ice in barrels for shipment. The Shaner family, owner of greenhouses in East Lexington, traces back to Joseph F. Shaner who is said to have moved to the county from Pennsylvania before the Civil War to grow vegetables for the VMI mess.[26]

Commercial dairy farming got under way in the county after 1900 with peak popularity in the 1940s and 1950s and perhaps fifty dairy farms in operation during the century. Improvements in transportation and sanitation and the growth of urban markets encouraged the specialization. One dairy farm was Sunnyside near Lexington, purchased in 1926 by VMI professor James Anderson, his wife, Isabel Webster Anderson, and Isabel's sisters. The antebellum Sunnyside house survives and has been restored but the farm has been developed as the Kendal at Lexington retirement community. Another farm was McCrum's Dairy Farm on South River which supplied the milk for the soda fountain at McCrum's Drug Store in Lexington. By 1938 the McCrum Farm featured a dairy barn of modern design with a capacious ventilated haymow in the gambrel roof (the iconic dairy barn roof form of the early and mid-twentieth century), a tile block silo, and a well-lit and ventilated ground-level milking parlor with a guttered concrete floor and smooth plaster wall and ceiling surfaces for ease of cleaning. Period photos show mechanical milkers and bottling machines. By-the-regs architecture and gleaming machinery assured McCrum's customers of the safety and healthfulness of the dairy's products.[27]

Today few dairy farms remain in operation in the county. As local dairy farming researcher Louise K. Dooley notes, the milk business has virtually "evaporated." Cattle raising and the growing of corn and hay to support cattle herds dominate Rockbridge County's present agricultural economy.[28]

Sunnyside Dairy Farm. The Lexington Water Tower stands on the ridge in the distance.
Courtesy of Arthur Bartenstein

FOUR

Churches

CEDAR HILL CHURCH clings to a rocky hillside above a branch of Buffalo Creek near Murat. Built in 1874 for local black families of various faiths (though predominantly Baptist), the small log chapel is the picture of simplicity. White-painted weatherboards protect the walls from the elements and contrast with the dark green cedars that give the location its name. Fieldstones underpin the building and stand as tombstones in the tall grass behind, unlettered mementos of a graveyard abandoned within a few decades of the congregation's founding. Another graveyard was established on a separate parcel to the south.[1]

The church members improved the interior early in the following century. Beaded matchboard sheathing covered the log walls and a handsome set of scroll-top pews, the handiwork of craftsman John Bolden, replaced what were likely simple benches. The church at this time doubled as a schoolhouse and social center, the scene of ice cream suppers, picnics, and fundraising "rallies." Edlow Morrison (b. 1918) grew up in the vicinity and remembers his father hitching up the wagon and team to take his family of seven children to services. "Those that could not fit in the wagon would ride on the backs of those horses," Morrison recalls. At Christmas Eve services the children of the congregation gave recitations and received gifts of nuts and candy for a job well done.[2]

Facing page: Timber Ridge Presbyterian Church. Photo (ca. 1885) courtesy SC, WLU

Above: First Baptist Church rose window. Photo by Dan Pezzoni

Morrison was among the last generation to attend regular services at Cedar Hill. His family moved to Lexington so he and his siblings could attend the newly-opened 1927 Lylburn Downing School. Other church members moved away to avail themselves of educational opportunities or to find work. Services dwindled in the 1930s and the church sat vacant for a quarter century until an annual homecoming was established in 1965. From that date on Cedar Hill Church has been preserved as a reminder of a vibrant tradition.[3]

Cedar Hill Church, though it does not number among the county's oldest houses of worship, is nevertheless broadly representative of the simple chapels built by the early settlers. The county's historic churches are heir to nearly two thousand years of architectural development. The Christians of Emperor Constantine's time adopted the versatile Roman basilica form as a model for great churches like the original St. Peter's. The form, usually simplified to a rectangular space known as the nave, entered at one end and focused on an altar or pulpit at the other, became the norm in the Middle Ages and survives to the present. Cedar Hill owes its gable-end entry and rectangular-plan interior to these prototypes, specifically the many hundreds of British parish churches that were familiar to the ancestors of the county's European settlers and also popular among African American congregations.

In the colonial period the Rockbridge area was officially part of Augusta Parish, formed in 1738 as an administrative unit of the Church of England or Anglican Church. Whether there was an Anglican chapel within the bounds of the present county seems doubtful, however. The Episcopal Bishop William Meade (1789–1862), a chronicler of the denomination, wrote that there may have been "a church or churches" of the Anglican faith prior to 1778 in Rockbridge, "but I have obtained no information of such." The county's earliest, positively identified church buildings were erected for so-called dissenting or nonconformist congregations, principal among them the Presbyterians. The strength of Presbyterianism in Rockbridge reflects the origin of many settlers in heavily Presbyterian Northern Ireland, home of the Scots-Irish.[4]

"The pioneer church in this county was always a log structure," county chronicler Oren Morton wrote with the first Presbyterian meeting houses in mind. "It was usually succeeded by a stone building, and then by a brick." Though the evolution of county churches may not always have followed Morton's exact sequence, the trend from simple, low-cost buildings to more expensive and durable ones is borne out by church histories. Most records date the first generation of Presbyterian chapels to the 1740s. One was Timber Ridge Presbyterian

Timber Ridge Presbyterian Church: original section to right, additions middle and left.
Photo by Maury Hanson

Church, attested to in a 1748 Augusta County court order which noted that area residents had "built a Presbyterian meeting house at a place known as Timber Ridge," possibly in 1746. By all accounts the congregation's starter church, which stood about two miles from the present building, was log. Details of its plan are unknown though it was probably a basic unmodulated space, a version of the stripped-down Anglican form known as the room or auditory church which came into vogue in the old country in the early 1600s and crossed the Atlantic with the first settlers.[5]

In contrast to the paucity of information on the first Timber Ridge chapel, a great deal is known about the congregation's present building, its second. The "house of stone and lyme, for the worship of God," so called in the specifications, was erected in 1755–56. A construction bond dated June 1755 obligated John Berrisford, Robert Houston, and Daniel Lyle to build the church 44 feet long, 34 feet wide, and 15 feet to the eaves. The specifications stipulated the number and placement of entries: "two large doors, in the end of the house, and a little door, by the pulpit." A door in the south gable, reached by a stone stair, is said to have provided access for a gallery, and in fact a "balcony" is mentioned in 1789 (the building's floor level was once lower). Nine windows, four to a side and "one in the gebal [gable] end above," brightened the interior. Doors and windows were arched (a walled-up jack-arched opening is visible), the stonework was pointed (the joints between stones mortared), and the roof was constructed with collar beams, the horizontal tension members that occupy the same position as the crossbar of an A in gable construction. Tradition claims the pews were split logs and the pulpit was equipped with a sounding board to help project the words of the preacher to his listeners. Timber Ridge Presbyterian was remodeled in 1871 and 1899–1900 but its original stone construction remains very much in evidence.[6]

Another important early Presbyterian congregation was Lexington's, which began construction of its first church, a brick building, in 1797. The building was far enough along to be used for services in 1799 although some accounts state it was not completed until 1802. The church stood in what is now Stonewall Jackson Memorial Cemetery, an airy elevated location outside the noise and bustle of the downtown. Most early western Virginia town congregations built on similar peripheral hilltop sites, which recalled Christ's description of a "city upon a hill" but also had numerous practical advantages such as space for horses and vehicles and the freeing of in-town lots for commercial use.[7]

In 1834 the Rev. Andrew Reed of London visited Lexington and preached in the building. "It was placed at the head of the town," he wrote, "on elevated ground, commanding a pretty view of it, and of the fine blue mountains in the distance." The building had five doors which "in consequence of the heat of the weather" were opened to the outdoors. "There were fans in motion every where, and small kegs full of water, with ladles, were placed in the window-seats and beneath the pulpit." Reed was struck by the fact that church-goers from the surrounding countryside arrived on horseback — "the horses are nearly numerous as the people in these parts" — and he noted that a paddock was provided for the animals.[8]

Reed also left a description of Lexington's antebellum African American church, which he noted was "without the town, and placed in a hollow, so as to be out of sight." "It is a poor log-house, built by the hands of the negroes," Reed wrote. "It is, perhaps, 20 by 25 [feet] with boarding and rails breast-high, run around three sides, so as to form galleries. To this is added a lean-to, to take the overplus, when the fine weather should admit of larger numbers. There were three small openings beside the door, and the chinks in the building, to admit light and air." The description suggests a hybrid building, a log core with an open-air adjunct something like the camp meeting tabernacles and brush arbors popular during the era.[9]

A camp meeting association is also suggested by what Reed called the "anxious seat," a cleared area in front of the pulpit where about a dozen attendees knelt "with great seriousness of manner." The arrangement recalls the mourner's bench of camp meetings though, perhaps with that analogy in mind, Reed emphasized there was "no extravagance" in the worshippers' behavior. (Rockbridge Presbyterians generally disapproved of the ecstatic forms of worship practiced at camp meeting revivals.) The Englishman was moved by his experience. "This was the first time I had worshipped with an assembly of slaves, and I shall never forget it."[10]

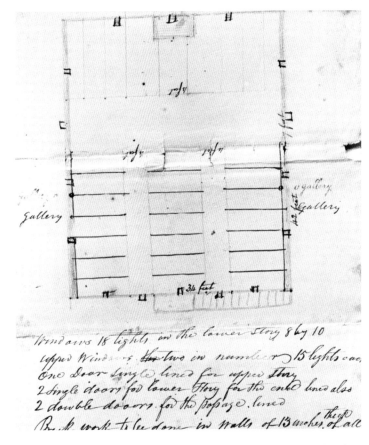

Fairfield's ca. 1818 Union Meeting House was similar in form and arrangement to many of the county's early churches.
Photo of church plan by James C. Foreman, courtesy SC, WLU

Neriah Baptist Church exterior and interior. The interior, now white, formerly featured brown paint on the chamfered posts under the galleries and ocher and later light gray paint on the walls.
Photos by Don Hasfurther and Dan Pezzoni

At its hilltop location, Lexington's Presbyterian church evolved continually over the years, as noted in session records and as documented by church historians. The brick building, extended in 1819, is described as fifty feet square with exterior stairs to an interior gallery and a sounding board over the pulpit. The original specifications are apparently lost but in 1833 the "committee on debts and repairs" made a report that implied a portion of the building was clad in lap siding and called for the building of a belfry, the procuring of new stoves and stove pipe, and the enclosing of the "church ground with [a] board fence." The construction firm of Jordan and Darst was to be paid, perhaps an indication that the work was already completed. The following year the session was permitted to "alter the Clerks seat; & to cut a door to the gallery from the inside." An 1840 reference to the "Western Gallery" suggests the gallery wrapped around the interior, a standard arrangement in period churches illustrated by the surviving gallery at the South River-area Neriah Baptist Church (1816).[11]

Double front entries like those mentioned in the 1755 Timber Ridge church specifications were popular with other denominations. The first building of the High Bridge Presbyterian congregation, a two-story meeting house, had them, as did the brick Fairfield Methodist Church built in 1842 (replaced by the present frame building in 1916). The doors of these examples were topped by transoms that admitted a little extra light into the interiors. The dual entries of the

Neriah Baptist congregation's Flemish bond brick church, built in the South River area in 1816 by John Jordan and John Moody, lack transoms. The double-entry arrangement is often explained as an indication of separate use by male and female worshippers, however there would have been other advantages such as enabling crowds of churchgoers to enter and exit without crowding.[12]

A church building was not the only recourse for religious assemblies. Before erecting its log chapel the Cedar Hill congregation met for a time under a spreading oak tree known as the Gospel Tree. A limb from the tree, which was destroyed by lightning, is preserved in the church as a keepsake. There is mention of a "pole structure" serving one early congregation, possibly a reference to a brush arbor, a semi-permanent construction of forked posts set into the ground and supporting a leafy roof of poles and foliage. Newly-formed congregations often worshipped under brush arbors or in groves until they acquired more permanent lodgings. Lexington's infant Presbyterian congregation met at first in oak groves on the outskirts of town and in 1792 raised money to purchase a tent. In the winter the congregation moved into the courthouse. It is also said to have met in the Hanna House which stood near the intersection of Main and Henry streets.[13]

Lexington Presbyterian Church with the R. E. Lee Hotel and other Main Street buildings.
Photo by Gail MacLeod

New Providence Presbyterian Church.
Photo by H. E. Ravenhorst

With the greater affluence of the antebellum era came a desire for edifices more ennobling than the plain log and masonry boxes of the early days. Classically conceived and ornamented churches were by then common in the nation's larger towns and cities and would have been familiar to area residents. Lexington's Grace Episcopal Church of 1844 is thought to be the first local church in the Greek Revival style, though it appears it was preceded by the Lexington Presbyterian Church Lecture Room, a Greek Revival temple-fronted building of religious function constructed on Main Street in 1835 (assuming the now-demolished lecture room's Greek Revival façade was original). Grace Episcopal, a brick church, stood where R. E. Lee Memorial now stands. It featured columns *in antis* (bracketed between brick stair towers at the corners) below a pediment and graceful steeple. Grace Episcopal's near contemporary, the second Lexington Presbyterian Church (1843–45; 120 South Main Street), was designed by nationally prominent architect Thomas U. Walter, whose credits include the dome of the United States Capitol. Minus the three-stage clock tower and spire—replicated after the 2000 fire that gutted the building—the Greek Revival Lexington Presbyterian Church with its uncompromising Doric portico would look at home on a rocky Aegean headland. The effect was even more pronounced in the nineteenth century when the building's stucco finish was painted to simulate blocks of massive masonry (the 1835 Lecture Room also had a faux stone finish). Walter designed another building in town: the former Rockbridge County Jail (ca. 1839) located on the courthouse square. Grace Episcopal, Lexington Presbyterian, and the other principal denominational churches to follow ranked among the finest buildings in their town and rural communities.[14]

More Greek Revival temple-form churches followed in the 1850s. Timber Ridge Associate Reformed Presbyterian Church adorned its 1856 brick church with columns *in antis* and added columns to the belfry that once perched above its temple front (the building now has a modern steeple). The New Providence Presbyterian congregation went through four church buildings—log, log, stone, brick—before completing its present brick church north of Brownsburg in 1859. New Providence features monumental white-painted Doric columns *in antis* in a projecting pedimented pavilion. The column theme carries through to the interior, to the supports under the galleries on the sides of the sanctuary and to a composition of pilasters and entablature, a flattened aedicula, on the wall behind the pulpit. From front to back the church is a series of nested temple-like spaces and frames. The Collierstown Presbyterian congregation, formed in 1842, hired Botetourt County brick mason Andrew J. Champ (or Champe) and Lexington carpenter James Archibald to erect its somewhat unusual church building in 1854–56. The building is cubical in appearance, capped by a pyramidal roof that rises to a louvered belfry. The elevations are articulated by wide pilasters which, on the front, neatly frame twin entries.[15]

The architect of New Providence is thought to have been Presbyterian minister Robert L. Dabney, the son-in-law of the church's minister at the time of its construction, James Morrison. Dabney designed the architecturally similar Tinkling Spring Presbyterian Church in neighboring Augusta County, completed in 1850, where he served as minister and which he described as "plainest Doric denuded of all

Oxford Presbyterian Church.
Photo (1909) courtesy SC, WLU

ornaments." There is some suggestion Dabney influenced the design of Timber Ridge Associate Reformed Presbyterian Church (1856), located a short distance from the 1755–56 stone church. Dabney drew a floor plan, roof section, and pedimented Greek Revival elevation study that were provided to Rockbridge County's Lebanon Presbyterian congregation in 1872 for use in the construction of its new church, though in the end the congregation opted for another design.[16]

Whoever the architect of New Providence may have been, he relied on church designs published by Asher Benjamin in his *Builder's Guide* of 1839. A notable feature of the building is its false windows. The perpetually shuttered windows at the front corners of the side elevations have only brick behind them. True windows were unnecessary at those locations since the stairs to the gallery rise behind them, but the architect felt windows needed to be suggested to complete the regular rows of side-elevation windows. False windows are also a feature of the 1844–45 Campbell House in Lexington (101 East Washington Street), headquarters of the Rockbridge Historical Society.[17]

Galleries enhanced the utility of the larger churches by providing space for more seating, and the way in which they were detailed often related to the architectural scheme of the church. Neriah Baptist's galleries are supported by thick chamfered posts with more slender turned posts above. The workmanlike treatment of the posts is in keeping with the austerity of the building and does not express a specific style. According to tradition, Neriah's galleries were used by slaves, a common arrangement before the Civil War. In Greek Revival churches the galleries typically received a characteristically classical treatment. Grace Episcopal's galleries stood on round columns, and though the specific order is unknown, the fact that the columns were round in section suggests they were Greek in inspiration in keeping with the building's Greek Revival style. The galleries had stepped floors so that people in the back pews could look over the heads of those in front for a better view of the proceedings in the space below. The front gallery of the church had space for an organ and twenty-five choir members. The gallery of the original 1797–1802 Lexington Presbyterian Church provided seating for slaves but it was altered in 1840 "to afford larger accommodations to the Cadets of the Virginia Military Institute and the Students of Washington College, and other persons

Falling Spring Presbyterian Church ca. 1900 and in 2013. *Historic view courtesy RHS/SC, WLU; modern view by H. E. Ravenhorst*

Gothic and Greek revival tabernacles behind the pulpits of Falling Spring Presbyterian Church *(above)* and New Providence Presbyterian Church *(right)*. Black and white photo courtesy DHR; color photo by H. E. Ravenhorst.

who have no regular seats in the church." Pews in the county's Presbyterian churches were often assigned to paying church members.[18]

Though county Presbyterians embraced the Gothic Revival style for manses—for example the Lexington Presbyterian Manse (1848) and the Buffalo Forge-area Falling Spring Presbyterian Manse (1856–57)—they at first neglected the style for their churches, despite Gothic's ecclesiastical associations. That changed with the construction of a new Gothic Revival Falling Spring Presbyterian Church by contractors John and William Poague who began work on the building in 1862 (some accounts state 1859 or 1860) and had it ready for dedication in 1864. The brick Falling Spring church has windows topped by lancet arches, the telltale arch form of the style, and a battlemented center entry and bell tower with corners defined by brick piers that rise above the roof in simplified reference to the buttresses

Churches

and pinnacles of medieval church architecture. The building's battlements and pinnacle-like features may have been inspired by the 1847 Smithsonian Institution in Washington, D.C., a design that influenced other area churches in the early postbellum period, namely Lee Chapel (1867) and First Baptist Church (1871 building; no longer extant), both in Lexington. The economic strain of Falling Spring church's construction during the Civil War is reflected in the arrangements for renting pews; cash-strapped members were charged in corn instead of money.[19]

Falling Spring is staunchly Gothic but it shares an oblique kinship with its Greek Revival contemporaries. On the pulpit wall is a

New Monmouth Presbyterian Church. The platform in the foreground may be for mounting and dismounting horses. Courtesy RHS/SC, WLU

tabernacle/aedicule, not of classical pilasters but lancet arches and pinnacles, and the gallery railings are paneled as at New Providence and Oxford Presbyterian Church (1867–69) but with a lancet motif rather than rectangular panels. Also of note is Falling Spring's brickwork, a rare "double-header" variant of Flemish bond: two headers between the stretchers instead of the customary one, in alternating courses. The bond may be otherwise without precedent in Virginia.[20]

Another early church in the Gothic vein is New Monmouth Presbyterian (1883), located in the Kerrs Creek area. The steep-gabled brick building is helpfully dated by projecting bricks at the apex of the front gable, above a trefoil vent, which form the numerals "1883," although there is some evidence the church is older and was heavily remodeled. Buttresses line the sides and front, positioned between door and window openings where they serve a true structural function as props for the walls. Paved weatherings, the sloping brickwork that caps the buttresses' double steppings, relate the features to medieval prototypes. Like Falling Spring, New Monmouth's windows are lancet-arched, and an old photo suggests a decorative aspect to the glazing, perhaps something as simple as translucent paint (Falling Spring's original window glass may have had a similar treatment). New Monmouth's front entry opening rises into the gable in the form of a tall transom cut into geometric forms by interlacing tracery. The lofty entry/transom gives the façade an upward-pointing verticality, leading eyes (and thoughts) heavenward—the hoped-for effect of Gothic Revival church architecture.

Among American denominations the Episcopal Church was an early champion of the Gothic Revival style. In this the denomination took its cue from its British counterpart, the Anglican Church, which preferred the style over others by the early nineteenth century. The Gothic Revival style emphasized Anglicanism's roots in medieval devotion and hence was popular with Episcopalians who valued the same tradition. Early Gothic churches in America have a superficial quality, the style appearing pasted on, but by the 1840s architects like Boston's Richard Upjohn had perfected a more academic or "correct" approach that paid authentic homage to medieval prototypes.

No wonder, then, that when the erudite parishioners of Lexington's Episcopal parish sought to replace their undersized 1840s Greek Revival church after the Civil War, they and their architects gravitated toward Gothic antiquarianism. The architects were at first

Ephraim F. Baldwin and Bruce Price of the Baltimore firm Baldwin and Price but the project was seen to completion by another Baltimore architect, J. Crawford Neilson. Robert E. Lee's death in October 1870 served as the catalyst for the new church, which was conceived as a memorial to him, although the decision to build anew was not made until 1871 and the decision to use stone, a defining feature of the building, was not made until the following year. A description of the plans published in June 1873 suggests the concept had achieved more or less its final form. Contractor E. J. Leyburn and "foreman of the masons" Matthew Sullivan set to work but fundraising woes delayed completion until the mid-1880s.[21]

R. E. Lee Memorial
Episcopal Church.
Photo by Carol M. Highsmith,
courtesy of the Library of Congress

R. E. Lee Memorial Episcopal Church (123 West Washington Street) is a work of considerable distinction. Like the local Gothic Revival churches that preceded it, the building is based on the nave plan and relies on lancet arches and wall buttresses to convey its style. The stonework, however, departs from local precedent. The blocks, rather than being smoothly tooled, are quarry-faced with a rough finish in keeping with the antiquarian theme. And whereas Falling Spring and New Monmouth are symmetrically balanced in composition, R. E. Lee is boldly asymmetrical, its offset corner tower a pile of ascending stonework with elaborately stepped corner buttresses and an octagonal belfry and spire.

The dramatic exterior is matched inside. A hammer-beam roof of carved and stained wood spans the nave, each bent supported by curved crucks that spring from stone corbels on the walls. In the lancet-arched chancel is displayed, like a jewel in a setting, a large stained-glass window divided by tracery into interlocking trefoil and cinquefoil forms (the three- and five-lobed shapes of Gothic ornament). Stained glass, also in the front rose window and the nave and accent windows tucked about the building, was something relatively new in the county's church architecture. Earlier generations of Protestants preferred clear glass for their windows, a practical and

budgetary expedient but also a legacy of the Reformation. Protestant iconoclasm, the destruction of medieval stained glass church windows and other material culture that smacked of "popish idolatry" decimated the British stained glass industry in the 1500s and 1600s. Stained glass was integral to the effect Gothic Revival church architects wished to achieve, however, and in the nineteenth century glass firms proliferated in Britain and, eventually, in America.[22]

As R. E. Lee Memorial neared completion, the vestry formed a committee to supervise the installation of stained glass windows, mostly memorials to major donors, Civil War dead, and venerated parishioners such as Robert and Mary Anna Custis Lee whose window occupies the place of honor in the chancel. The window committee commissioned the Lee window from Edward Colgate of the prestigious New York City glassmaker Sharp and Colgate. The vibrantly hued window features Christ with angels at his sides and cowering Roman soldiers at his feet, and its dedicatory inscription includes the line "Numbered with thy saints in glory everlasting." At churches like R. E. Lee Memorial, memorial windows were installed over time as donors stepped forward. At other churches, like Bethany Lutheran north of Lexington, stained glass windows were ordered in one go, in the case of Bethany from the B. F. Biehl glass firm of Audubon, New Jersey.[23]

Episcopal congregations sprang up in county boom towns of the late nineteenth century and, like the Lexington congregation, chose Gothic Revival for their churches. Buena Vista's Christ Episcopal Church (ca. 1890) features lancet windows with diamond panes and ornate pierced detail in its belfry vents. Glasgow's Episcopal congregation, St. John's, was established in 1886 before the inception of the town and met at first in a chapel on the Robert Echols farm. The

Beechenbrook Chapel was built in 1873 for workers at Jordan's Point as an outreach mission of Lexington Presbyterian Church. The gable vent combines three lancet forms in a pinwheel design. Falling Spring Presbyterian Church has a similar design in its tower window.
Photo by H. E. Ravenhorst

The Rev. Lavert Taylor bids farewell to churchgoers at First Baptist Church.
Photo by Carol M. Highsmith, courtesy of the Library of Congress

congregation's second church, a finely detailed brick building with a corner entry tower and a large lancet-arched front window that incorporates a rose window motif, was built between 1895 and 1900 during the slow revival that followed Glasgow's near extinction in the early 1890s. According to tradition, St. John's was constructed of bricks salvaged from an abandoned factory.[24]

By the early twentieth century most of the county's newly constructed town and rural churches bore the mark of Gothic Revival influence. Lexington's First Baptist congregation, within thirty years of its organization in 1867, completed one of the town's most distinguished landmarks, the loftily-steepled First Baptist Church at 103 North Main Street. The congregation erected a log chapel which it replaced with a frame church before hiring Lexington builder E. N. Bogher (or Boogher or Booker) to erect its present brick building in 1894–96. Construction was a joint effort. "Men of the congregation," writes one church chronicler, "friends, and paid laborers worked nights while women held lanterns and brought baskets of food." Ranks of lancet-arched windows, filled over the decades with commemorative stained glass, line the sides of the nave and a rose window with brilliant blue and gold glass decorates the street front, echoed by round windows in the corner tower, with an ornamental weathervane at the tower's top. The interior is spanned by a barrel-vaulted ceiling with molded wood ribs and beaded matchboard finish.[25]

Gothic influence might be subtle, a thin overlay on otherwise vernacular structures. Triangular window heads, inexpensive to construct, approximated curved lancet arches. Otherwise plain entry and bell towers betrayed their Gothic sympathies by off-center placement. Some churches started out relatively plain and evolved toward complexity. Bethesda Presbyterian Church in Rockbridge Baths, for example, began with a simple nave-plan brick sanctuary in 1876, its chief decorative feature a pair of tall segmental-arched entryways on the front. A 1909 remodeling walled up the entries and added in their stead a corner entry tower with an arcaded belfry. The round arches in Bethesda's belfry may have been intended to harmonize with the rounded arches of the original building and additions, or they may reflect the influence of the Romanesque Revival style, which like the Gothic Revival was based on medieval precedents. The same Romanesque stylistic impulse is seen in Lexington's Trinity United Methodist Church (1926; 147 South Main Street) with its arcaded porch, round and segmental-arched windows, and vaguely Italian campanile-like main tower.[26]

A Gothic Revival corner tower graces Bethany Lutheran Church.
Photo by Michael Pulice, courtesy of DHR

Bethesda Presbyterian belongs to a group of Rockbridge County Presbyterian churches that were built with or obtained arcaded porticos during the nineteenth century. The idea appears to have started with Timber Ridge Presbyterian which acquired a three-arched front in 1871. Lebanon Presbyterian, as built, also had three arches, and Bethesda originally featured two somewhat ungainly arches. In each church the arches formerly opened into open-air porches but they have been enclosed in various ways. The interest in round arches may have come from Lee Chapel, built facing the Washington and Lee Colonnade in 1867 and notable for its round-arched Italianate entry and windows. Lee Chapel was designed by VMI engineering professor Thomas Williamson who may have been inspired by John Renwick's design for the Smithsonian Institution (1847). The Smithsonian Institution, an early American example of Romanesque influence (blended somewhat with Gothic and Italianate), was published in a pattern book available in the Franklin Society and VMI libraries in Lexington. (Falling Spring Presbyterian

St. John Methodist Church *(left)* and Christ Episcopal Church *(right)* are two representative Gothic Revival churches in Buena Vista.
Photos by H. E. Ravenhorst

Church may also have influenced Lee Chapel.) The Smithsonian-Lee Chapel vector headed in an additional direction, to First Baptist's 1871 building which formerly stood next to the present 1894–96 church. The 1871 building featured round-arched windows and a center tower with a finial-spiked concave pyramidal roof like Lee Chapel's.[27]

Church towers were a favorite focus of the gingerbread ornament so cherished by the Victorians. Immanuel Presbyterian Church (1879), located in the north part of the county, has a tower capped by a wood-shingled gabled element flanked by Gothic-inspired pinnacles. Angled façade projections, another staple of the era, served as apses at the ends of naves or simply enlivened an otherwise straight-laced exterior. Such is the case with two congregations of different denominations but the same Biblical name: Ebenezer Associate Reformed Presbyterian Church west of Lexington and Ebenezer United Methodist Church in Rockbridge Baths. The congregations not only share the same name, but their buildings share the same plan, with a broad angled front projection flanked by entry towers with pyramidal roofs. The Presbyterian Ebenezer was built first (1898–99) followed by the Methodist Ebenezer in 1908.[28]

Fashions changed again in the early twentieth century when local congregations and their builders rediscovered classicism. Lexington's Manly Memorial Baptist Church (202 South Main Street), designed in 1917 and completed in 1920, is loosely modeled on the Roman Pantheon with a probable boost from the University of Virginia Rotunda, also inspired by the Pantheon. Richmond architect Herbert Levi Cain gave Manly Memorial an Ionic portico, round-arched windows, and a dome on an octagonal base. The Roman Maison Carrée in France or its image, the Virginia State Capitol, may have been on the mind of the architect for Buena Vista Baptist Church (1926–27; 2174 Chestnut Avenue). Broad steps rise to a commanding portico on Doric-inspired columns. The triple entries behind are surmounted by pediments and have Roman reticulated patterns in their door panels. At Buena Vista Baptist's dedication in 1927 a local newspaper lauded the building for its "strict adherence to the classical simplicity and restful grandeur handed down by Greek and Roman precedence."[29]

Same name, same design: Ebenezer Associate Reformed Presbyterian Church *(top)* and Ebenezer United Methodist Church *(immediately above)*. Photos by Dan Pezzoni and Don Hasfurther

Buena Vista Baptist Church. Photo by Dan Pezzoni

Tiffany, the glassmaker whose name is associated with excellence, supplied this circular stained glass window for Bethesda Presbyterian Church, probably in conjunction with a 1909 remodeling. Christ Episcopal Church in Buena Vista also has a Tiffany window. Photo by Maury Hanson

A marbled glass window on the front of the Stone Church of the Brethren in Buena Vista. Photo by Dan Pezzoni

By the mid-twentieth century Rockbridge congregations could choose between two basic stylistic approaches, historicism or modernism. Lexington's St. Patrick Catholic Church (219 West Nelson Street) went the traditional route. After World War II the parish outgrew its 1873–74 building, located in the working-class neighborhood on the east side of the downtown, and acquired a site for a new building on US Route 60 West, then one of Lexington's principal automobile entryways. The Philadelphia architectural firm Gleeson and Mulrooney designed a broad nave-form building of concrete block faced with Catawba sandstone. The church, completed in 1953, is a near twin of Huntington Court Methodist Church in Roanoke, suggesting either reuse of the plans or close copying. In addition to the buttresses and lancet arches of the Gothic Revival style, ranks of lancet-form laminated Douglas fir trusses span St. Patrick's interior, an old form in a new material.[30]

Buena Vista's Church of Jesus Christ of Latter-day Saints (Mormon) congregation also chose a traditional approach. In 1953 the congregation dedicated a Colonial Revival brick-veneered church that was an almost exact duplicate of a church in Tarboro, North Carolina. The building features a tall and deeply recessed segmental-arched entry, round accent windows on one side elevation, and a recreation hall wing with (formerly) a front porch on the other. According to a period newspaper report, the chapel was separated from the recreation hall by "soundproof doors which when opened doubles the seating capacity." Such auxiliary spaces that could be combined with or separated from the sanctuary by hinged or sliding doors were a common feature of church planning beginning around the turn of the twentieth century. The architect and contractor for the Buena Vista Church

Good Shepherd Evangelical
Lutheran Church exterior
and interior. Photos by
Dan Pezzoni

of Jesus Christ of Latter-day Saints was Frank Leake, a Mormon from
Richmond, assisted by Meredith J. Ramsey of Buena Vista.[31]

Lexington's Lutheran congregation opted for a modern approach,
tapping Charlottesville architect Milton Grigg to design Good Shepherd Evangelical Lutheran Church (1963; 617 South Main Street)
in the modern idiom. Grigg's arresting composition, built by W. W.
Coffey & Sons, employs a monumental cross to support a projection
of the gable roof over the front entries. Gridded honeycomb windows
flank the altar end of the sanctuary, their colored glass rich with sym-
bolism: purple for the emptiness of the human condition without
God, red for God's grace, and "an effulgence of yellow" to represent
the "Christ event." As with the best of modernist design, inspiration
extends to the detail level, seen in the front door handles which are
made in the form of the chi-rho, the anagrammatic Greek letters that
stand for Christ. Good Shepherd, though a harbinger of the modernist style in local church construction, is essentially a nave-plan church,
a testament to the enduring power of tradition in the county's religious architecture.[32]

FIVE

Schools

"THE ABILITY TO READ THE BIBLE and the catechism was almost an axiom in the Presbyterian practice," historian Oren Morton wrote in his lead-in to the history of education in Rockbridge County. John Knox, a founder of the denomination in Scotland, was a firm believer in education. "For as the youth must succeed us," he wrote in the *Book of Discipline* (1560), "so we ought to be careful that they have the knowledge and erudition to profit and comfort that which is most dear to us." The Scots-Irish brought this zeal with them and there is record of Presbyterian schools in the Valley of Virginia by the end of the 1740s and within the borders of present-day Rockbridge by the 1770s. Mount Pleasant School, a precursor of Washington and Lee University, was established near Fairfield by 1773. (A school in existence in Augusta County in 1749 is traditionally cited as the original precursor of Washington and Lee but in recent decades several researchers have questioned the association between the institution, known as Alexander's School, and the Fairfield school that developed into the university.) In 1774 the Presbytery of Hanover provided support to the Mount Pleasant School to help it train ministers for the region's Presbyterian congregations. Princeton graduate and Presbyterian minister William Graham took the helm as rector of the school. Graham upgraded the curriculum, transforming the school into an academy modeled on the Presbyterian-affiliated College of New Jersey at Princeton.[1]

Facing page: The VMI Barracks from the Parade Ground. Photo (ca. 1900) from the Miley-Burns Collection courtesy Sally Mann and SC, WLU

Above: A wrought iron boot scraper on the Colonnade, W&L Photo by Dan Pezzoni

Liberty Hall Academy, photographed
by Michael Miley and as reconstructed
to its conjectural original appearance
by Larry Drechsler. Photo
courtesy SC, WLU

In 1776 Graham moved the program to Timber Ridge where local
Presbyterians had erected their stone church in 1755–56. The move
came with the blessing of the Hanover Presbytery which met at the
church in May 1776 and considered the location "convenient" for a
school. An offer of land by Alexander Stuart and Samuel Houston
(father of Sam Houston of Texas fame) to support the school swayed
the Presbytery's decision, as did subscriptions from Timber Ridge-
area residents and an offer by those residents to build "a hewed log-
house, twenty-eight by twenty-four feet, one story and a half high" for
a schoolhouse. With the move came a new name: Liberty Hall. Recent
events at Concord and Lexington, Massachusetts, presumably influenced the choice of the name, although it is said that Liberty Hall was
also the name of a house in Ireland that was the ancestral family home
of the Rev. John Brown, head of the school prior to Graham. With
the economic dislocations of the American Revolution, the school's
prospects dimmed and in 1779 Graham suspended the program and
moved to Mulberry Hill near Lexington in order to support his family
through farming. But he continued to teach, boarding a few students
in his home. In 1782, after the American victory at Yorktown, Graham

and two neighbors donated acreage for a campus near Mulberry Hill and erected a small frame academy building, the concrete beginning of the Lexington association for what would become Washington and Lee University.[2]

A second frame academy, 24 by 16 feet, followed in 1783. The second building burned in 1790 and was replaced in 1793 by the impressive stone building now known as the Liberty Hall ruins. The architectural evidence of the ruins, coupled with detailed specifications in the school records, permitted Lyle and Simpson and artist Larry Drechsler to create a drawing that shows how Liberty Hall might have looked before it burned in 1803. It was a three-story building approximately 34 by 42 feet in dimension with a cupola or belfry at the apex of its hipped roof. Chimneys rose at each of the four corners — their segmental-arched fireplaces are still visible — with neatly finished stacks above the roof line that appear to have been crowned with stone moldings, a refined detail. Lyle and Simpson noted Liberty Hall's similarity to the first Kentucky Statehouse, a 1793–94 stone building of similar proportions which, like Liberty Hall, featured a five-bay façade, two windows to each side of a center entry. Enough of the interior plasterwork shows in a late nineteenth century photograph of the ruins to deduce that the academy had a two-room-deep center-passage plan, the plan of the large and architecturally sophisticated plantation houses and many civic buildings of the era. Chair rails crossed the walls at hip height and high mantels, presumably of paneled Georgian design, decorated the fireplaces.[3]

The outer corner placement of the fireplaces was another feature that linked Liberty Hall to elite domestic construction. Outer corner fireplaces were a rare local treatment documented by Lyle and Simpson only in the 1780s Alexander-Withrow Building and the contemporaneous Moore House which survives in ruinous condition a mile west of the academy. The fireplaces are angled, a somewhat more common feature in the region's domestic architecture. Washington and Lee has stabilized Liberty Hall to slow its deterioration, but part of the building's enduring presence owes to the skill of its builder, Rockingham County stone mason William Cravens. Cravens was also a Methodist minister known as the Son of Thunder for his fiery preaching. Anecdotes of his life suggest he was also a roof framer so he may have been involved in that capacity at Liberty Hall as well.[4]

Archaeological remains thought to be the Liberty Hall stable with the academy ruins beyond. Photo (ca. 1976) courtesy of the Laboratory of Anthropology, Washington and Lee University

Liberty Hall formed the nucleus of a small campus, a cluster of buildings documented in construction contracts and other sources. The 1799 Rector's House, for example, was a two-story brick dwelling on a stone foundation with a "handsome dentil cornice." The detailing and use of brick suggest it was one of the better Georgian houses in the county at the time of its construction. Louisa Baxter (b. ca. 1820), the daughter of George A. Baxter who came to head the academy in 1799, recalled that the library was kept in the Rector's House "as the Academy [stone building] was very much crowded." In the 1970s Washington and Lee archaeologists discovered a foundation that agrees well with the house's 20 by 25 foot dimensions.[5]

The archaeologists' investigations also revealed a stone foundation for a relatively large building which is thought to have been the Steward's House, built in 1793 along with the academy building. The building had fireplaces at each end of a brick-paved cellar. One of the fireplaces was seven feet wide, the size of the era's capacious cooking fireplaces, which may indicate meals for the students were prepared and eaten in the building (the school had very few students at the time). The stonework is similar to that of the Liberty Hall ruins which suggests contemporaneous construction by William Cravens. An approximately 68 by 21 foot stone foundation, dubbed Structure 1 by the archaeologists, may represent the remains of the academy's stable, constructed in 1800. The building's proportions are commensurate with barns described in Mutual Assurance Society declarations of the period. The school abandoned the Liberty Hall campus for academic use after the fire of 1803 and moved to the present Washington and Lee campus, more convenient to town.[6]

The small wooden academy buildings that preceded the stone building at Liberty Hall were probably representative of the county's early schools, those that operated separately from churches. Details of one of the earliest, the 1753 Campbell Schoolhouse near Lexington, are sketchy, but something is known about others from the Mutual Assurance Society records. In 1802 William Tidd insured a one-story wooden schoolhouse in Lexington that measured 20 by 30 feet. Three years later Hugh Wilson insured another, a one-story wooden building of 16 by 20 feet located on Washington Street. As the descriptions in the insurance declarations suggest, these were simple buildings. Their plainness is illustrated by a slightly later schoolhouse, from 1819, which formerly stood beside Randolph Street Methodist

Church in Lexington. In enlarged form the gabled and weatherboard-sided frame building served as the town's African American schoolhouse from 1865 to the 1920s.[7]

Amazingly, a school from these early days survives. The Hamilton Schoolhouse, built in 1823, stands on the bank of South Buffalo Creek in the sparsely settled southwest corner of the county. The one-story building measures 22 by 24 feet and is constructed of hewn yellow poplar logs joined with half-dovetail notches at the corners. Hamilton Schoolhouse received assistance from the Literary Fund, established in 1810 to provide state money for schools, and was built to educate the children of Robert Hamilton, who gave the land for the building, and his neighbors. William H. Letcher, the brother of Robert Hamilton's wife, Sally Letcher Hamilton, is said to have been the builder. The schoolhouse is an example of what was once known as a "field school," shortened from "old field school" with the suggestion that these simple public or "common" schools were built on exhausted cropland considered no longer fit for cultivation. In 1838 Hamilton Schoolhouse would likely have been one of the forty-four common schools reported in operation in the county. When Virginia established its modern public educational system in 1870, Hamilton Schoolhouse made a smooth transition and it served as a public school until it closed in 1928. Michael Pulice noted in the National Register nomination for the schoolhouse that it is "the last of the old log field schools built before the Civil War in the area" and it appears to be one of the few to survive in the state.[8]

Hamilton Schoolhouse. Photo by Michael Pulice, courtesy DHR

The most prominent local educational developments of the nineteenth century were the growth of Liberty Hall into Washington College (later Washington and Lee University) and the establishment, in 1839, of the Virginia Military Institute. In 1798 Liberty Hall's trustees changed the name of the school to Washington Academy in recognition of a previous gift of $20,000 worth of James River and Potomac Canal Company stock shares from George Washington. They used the financial infusion to construct three buildings: a steward's house and twin classroom and dormitory buildings, Graham Hall and Union Hall, two-story brick buildings completed in 1804. Construction of the imposing Center Building, the present Washington

Old George gazes from his perch on Washington Hall at the center of Washington and Lee University's Colonnade. Photos by Sally Mann

Hall, followed in 1822–24. The three-story brick edifice, fronted by a classical portico, referenced through its architecture the classical ideals that were the paradigm of higher education during the era. In 1831 the school built Payne Hall, originally known as the Lyceum, to the left of Washington Hall, followed in 1840 by Robinson Hall on the right to form a tripartite symmetrical arrangement. In 1842 two-story hyphens connected the three buildings and the Washington and Lee Colonnade essentially achieved its present appearance. "No more impressive expression of the educational ideals of the time could be imagined than this Classic group," wrote Talbot Hamlin of the grouping in *Greek Revival Architecture in America* (1944), "its pediment and orders seen through embowering trees, over swelling American lawns, its cupola crowned with the image of the *Pater Patriae*." The cupola, modeled on the Tower of the Winds in Athens, was an 1840s addition to Washington Hall, and the image of the Father of the Country was Old George, the statue of George Washington carved by local cabinetmaker Matthew Kahle and installed in 1844. The present statue is a replica; the original is displayed in the Special Collections of Washington and Lee's Leyburn Library.[9]

In counterpoint to Washington and Lee's classical orders are the Gothic battlements of Virginia Military Institute. At first VMI bore no resemblance to the school of today. When it opened in 1839 with twenty-five cadets it occupied the former Lexington Arsenal on the high ground between Washington and Lee and Jordan's Point. Major John Staples, superintendent of the state arms factory in Richmond, designed the arsenal and Lexington's John Jordan built it in 1816. The arsenal stockpiled munitions for the defense of the western part of the state and was an impressive if somewhat forbidding complex. It was "a large and substantial brick building, in the center of a small courtyard," wrote Francis H. Smith, first VMI Superintendent, in 1839:

> In front were the soldiers' barracks, embracing a small two-story brick building in the center, with five rooms; and two wings of one-story each having two rooms. The sally-port was closed by a large iron-bound gate, and the court was enclosed by a brick wall fourteen feet high. The windows of the first story of the barracks were guarded by substantial iron bars; the whole establishment presenting the appearance of a prison, and such it was to the old soldiers.

In an 1873 Lexington newspaper article, an elderly Lexington citizen recalled that the buildings formed a "large quadrangle" with the barracks for the guard and the commandant's residence in the front building. "A high brick wall [ran] from the back corners of this front line" to enclose the armory building in a walled courtyard. "I well remember its nicely cleaned floors and the multitudinous rows of burnished muskets, through which I used to walk, when I visited," the old-timer recalled with evident fondness. Soon after the Institute acquired the arsenal buildings in 1839 it added a third story to the central barracks buildings and perhaps enlarged the side wings so that the complex that appears in early illustrations shows a mix of features from before and after the establishment of the school.[10]

The Lexington Arsenal, altered for use by VMI, appears in this detail of a drawing by Charles Deyerle. Courtesy of VMI Archives

Executive Mansion Va. Military Inst. Lexington. Va.
1860.

A. J. Davis's 1860 design for the VMI Superintendent's Quarters.
Courtesy of VMI Archives

Superintendent Smith was eager to improve VMI's appearance and in the late 1840s he found an ally in Philip St. George Cocke, a wealthy Powhatan County planter and West Point alumnus who, as a member of the VMI Board of Visitors, hoped to make the new school a model of "distinctive architectural excellence and taste." Cocke built his plantation house Belmead in the Gothic Revival style in 1845–48 and was in a position to recommend its architect, the nationally-known Alexander Jackson Davis of New York, for the work of remaking VMI.[11]

In 1848 Smith and A. J. Davis began to plan a new barracks. Smith provided the basic concept: a four-story building forming a quadrangle with accommodation for two hundred cadets. Davis handled the design, specifying stuccoed masonry scored to suggest stone and crowning the walls with battlements. Octagonal turrets guarded a Tudor-arched entry, shown with what appears to be a medieval portcullis in Davis's 1850 presentation drawing, and slightly lower octagonal turrets defined the building's corners. To lend his composition monumentality Davis used a trick of scale. He grouped the windows of the first and second stories and the third and fourth stories into conjoined vertical compositions so that the building has an appearance of two very large stories. John Jordan built the massive stone foundations and Superintendent Smith supervised the rest. The Main Street-facing Washington Arch side of the barracks was completed and ready for occupancy in 1851. The rest followed in subsequent years.[12]

Davis went on to design faculty houses that in altered form now define the north side of the Parade Ground. The houses are variations on the theme of the Barracks: stuccoed, turreted, and battlemented with such Gothic details as diamond-paned windows, label moldings, and oriel windows. Most imposing is the Superintendent's Quarters (1860), a symmetrical composition with two three-story octagonal towers linked across the front by a bowed porch with three Tudor-arched openings (the porch is labeled "arcade" in Davis's drawing). A circular dining room at the back of the house echoes the curve of the front porch. The dining room affords panoramic views of the ravine of Woods Creek which flows on the north side of the Post, as the VMI campus is called.[13]

In June 1864 the Superintendent's Quarters hosted an unwelcome visitor: Union General David Hunter, who occupied Lexington during the operation known as Hunter's Raid and burned the Barracks, professors' houses, and other VMI buildings. Hunter made the superintendent's residence his headquarters during his time in Lexington, consequently sparing the house. Francis Smith returned after the war and began the process of rebuilding, aided by Davis who designed a new principal façade for the Barracks facing onto the Parade Ground (his original drawings for the façade predated the war). The school rebounded in the decades that followed and in the early twentieth century its facilities were greatly expanded from designs by a new architect of national renown: Bertram Goodhue, architect of the Nebraska State Capitol and the Chapel at West Point, who designed VMI's Jackson Memorial Hall (1915–16) and additional houses fronting on the Parade Ground.[14]

W&L and VMI were male preserves, as were most early Lexington schools. An exception was the Ann Smith Academy, constructed in 1808–09 by Lexington families who had "daughters ready to be

The VMI Barracks as a burned-out shell after the Civil War. Courtesy of Seth McCormick-Goodhart

Ann Smith Academy. Courtesy RHS/SC, WLU

educated" in the words of the first chairman, James McDowell. The two-story brick academy building, which was apparently planned by a committee of parents, was built by John Jordan in the Federal style with a large lunette in the decorative front gable. Lexington businessman William Caruthers was proud enough of the new undertaking that he mailed Thomas Jefferson a progress report in July 1809, noting that the builders had "got up the Walls of a large & commodious house to finish." Caruthers also sang the praises of headmistress Ann Smith in the letter. In its prime the Ann Smith Academy taught geography, natural philosophy, chemistry, astronomy, and French in addition to the three Rs. The 1808–09 building, which stood in Lexington's early Lee Avenue suburb, was replaced in the early twentieth century by the Ann Smith School, built as the high school and now the Chi Psi Fraternity House.[15]

The nineteenth century was the heyday of the private academy in the county. In 1850 the Brownsburg Academy opened outside the village in a two-story brick building of pedimented Greek Revival design built by contractors John and James Withrow with carpentry by Abraham Supinger. In lieu of a portico the no longer extant building had a quartet of pilasters, painted white to contrast with the red brick in a suggestion of freestanding columns. A drum-like octagonal cupola, possibly an early addition rather than an original feature, rose above the side-gabled roof, in it a bell to summon children to class

Brownsburg Academy.
Courtesy RHS/SC, WLU

and citizens to public meetings. Private schools were also conducted in private homes and could be quite small. Ingleside, a Gothic Revival brick house built in the Spring Branch area by W. B. F. Leech in the 1870s, had an upstairs room used as a schoolroom for the Leech children and children from neighboring farms. Leech's "home school" is reminiscent of the old practice of wealthy farmers hiring tutors for their children and lodging the tutors in their homes. A late reference to the traditional in-home arrangement dates to July 1888 when Ollie Massie of Fluvanna County, "who has been teaching in the family of Mr. J. H. Whitmore" in the South River area, returned home for the summer break.[16]

After the Civil War, Lexington civic leaders seized on education as a catalyst to revive the town's economy. They successfully recruited General Robert E. Lee for president of Washington College, a public relations coup (Lee's name was added to the school after his death in 1870), and education-related economic development efforts of the post-war era took on a scientific aspect in the spirit of the age. In 1870 architect A. J. Davis suggested the creation of a Rockbridge Park in the lower Woods Creek ravine as part of his continuing involvement in the physical development of VMI. He proposed "a nursery or botanic garden for exotic hardy shrubs and trees be got up under the auspices" of the school. Davis's proposal reflects the growing influence of landscape architecture and park creation in American community development. A year earlier his design for an addition to the VMI Barracks included a museum with specimen cabinets and what appear to be sky-lit two-story circular or octagonal galleries.[17]

Neither the park nor the museum developed in the form Davis imagined them, although in 1881–82 Washington and Lee achieved something along the same lines as the museum galleries with the construction of a sky-lit art gallery on the top floor of Newcomb Hall. This art gallery, with its decorative trusswork revealed by a modern rehabilitation, served at first as a gymnasium until 1890 when the athletes moved out and the artists moved in. A period photograph suggests a relatively sedate paint scheme with a dark-toned wall as a backdrop for the portrait and landscape paintings hung on it and a light-toned ceiling to reflect light from the skylight. The ceiling and trusswork preserved historic-period light buff paint at the time of rehabilitation.[18]

In the 1870s Washington and Lee aimed considerably higher than an art gallery. Chicago industrialist Leander J. McCormick, brother

and business partner of the famous Cyrus, and like Cyrus claimed
as a native son of Rockbridge County, announced in 1870 that he
wished to donate a twenty-six-inch Clark refracting telescope to a Virginia college. The Clark was the largest "light cannon" of its day; in
1877 astronomer Asaph Hall used the model to discover the moons
of Mars. Washington and Lee and the Lexington community lobbied
hard for the gift. Funds were pledged and an observatory building
was (allegedly) designed, but in the end McCormick chose the University of Virginia for the massive instrument.[19]

Washington and Lee fared better with the earth sciences. In the
mid-1870s Northern philanthropist Lewis Brooks donated to the
school a collection of plaster casts "of the most celebrated specimens
of the organic remains of the old world." Museum supplier Henry A.
Ward of Rochester, New York, whose firm made the casts, arranged
with Washington and Lee President G. W. Custis Lee for their exhibition, and architect J. Crawford Neilson drew up plans that converted
the lower floors of Robinson Hall into what became known as the
Brooks Museum.[20]

The museum was a "cabinet of curiosities," a miscellany of paleon-
tological casts, fossils, taxidermy, and other artifacts mounted on walls
and protected behind glass in the manner such collections were displayed in centuries past. Ward placed the largest exhibits at the center of the two-story exhibit hall. At one end stood the skeletal cast of
a *Glyptodont*, an armadillo-like creature the size of a riding mower;

Buffalo Forge Schoolhouse in a late 19th century drawing. The drawing suggests a building of "boxed" construction, a technique that minimized framing, and shows a flue projecting from the roof ridge, a log footbridge (over a millrace?), and a pentagonal ring of logs that may have served as seating for outdoor activities.
Courtesy RHS/SC, WLU

Buena Vista Colored School.
Photo by H. E. Ravenhorst

next to it loomed the skeletal cast of a *Megatherium* ground sloth mounted so that it grasped a tree trunk with a clawed forelimb. At one point in design development the museum was to have a gallery reached by a spiral stair, though whether this feature was built is unclear.[21]

Historian Ruth Anderson McCulloch recalled a popular Brooks Museum exhibit: the skeleton of Robert E. Lee's horse Traveller, deceased not many years before and mentioned in the correspondence between Custis Lee and Ward. The skeleton of a colt stood next to the famous remains, and according to McCulloch, guides told visitors, "This is a skeleton of Traveller when he was a colt." The Brooks Museum exhibits were removed in the 1930s and Robinson Hall converted back to classroom space but many of the animal specimens survive in exhibits in Washington and Lee's science building.[22]

By the end of the nineteenth century the Commonwealth's public school authority, created in 1870 amid the tumultuous politics of the era, watched over a growing roster of public schoolhouses in Rockbridge and other counties. These were mostly modest log and frame buildings, the one-room schoolhouses of legend, but they held great meaning for the rural communities they served and were especially cherished by the county's newly emancipated African American population. The log 1874 Cedar Hill Church doubled as a school and in its original form was probably representative of the county's early black schoolhouses. The interior was exposed log too as indicated by an anecdote. In the 1880s or 1890s, when the church still served as a school, a "mischievous boy . . . would pick the daubing out of the wall and throw it" at the head of the teacher. Another building from the era of small rural schools is the Laurel School, located near Bells Valley Depot and possibly built ca. 1885.[23]

Facilities for black students were somewhat better in the towns. The original Buena Vista Colored School, built in 1891, was a modest one-room building but constructed of frame instead of log. The 1891 schoolhouse burned in the 1910s; the original section of the brick school that stands today near the intersection of 30th Street and Aspen Avenue dates to ca. 1915. In 1924 the black community, motivated by the construction of a new up-to-date school for Buena Vista's white children, formed an Improvement League to petition the school board for improvements. A much-needed addition resulted in 1926. The Buena Vista Colored School closed in 1957 with the opening of the Park Avenue School and the building stood vacant for many years. In 2002 the Buena Vista Colored School Historical Society formed to preserve the building and explore options for its reuse. For the entire period it was in use the Buena Vista Colored School operated during the era of segregation, which did not end in the area until the 1960s.[24]

Near the Buena Vista Colored School, on the hill occupied by the 1890–91 Hotel Buena Vista, Rockbridge County's third institution of

Hotel Buena Vista, the main building of the Southern Seminary/Southern Virginia University campus. Photo by H. E. Ravenhorst

The Peristyle on the Southern Seminary/Southern Virginia University campus. Photo by H. E. Ravenhorst

Activities on the Kimball Student Center sundeck, Southern Seminary/Southern Virginia University campus. Photos from 1930s editions of the *Maid of the Mountains* yearbook. Courtesy SC, WLU

higher learning developed in the early twentieth century. The female Southern Seminary, fondly known to generations of students as Southern Sem, opened in the former hotel building in 1901. The school abandoned the Queen Anne style of the hotel in favor of the classicism popularized by the World's Columbian Exposition held in Chicago in 1893, the style of choice for civic architecture during the early twentieth century. As new buildings went up on "Seminary Ridge" they were classical in spirit and created an air of established gentility considered appropriate for a girl's finishing school. An early addition to the grounds was the Peristyle, a graceful arc of Doric columns that formed the perfect backdrop for Mayday festivities and class photos. The structure may have been inspired by the New Orleans Peristyle, a freestanding colonnade built to ornament a park beside the Bayou Metairie in 1907.[25]

The present Kimball Student Center behind the hotel began in 1925 as a simple neoclassical brick enclosure for an indoor swimming pool. In its original form the building faced a rose garden and had globe light fixtures at the corners of its parapeted flat roof. In 1933 an upper story was added for a gymnasium, a pedimented entry pavilion grafted on as an architectural focus, and a sun deck created on the new flat roof. "Sun worship is a cult at S. S.," explained a 1930s yearbook alongside pictures of students playing shuffleboard and badminton on the roof with spectators perched on the parapet and lounging under a pergola.[26]

The construction of the Durham Hall classroom building to the left of the hotel in 1939, followed by Chandler Hall auditorium and library

CHANDLER HALL, LIBRARY AND AUDITORIUM, SOUTHERN SEMINARY AND JUNIOR COLLEGE, BUENA VISTA, VIRGINIA

Chandler Hall, Southern Seminary/ Southern Virginia University campus. Courtesy SC, WLU

to the right in 1940, marshaled growth into a linear composition that maximized the apparent size of the campus when viewed from town. The two new buildings demonstrated that the generic classicism of the school's early years had given way to the more specific Colonial Revival style, which evoked Virginia's architectural heritage and furthered the administration's efforts to create a sense of tradition in the image of such venerable Virginia institutions as the University of Virginia and the College of William and Mary. Durham and Chandler halls, white-trimmed buildings of brick, were fronted by shallow porticos with roof balustrades and attenuated square columns, and each building had an elaborate scrolled pediment over its front entry. Durham Hall's portico was later removed, as was the auditorium's, in the latter case replaced by the present temple front in the 1960s. Other classroom buildings, dormitories, a separate library, and an indoor riding arena were added after World War II. In 1996 Southern Seminary became Southern Virginia College (now University), which has perpetuated the Colonial Revival theme in new construction.[27]

The private academies continued into the early twentieth century but with the ascendency of public education they gradually shut down or reorganized as public schools. Palmer Academy (1903) is a case in point. The two-story building, which served children in the upper Buffalo Creek valley, resulted from a sophisticated fundraising campaign that included a stock offering and a brochure with testimonials from Washington and Lee educators. After three years of private operation

Above: Effinger High School.
Photo by Dan Pezzoni

Right: An Effinger High School classroom used for Future Farmers of America instruction. Photo from a 1952 "Buffalo Community Improvement League" scrapbook. Courtesy SC, WLU

the academy became the public Palmer High School and Graded School. It lost its high school program to Effinger High School in the 1920s but continued as an elementary school until closing in 1956. Unlike some other disused rural schoolhouses of the era, the Palmer building was not filled with hay bales or otherwise set on the path to eventual demolition but was instead made into a community center and meeting space for the Effinger Ruritan Club. Palmer School, renovated in 1999–2003, continues to play an important role in its community, hosting an ice cream supper that draws hundreds to the rural landmark every August.[28]

The former Collierstown Graded School, built in 1906–1907, was similar to Palmer School in its frame construction and weatherboard siding but its carpenters added to it a few sparing decorative touches such as round windows in the front gables and a hip roof capped by a pyramidal-roofed belfry. Construction of the Collierstown school coincided with passage of the 1906 Mann High School Act which established and maintained a system of public secondary schools. Goshen's first public school, a two-story frame building, housed a temperance hall in its upper story. It was replaced in 1916 by another two-story school building with banks of triple windows that point to the importance of natural light in an era before widespread rural access to artificial illumination. Windows were a prominent feature of the original

Schools

Mountain View School, built by carpenter Frank D. Lowe in 1919. Originally L-shaped in plan, the school was enlarged by filling in the angle of the L to create a total of six classrooms and an auditorium with a stage. A survivor from this era of large multi-windowed frame schools is Highland Belle School in the Kerrs Creek valley, a two-story weatherboard-sided building from the early twentieth century that preceded the present brick school of the same name.[29]

The laissez-faire approach to public school design followed by state school authorities in the nineteenth century changed in the new century. The Strode Act of 1908 promulgated guidelines for ventilation, lighting, and toilet facilities, and starting in 1911 the Virginia

Lylburn Downing
School (1927 section).
Photo by Dan Pezzoni

Department of Public Instruction provided free schoolhouse designs to local districts. The designs ranged from two to eight classrooms and featured large windows for natural lighting and ventilation. The Division of School Buildings, created in 1920, furnished plans, advised on sites, wrote building specifications, and supervised construction projects through its School Building Service.[30]

Consolidation was the mantra of early twentieth century school authorities. Reformers touted economies of scale and enhanced learning and socialization opportunities as the chief benefits but they also saw a broader purpose, the strengthening of rural communities. Larger, better staffed, modern rural school facilities might induce "persons of means and influence" to remain in the countryside rather than move into town to educate their children. Effinger High School (1939) is a product of these philosophies. The two-story brick building consolidated the high school programs at the Palmer and Collierstown schools which then became elementary schools. Effinger School itself experienced the consequences of consolidation, first when its high school program was transferred to the newly constructed Lexington High School (the present Maury River Middle School; 600 Waddell Street) in 1960, and then in 2010 when its children were transferred to Central Elementary School in Lexington and the 1939 building closed. Fortunately the attractive Colonial Revival building has reopened as county school offices. Across Colliers Creek from the 1939 building stands its predecessor, a four-room frame high school built in 1923.[31]

The Virginia School Building Service provided plans for most, if not all, of the large schools of the consolidation era. Lylburn Downing

Lexington High School (Harrington Waddell Elementary School) soon after completion in 1927. Courtesy of the Library of Virginia

Ruffner School, the current
Lexington City Hall.
Photo by Dan Pezzoni

School (302 Diamond Street), Lexington's African American public
school completed in 1927, illustrates one of the more popular state
designs: classrooms arranged around a high auditorium, gymnasium, and circulation space with clerestory windows illuminating the
interior. Lylburn Downing's exterior combines Colonial Revival and
Craftsman-influenced details such as an entry porch with paired classical columns, brick walls articulated by pilasters with simple concrete
capitals, and decorative façade panels outlined by projecting header
bricks. Lylburn Downing was built with aid from the Rosenwald Fund,
a philanthropy that funded African American school construction
throughout the South in the 1920s and 1930s. The school was the only
"Rosenwald School" in the county. When it opened in 1927, Lylburn
Downing accommodated grades one through nine, the eighth and
ninth grades considered high school-level grades at the time. By 1942
a full twelve-grade curriculum had been instituted.[32]

Similar to Lylburn Downing in style and basic form were the designs
for Fairfield High School (1925) and Lexington High School (1927;
later Harrington Waddell Elementary School), both built for white
students. In 1925 Lexington educator Harrington Waddell urged the
construction of a white high school which would be "modern and

The former Parry McCluer High School (now Parry McCluer Middle School). Photo by H. E. Ravenhorst

up-to-date in every respect, and large enough to accommodate all students from Rockbridge County who wish to come into Lexington, if prepared to enter." Raymond V. Long, a Richmond architect associated with the Board of Education during the 1920s and 1930s, adapted an off-the-shelf central auditorium concept to a challenging steeply sloped site in the "sequestered vale" of Woods Creek, near newly created residential neighborhoods on the west side of town (the Lexington Playground and Park Association provided the site). Long gave Lexington High School a colonnade of monumental fluted Doric columns that emphasized the importance of education to the civic life of the community.[33]

When it was completed in 1927, Lexington High School was the latest in a succession of white high schools in the town. An early link in the chain was the 1892 Ruffner School at 300 East Washington Street, a handsome brick and stone building with large windows and a modillion cornice. The historic windows, their height augmented by transoms, represent an early local example of the importance placed on ample natural lighting in progressive school planning. Ruffner School was designed by the Lexington firm of Rose and Willis and serves today as the Lexington City Hall. The Ruffner School was superseded by the Ann Smith School, not the 1808–09 academy but a high school named in its honor and built on the same Lee Avenue site in 1910. Prolific Richmond school architect Charles M. Robinson designed the two-story Classical Revival brick building which features a high stone base and a broad round-arched entry under a monumental Doric portico. Both the Ruffner and Ann Smith high schools later served as elementary schools.[34]

Raymond V. Long designed the former Parry McCluer High School (now Parry McCluer Middle School; 2329 Chestnut Avenue) in Buena Vista in 1923. Historian Francis Lynn notes that prior to construction the school authorities displayed a rendering of the proposed building in a downtown shop window so that citizens who would be footing the bill could see what they were getting for their money. When Parry McCluer opened, writes Lynn, the students were delighted by its modern bells and whistles: one desk per pupil, central heating, water fountains instead of a common bucket and dipper, and *"indoor plumbing . . . no more bundling up to run outside and 'be excused!'"* The former Parry McCluer High School is graced by a Doric colonnade. The ca. 1940 Natural Bridge High School is another product of the era's drive for school consolidation and new construction. By the eve of World War II Rockbridge County boasted large, up-to-date consolidated public schools that anticipated educational trends of the post-war era.[35]

SIX

Resorts

O N June 7, 1855, the steamer *Ben Franklin* entered Norfolk harbor en route from the Caribbean island of St. Thomas to New York. On board with the crew and cargo, lurking in the bilge, were mosquitoes infected with the virus that causes yellow fever. The dreaded malady induced fever and nausea and worse — in the era before modern medicine, up to eighty-five percent of yellow fever cases led to hemorrhaging and death. A crewmember died in July and the disease spread to Norfolk with terrifying swiftness. As many as eighty people succumbed daily at the peak of the epidemic, their coffins piling up at the cemeteries for want of anyone to bury them. When it was all over in October an estimated two thousand Norfolk citizens had perished.[1]

Yellow fever and cholera, another killer, routinely ravaged Tidewater Virginia until their causes were understood and effective treatments devised around the turn of the twentieth century. In the meantime the Tidewater's bane was Rockbridge County's boon, for though death and disease were no strangers to Rockbridge its highland location spared it from the coastal epidemics. Every summer wealthy Tidewater urbanites and planters decamped by the thousands to Rockbridge and other mountain counties where a constellation of fashionable springs resorts catered to their needs and plied them with allegedly restorative mineral waters while they waited out the sickly season. "Taking the waters" was the social event of the summer and an economic opportunity for resort owners and the many local people who built, ran, and supplied the resorts.

Facing page: The lawn at Rockbridge Alum Springs, late 1800s. Grace Lewis, the wife of novelist Sinclair Lewis, visited Rockbridge Alum in 1919 when the resort was on the decline. She described the lawn as "a parade ground with circular beds of tired cannas and a hazardous croquet patch." Courtesy RHS/SC, WLU

Above: Hotel Buena Vista porch. Photo by H. E. Ravenhorst

Barclay's Tavern, an early hostelry, with Red Mill beyond. Photo by Michael Pulice, courtesy DHR

The springs resort phenomenon started slowly in Rockbridge and in its early phases was not very different from traditional hostelry and entertainment businesses. Taverns and ordinaries were present from the early years of settlement and were particularly numerous in the county's towns and villages. Lexington's Blue Hotel illustrates the finer establishments. Jacob Clyce purchased a lot at the foot of Lexington's Main Street hill in 1817, in the process acquiring, or soon thereafter building, a handsome two-story brick hotel. If Clyce was the hotel's original owner he may have been his own builder since he had entered the trade of "house joiner" in 1803 and contractor in 1809. In 1829 the county court granted Clyce permission to keep an ordinary, certifying that he was a "man of good character not addicted to drunkenness." The Federal style gabled building seen in old photos was sure to have been built by that time. The hotel was graced by a two-tier porch with slender columns and a bull's-eye window in its gable. A dining room and lobby occupied the basement level, the haunt of local patrons and travelers who tippled from a selection of wines, brandy, "common" whiskey, and "Good West Indies Rum." The two upper floors contained parlors and bedrooms. In its heyday the Blue Hotel "gave the impression of quiet elegance," wrote Ruth McCulloch around the time of its demolition in 1947, and the experience of staying in a genteel residence certainly seems to have been the point Clyce wished to convey to his patrons.[2]

The Blue Hotel is gone, as are other early Lexington inns such as Shields Tavern (also known as the Eagle Tavern) where William Clark breakfasted in 1809 on his way to Monticello to give his report on the success of the Lewis and Clark Expedition to Thomas Jefferson, and rural establishments like Steeles Tavern which lent its name to the community on the Rockbridge-Augusta county line. Something of the feel of the hostelries is preserved in the relatively untouched village of Brownsburg. Nicholas Spring's Tavern is an antebellum log building of domestic form and appearance sided with weatherboards. The two-story brick Lavelle's Tavern, named for a family that resided in it beginning in 1852, is also domestic in character.[3]

As Brownsburg's taverns suggest, private homes, if they were located on a main road, could be run as profitable lodgings. Fancy Hill (ca. 1821), the Federal style house in the community by the same name, was one of these residence-taverns and was known as Welch's Tavern after its owner, Benjamin Welch. Fancy Hill's location between Lexington and Natural Bridge also suited it as a stagecoach stop and in the antebellum period it acquired some of the trappings of a community with the opening of a post office and Dr. Washington Dorsey's office, either in the mansion or nearby. Tradition asserts a balcony on the house was formerly enclosed with bars to keep prisoners being transported by stage coach.[4]

Dramatically sited at the crest of the Blue Ridge was Alexander's Tavern, located on Jordan Road where it passes through White's Gap northeast of Buena Vista. According to an 1896 newspaper account, "A great many people passed there years ago crossing the mountain going to and coming from East Virginia." The brick house in which the tavern operated was said in 1896 to have been built over a hundred years earlier, though it may actually have dated to the early nineteenth century when Jordan Road was constructed to provide Rockbridge with an improved land connection to the Piedmont.[5]

Later in date but in many ways similar to earlier establishments is Tankersley Tavern, named for bachelor brothers Benton and Frank Tankersley and their maiden sister Annie who in 1886 acquired an antebellum house at the east end of the East Lexington covered bridge and opened a tavern in it. A whiskey label of the period described Benton Tankersley as a "leader in fine wines, liquors, cigars & tobacco." The original part of Tankersley Tavern was once believed to have served as the tollhouse for the covered bridge although research by archaeologist Donald Gaylord has documented the existence of a building on the opposite, Jordan's Point side of the bridge that is a more likely candidate. (At one point during the antebellum period the toll-house at the Point was occupied by toll-keeper and clerk William Lewis who received for his services use of the house, a garden plot, an annual salary of $200, and three months of leave time.) Tankersley Tavern closed its doors in 1900 when Rockbridge County "voted dry," prohibiting the sale of liquor. However the barroom was preserved, at least until 1946 when a newspaper described its 1880s oak

The spring pavilion at Rockbridge Alum Springs.
Photo by Arthur Bartenstein

and walnut counter, "made entirely by hand by an old pattern-maker, Ned Booker," and "double swinging doors, covered with tooled and dyed leather."[6]

Compared to the taverns and other lodging and entertainment venues in operation back into the colonial period, the county's springs resorts are a late phenomenon, although the mineral waters that were the basis of their prosperity were known from an early date. Rockbridge Alum Springs may have been the first. According to Lexington historian Leslie L. Campbell, whose memory reached back to the early postbellum period, the resort developed in a remote vale on the headwaters of Brattons Run at a complex of alum (sulfate) and chalybeate (iron) springs that acquired their minerals from the shaly strata through which the water flowed. The mineral residues formed a "lick," a concentration of salts that attracted deer to the location. The deer in turn attracted hunters who, according to Campbell, found the waters beneficial for their "diseased glands and stomach troubles." Alum, an astringent, can in fact be used in water purification, but regardless whether the waters worked the cures claimed for them, Campbell wrote that "the fame of the Alum Springs Deer Lick began to spread and people came and camped in tents."[7]

An 1847 deed noted that the "Alum Spring" property embracing 2,008 acres was originally patented to Alexander Campbell in an arrangement with John Dunlap. Tax records suggest no substantial development on the tract as late as 1836 but by 1846 $2,000 worth of buildings had been constructed. According to some accounts a "house of entertainment" stood at the springs, perhaps the same building described as a small hotel said to have opened in 1834 and to have operated for six years before burning down in 1840 (the accounts do not jibe well with the tax record evidence). By 1852 the resort boasted "hotels and cabins" that presumably included the three-story brick building at the center point of the complex, a building known in after years as the Central Hotel.[8]

The resort's major development commenced after John W. Frazier purchased the property in 1852 and initiated an ambitious building program with the goal of challenging White Sulphur Springs and other flagship springs resorts of the region. John's brother William visited in 1853 and penned a detailed account of the transformation. "Arriving after midnight," William Frazier wrote, "I found the lawn covered with stacks of lumber, and the next day found at least fifty

Edward Beyer's lithograph of
Rockbridge Alum Springs in the
Album of Virginia (1858). Courtesy
of the Library of Virginia

or sixty workmen — brick and stone-masons, carpenters, plasterers, tinners, painters — all busily plying their several trades; many new buildings going up and old ones being enlarged and extended; none of them in a completed state and some only just begun." To keep his builders stocked with lumber, John Frazier scoured Rockbridge and adjacent counties, even contracting with a sawmill in distant Pocahontas County. William noted the teams of horses and mules employed in "continuously hauling lumber from the mills, sand from the mountain, lime from Kerr's Creek and saw logs from our own land to our own saw-mill, which was kept running daily and most of the night." Two brick kilns were burned the previous fall and "preparations were now making for burning a third." Rockbridge Alum Springs officially opened on June 1, 1853, but construction continued, the workmen not departing until mid-July.[9]

The result of John Frazier's construction blitz was a veritable city in the wilderness, an assemblage of hotels, cottages, and auxiliary

The Central Hotel and adjacent Ladies Hotel (seen in part on the right) at Rockbridge Alum were detailed in the Greek Revival style. Courtesy RHS/SC, WLU

buildings in a diversity of forms and styles. Predictably, given the times, the styles were Greek and Gothic revival. At the heart of the resort a northward-opening horseshoe arrangement of four-room cottages wrapped around a park with an octagonal "music stand" at its center. Across the front of each hip-roofed cottage spanned a veranda on delicate wooden lattice supports, the railings between with zigzag picket designs. The cottages were brick, essentially Greek Revival in character with four rooms arranged around a center chimney. They were designated "Baltimore Row" on the west side of the horseshoe and "Kentucky Row" on the east side.[10]

At the bend of the horseshoe stood the Central Hotel with a triple-decker porch and an L-shaped rear wing containing a dining room. Edward Beyer, artist of the lithograph set *Album of Virginia*, visited in the mid-1850s and portrayed the "large and commodious Hotel" and the cottages with white-painted or whitewashed walls, though in later depictions they have red brick exteriors. The star attraction, the springs, may have been at the time of Beyer's visit relatively undeveloped; at least he does not show a spring pavilion or other enclosure at the location. He does, however, show a long building by the springs elsewhere identified as the bowling alley, a fixture of period springs resorts.[11]

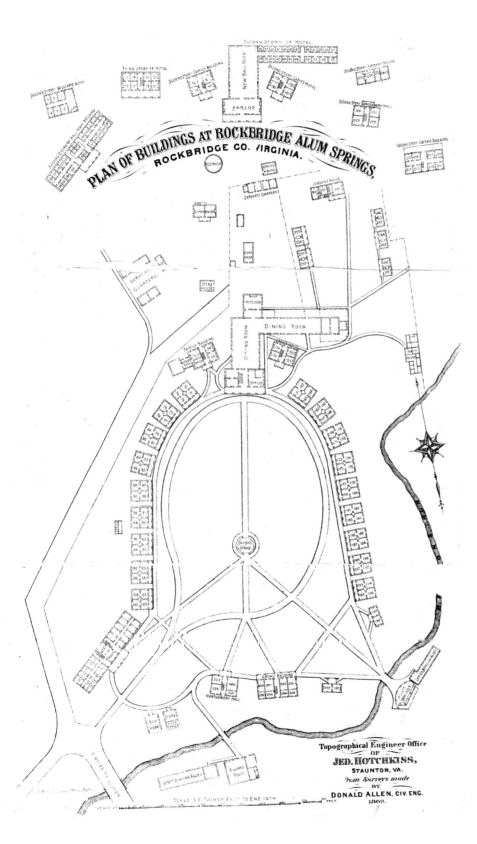

In this 1869 site plan of the Rockbridge Alum complex the floor plans at the top represent the upper stories of buildings shown below.
Courtesy SC, WLU

A surviving 1850s cottage
at Rockbridge Alum.
Photo by Arthur Bartenstein

Beyer's lithograph shows an assortment of buildings behind (south of) the Central Hotel, some of which appear on the 1869 Jedediah Hotchkiss map of the resort which reveals the buildings to have been a service complex, analogous to the outbuilding complexes that stood behind plantation houses of the era. Store (storage) houses are shown as are a linen house, an engine house, "servants quarters," a reservoir, and a scattering of guest cottages. Three of the servants quarters are arranged in an open quadrangle. The engine house, tucked behind a pair of two-room servants quarters, probably housed a hand- or horse-drawn fire engine. At the opposite end of the grounds, between the cottage horseshoe and the shaly hillside from which the springs issue, stood a quasi-commercial district consisting of a barroom, store and post office, and the Gothic Building, today one of the few vestiges of the resort. Another vestige is Rockbridge Alum's spring pavilion, built by the end of the 1850s. The curved and bracketed cornice of the open-fronted Italianate structure is supported by fluted square columns. On the roof, dispensing good health to all, perches a statue of Hygeia, the Greek goddess of health and hygiene.[12]

According to memoirist John Seymour Letcher, the "springs were numbered from left to right as you entered the springhouse pavilion, from one to five," each successively more potent. Number one was "only very slightly impregnated with alum" but the water from number five "puckered your mouth." Guests were cautioned to work their way up to spring number five over the course of a week or more, and while they were building up their tolerance they partook of a range of activities, from croquet on the grounds and bowling in the bowling alley to horse and carriage rides in the surrounding mountains. An orchestra performed twice daily in the bandstand—which acquired a blue and crimson paint scheme by the end of the century—and the management hosted full dress and masquerade balls in the Central Hotel's second-story ballroom. A staff of black workers sustained it all.[13]

The Civil War brought a halt to the music and balls and the resort was pressed into service as a military hospital, although a trickle of guests continued through the war, among them members of Robert E. Lee's family. When the war ended and full operations resumed, Rockbridge Alum was a changed place. The black staff dispersed at the end of the war and was replaced by local whites desperate for paying work. Eighteen-year-old B. A. Braur, for example, worked in the resort's slaughterhouse and recalled the day in 1866 when Robert E.

Lee showed up riding Traveller. In later decades the work force had a mixed composition. Both blacks and whites are shown working in the laundry, kitchen, and ice plant in photos from the early twentieth century. John S. Letcher recalled that in the 1910s, "The Negro cooks, kitchen helpers, chambermaids and bell boys came from Lexington after the closing of Washington and Lee and V.M.I. released them from their duties in student boarding and fraternity houses and from the V.M.I. mess hall."[14]

Another change was the opening of a competing resort literally next door to Rockbridge Alum. Jordan Alum Springs was the brain-child of John W. Jordan of the local iron furnace dynasty, and though Jordan transferred the new resort to Fred Effinger of Staunton prior to the gala opening in June 1873, the resort retained his name. Jordan Alum's crown jewel was the Grand Hotel, a three-story building in the mansarded Second Empire style. The U-shaped building was said to contain 150 guest rooms, some presumably wedged into the mansard roof which sprouts a profusion of barrel-vaulted dormers in old pictures. (Some of the rooms may have been dispersed among other

Grand Hotel, Jordan Alum Springs. The hotel as built was smaller than pictured here. Courtesy SC, WLU

Jordan Alum Springs gazebo.
Photo by Arthur Bartenstein

buildings.) Guests strolled along a "piazza" or veranda that wrapped around the hotel's first story. They could also stroll on the flat roof; a promotional brochure described "a delightful promenade around the Mansard roof [which] gives a most commanding and extended view, grand and beautiful." The hotel theater was lavishly decorated with wall and ceiling papers and possibly also stenciling. Around 1940 the ballroom had a blue ceiling, presumably a decorative scheme from earlier in the century.[15]

The two resorts went toe to toe for guests during the 1870s, Rockbridge Alum gradually losing ground to the upstart Jordan Alum, until they were brought under joint ownership in 1880. That was the year Richmond novelist James Branch Cabell first summered at the resort as a hearty one-year-old. In later life he recalled his romantic adventures in the hotel as a young beau, sneaking at midnight "through the dim hallways, over the red and brown matting, and past many closed dove-colored doors [each with] a number painted on it in fat, black figures, until you reached the appointed door, which was ajar . . ."[16]

Cabell was among the last to experience the resort as a going concern. The nation's involvement in World War I and the changes that followed were a one-two punch. The resort was "crushed," as Cabell put it, "by the rubber tires of the automobile" and the wider horizons car travel opened to vacationers. "Even building a golf links," writes newspaper publisher Matthew W. Paxton Jr., "to take advantage of the newest craze in sports, failed to arrest the downward trend." Tourist brochures from the last years showed motorists happily tootling over mountain roads to the resort, but after 1919 the end came swiftly. In

The bathing pool
at Rockbridge Baths.

recent years the Rockbridge Alum Springs Young Life Camp opened on the grounds, and its expansion has resulted in a facility that rivals the antebellum resort in square footage under roof. Most of the historical buildings that had survived long enough to be listed in the state and national registers in the late 1980s have since been torn down but important vestiges survive.[17]

Other resort development focused on Goshen Pass and its scenic approaches, appreciated as a natural attraction from an early date. Rockbridge Baths, located in the community of the same name, centered on a pool of pure water touted as "peculiarly beneficial to females." Robert E. Lee visited as did his wife, Mary, who found relief from her crippling arthritis in the waters. Like the later Jordan Alum Springs, Rockbridge Baths had an association with the Jordan family and was known for a time as Jordan's Spring. In June 1856 proprietor William Jordan announced the construction of "large and expensive buildings" for guests, promising to have them "*sufficiently* completed by the *4th July*." Lording over Jordan's complex was a two-story hotel with a capacious bracketed double veranda in the Italianate style. A belvedere with round-arched windows afforded views of the Maury River and the notch in Hogback and Jump mountains that formed the entrance to Goshen Pass. In 1873 the bathing pool was described as measuring 40 by 60 feet "with water as clear as crystal, and a temperature of 74 degrees."[18]

Ruth Anderson McCulloch first visited Rockbridge Baths with her family as a child in the 1880s, and according to the Lexington preservationist more women frequented the baths than men. The women were tended to by Nancy Steptoe, a black woman who "rubbed down the people who needed rubbing." McCulloch wrote that Rockbridge Baths cultivated a family atmosphere. "It was not a place where you went and socialized or where you enjoyed the dances," as at Rockbridge Alum. Dinner was in a dining hall overlooking the river. McCulloch recalled a menu of cold beef and bread, "huge pitchers of milk and water on the table, and also buttermilk," with cake and preserves after. "Everybody helped themselves." The Rockbridge Baths hotel is gone but vestiges of the resort survive in the weatherboarded sheds that flank the bathing pool and, on the opposite side of State Route 39, the community store and post office building, adapted from the resort's former dance hall. In the mid-twentieth century artist Pierre Daura and his wife, Louise, lived at what had been the resort.[19]

The Green at Wilson Springs in a 1939 photograph by William Hoyt. The road continued into Goshen Pass.
Courtesy SC, WLU

Also nearly vanished is Wilson Springs at the mouth of Goshen Pass. The site was earlier known as Strickler's Springs after owner Daniel Strickler, who may have built the log core of the surviving hotel, a linear two-story building with board-and-batten siding and a double-tier porch. According to tradition, later owner William A. Wilson was responsible for the construction of a matching building which was joined to the first by a connecting infill element with a gable front (the addition and connector were removed in the 1940s). Graffiti hint at goings-on in the hotel; in 1898 a group of girls wrote on the plaster wall of one room "Anyone who stays in this room will have a jolly time." As at other resorts, cottages populated the grounds, but here they were crudely constructed with unpainted board siding and rustic touches like crooked log porch posts. According to John S. Letcher, beginning shortly after the turn of the twentieth century the resort management allowed people to build cottages on the ground free of charge. The area became known as the Green.[20]

Campground use of the springs property dated back at least to 1822 when a religious revival was held on the grounds. Henry Boley, drawing on the recollections of attendee and future minister William Brown, described the 1822 meeting as a "great gathering [of] newly convicted sinners, the stricken penitent, the rejoicing converts and the older Christians." A century later the scene had become decidedly more secular. Photos show a raised, roofless dance platform where guests could dance under the stars. Letcher recalled dances to the tunes of a string band composed of black musicians from Lexington and, during Prohibition, dancers slipping off to refresh themselves from Mason jars of moonshine hidden about the grounds.[21]

A scenic attraction of a different sort — Natural Bridge — developed as a tourist destination and resort beginning in the antebellum period. The Bridge, formed over the millennia by the erosive action of Cedar Creek which flows under it, was once owned by Thomas Jefferson, who described it as "the most sublime of Nature's works" in his *Notes on the State of Virginia* (1787). "So beautiful an arch," the future president wrote, "so elevated, so light, and springing, as it were, up to heaven, the rapture of the Spectator is really indescribable!"[22]

Jefferson purchased the Bridge in 1774 and considered building "a little hermitage" by it for extended visits but instead in 1817 he gave his consent for Patrick Henry, "a freeman of colour," to live there and "cultivate the cultivable lands" granted that Henry pay the taxes and discourage surrounding property owners from cutting timber on the tract. Henry built a house where he lived until his death in 1831; his widow, Louisa, resided there or in the vicinity into the 1850s. Nothing is known about this house other than it stood 150 yards from the bridge and was adjoined by a garden where Henry requested, in his will, he be buried. Henry's house is often described as a "cabin" which in turn implies it was log — a fair assumption considering building practices of the era. Natural Bridge attracted a stream of visitors during Jefferson's day and although they apparently did not lodge at the Bridge

Natural Bridge and associated development as pictured by Edward Beyer in the *Album of Virginia* (1858).

they may have stayed nearby in a house known as the Stone Castle but referred to in old deeds as "the old Natural Bridge tavern."[23]

The first major tourist development at the Bridge dates to the 1830s. A jump in the value of buildings on the tract in 1834 probably represents construction of the first hotel. The property still belonged to Jefferson's heirs at the time so the hotel may have been built by or in coordination with a concessionaire. Hotelier Joel Lackland came into ownership by the end of the 1830s and it is he who is most remembered in connection with the first hotel. Edward Beyer portrayed the extent of development in his lithograph of the Bridge, published in 1858, in which he shows a long two-story building with a double veranda which appears to have been situated upslope from the present hotel, closer to the Bridge. Nearby are one-story cottages, perhaps guest cabins, and to the north are a large stable-like building and other farm buildings. A carriage approaches on a road lined with worm fences; then as now US Route 11 and its predecessors crossed the Bridge. A photograph from about 1870 suggests the hotel was enlarged after Beyer's visit.[24]

Henry C. Parsons acquired Natural Bridge in 1881 and made substantial improvements, enlarging Lackland's antebellum hotel and building the Appledore Hotel (or Cottage) as well as expanding the stable facilities and opening a store. An 1882 map shows the hotels surrounded by cottages and landscaped grounds. The Forest Inn, one of the hotels, was a rambling frame building, three stories with a three-tier porch across the front. A livery office for arranging transportation by carriage or hack operated out of a partial basement story, and across the road was a reflecting pond bordered by weeping willows and enclosed by neat whitewashed fences. The resort expanded again in 1892. The A. F. Withrow Lumber Company of Lynchburg was responsible for the 1892 construction projects, and the architectural firm of Rose and Wills designed the addition to the Appledore

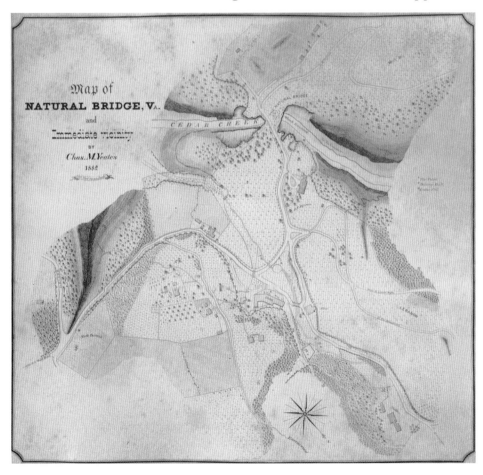

Development at Natural Bridge in 1882. Courtesy SC, WLU

The Forest Inn, Natural Bridge.

Hotel built at that time. The Rose half of Rose and Wills was Isaac E. A. Rose, an 1883 graduate of VMI who practiced in Lexington before moving on to New York City. An architectural highlight of the resort was the Jefferson Cottage, a Queen Anne-style confection of tiered porches, arched balconies, paneled wall surfaces, and a tower with a steeple-like pyramidal roof. The Natural Bridge resort would continue to prosper into the twentieth century by exploiting its automobile accessibility whereas other rural resorts declined.[25]

A new era of the Rockbridge resort economy dawned with the urbanization boom of the 1880s. Promoters in Buena Vista, Glasgow, Goshen, and a revivified Lexington erected hotels of a scale and sophistication on a par with the Rockbridge Alum and Natural Bridge resort buildings. Today the only boom hotel to survive is the 1890–91

The second Hotel Buena Vista
(1890–91), exterior detail
and hallway. Photos by
H. E. Ravenhorst

Hotel Buena Vista, later home of Southern Seminary and then Southern Virginia University. The sprawling turreted hotel was built on a ridge overlooking the rapidly filling grid of Buena Vista, platted in 1889, and stands near the site of a first Hotel Buena Vista, designed by architect Walter P. Tinsley of Lynchburg and opened in July 1889. The original hotel was a gambrel-roofed Colonial Revival building, relatively sedate by boom hotel standards, to which a matching addition was added in 1890. In July 1890 a fire in the hotel bakery spread to the rest of the building and burned it down. A. T. Barclay, head of the development company that operated the hotel, promptly telegraphed the contractor who had built the addition, John P. Pettyjohn of Lynchburg, who put Barclay in touch with Pennsylvania architect Sidney W. Foulk to begin planning a replacement.[26]

Foulk conceived a three-story brick building organized around a five-story cylindrical tower with a bell roof. A three-tier porch curves around the tower's lower stories and breaks at the building's main entry to form a three-story volume spanned at the top by an archway and gable roof. At the base of the composition is the entry, contained in a broad stone-trimmed archway that is repeated in the arched windows above. The style is Queen Anne with a riot of gabled roof forms, turned and sawn ornament, and windows of clashing shapes and sizes. Inside are winding hallways with cove ceilings and intricately paneled wainscots. The newel post at the base of the grand stair is a masterpiece of Victorian-era carved and turned detail.

The Alleghany Hotel overlooks
downtown Goshen in this ca. 1900
photo. Courtesy RHS/SC, WLU

The second Hotel Buena Vista opened for business in the summer of 1891 but guests dwindled during the depression year of 1893
and in 1894 the hotel was repurposed as a Lutheran-affiliated girls'
school, the Von Bora College for Women, named for Martin Luther's
wife Katerina Von Bora. Von Bora College was not a success and in
1901 Methodist minister Edgar H. Rowe, head of the Bowling Green
Female Academy in Caroline County, opened a branch of his academy in the hotel. The branch prospered and by 1907 Rowe had consolidated the academy programs in Buena Vista. Renamed Southern

Seminary, the school grew into one of Virginia's leading preparatory institutions and junior colleges. In 1996 Southern Seminary became Southern Virginia College, now Southern Virginia University, affiliated with the Church of Jesus Christ of Latter-day Saints.[27]

Goshen's pride and joy was the Palace Hotel, better known as the Alleghany Hotel, built on an eminence on the south side of town. In 1890 the Goshen Land and Improvement Company tapped Philadelphia architects Albert Yarnell and William Goforth for the project. The Alleghany appears to have weathered the economic downturn of the early 1890s better than other boom hotels but it experienced difficulties later and was destroyed by fire on Thanksgiving Day 1923. The Alleghany Hotel is explored in more detail in the Cities chapter.[28]

The ill-conceived boom metropolis of Cornwall, platted in 1890 at the confluence of Irish Creek and South River, managed to produce before its demise the Cornwall Hotel (1892), a two-story frame building of Colonial Revival character with a third story in its dormered gambrel roof. The attic story housed, in addition to some of the hotel's forty-eight rooms, wooden water tanks replenished by a Rife ram, a mechanism manufactured in Waynesboro by the Rife Hydraulic Engine Manufacturing Company that used the force of flowing water and a system of valves and air chambers to raise water. A period illustration shows the Cornwall Hotel to have had brick chimneys with clustered stacks and a bay window, veranda, and possibly varied wooden claddings in the Queen Anne mode. The builders left native trees standing around the hotel to provide shade, locally a novel approach to landscaping during the era that suggests, like the advanced Colonial Revival style of the hotel, the involvement of professional designers. Cornwall's town prospectus, which lists R. E. Lee (Robert Edward Lee Jr., son of the general) as president, notes the presence of two chalybeate and twenty-five "freestone" springs on the town site. Despite the health-giving springs, Cornwall failed to develop and its hotel is long gone.[29]

Glasgow had its Rockbridge Hotel, a gambrel-roofed hulk announced to great fanfare in the inaugural May 21, 1890, issue of the *Glasgow Herald*: "A boundary of land, containing 125 acres, and sufficiently elevated to afford one of the grandest views to be obtained in Virginia, has been surveyed off and set apart for a park. In this park a 200 room hotel, planned by Mr. Edgerton Rogers, the well known Richmond architect, will be built, at a cost of $60,000."

The Gothic Building (left) and
Montgomery Hall (right) at
Rockbridge Alum Springs.
Photo by Arthur Bartenstein

The July 5, 1890, *Herald* reported the building's dimensions — 280 feet long with three wings — and counted an office, bar, billiard room, and parlors in addition to the two hundred rooms. "The brick, tiling and wood work are all products of Glasgow manufacturing concerns," the editor added, assuring his readers of business for the community's new factories and employment for its burgeoning population. Photographs show a six-story observation tower and an oddly scalloped stone railing-wall under the supports of the wraparound verandas. The grand opening was delayed until 1893, and the hotel promptly closed amid the depression of that year. A new owner made a go of it in 1904 but was ultimately unsuccessful and most of the building was later salvaged for materials. A wing survived as late as the 1950s.[30]

Lexington, though an established community, was not immune to boom fervor, and in 1891 the Lexington Development Company completed the Hotel DeHart (or deHart) on Castle Hill west of the downtown. The hotel was "immense in scale," wrote Lyle and Simpson, "as aggressive as the others and just as fanciful in its combination of Norman towers and onion-shaped domes over a rambling, jutting wooden profile." There were architectural affinities with the Hotel Buena Vista, not surprisingly since the Hotel DeHart was also designed by

Sidney W. Foulk. In Lexington's downtown the taverns of the early years had given way to hotels, prominent among them the Central Hotel which opened in 1907 in a building with the ca. 1809 brick house of John McCampbell at its core. The Central Hotel closed in the 1930s but was acquired by Historic Lexington Foundation in 1971 and later rehabilitated as the McCampbell Inn. The hotel was renovated again in 2014 and reopened as half of The Georges Inn (the other half being the Alexander-Withrow Building).[31]

In Buena Vista the Hotel Colonnade opened in 1890 on the busy intersection of Sycamore and 21st streets, and the Hotel Marlbrook opened at about the same time on Magnolia Avenue. The three-story Marlbrook featured a cast iron façade with decorative pilasters, a tall wedding-cake bracketed cornice, and a peaked cresting with urn-like finials and the embossed hotel name. Lavish iron fronts were a hallmark of boom construction nationwide; many were produced at the Mesker Brothers ornamental ironworks in Indiana. Boarding houses, a majority operated by women, provided rooms for long-term lodgers. The two-story brick Advocate Building, completed in December 1889 at the corner of Magnolia Avenue and 21st Street, another major intersection, housed Mrs. W. H. Wolfe's boarding house and once boasted a balcony on its 21st Street elevation.[32]

Most of Buena Vista and Lexington's downtown hotels gradually disappeared in the twentieth century or were converted to different uses, victims of the societal changes ushered in by the automobile. But the automobile created as well as it destroyed, and a new chapter opened in the county's resort history after World War I.

SEVEN

Industries

The historical Rockbridge County landscape was dotted with buildings and structures devoted to industrial pursuits of various kinds, among them iron making, distilling, and textile processing, but perhaps the most iconic was the country gristmill with its creaking, splashing waterwheel. Beginning in the earliest years of settlement, mills were constructed to grind corn into meal and grain into flour for home consumption and sale. The county was especially suited to water-powered milling; its hilly terrain and swift-flowing watercourses created an abundance of mill "seats" for development by settlers.

Mill owners and their millwrights constructed mills in a range of types and sizes. One of the earliest mills known to county historian Oren Morton, who wrote in the 1920s, was the John Hays Mill which was probably located on Hays Creek near Brownsburg. Morton dated the mill to 1740 and he speculated that it was "a specimen of the primitive affair known as the tubmill." A tubmill, essentially a water-powered version of a hand-powered quern, was driven by a simple turbine wheel consisting of paddles attached to a vertical shaft that turned the millstones above. The paddled wheel sat in a tub-like cylindrical wooden enclosure through which the water flowed. Though tubmills were inefficient compared to mills powered by overshot or undershot wheels (that is, vertical wheels driven by water from above or below), they did not require dams, races, or flumes and they dispensed with the gearing needed to transmit the motion of a vertical water wheel to

Facing page: Glenwood Furnace in a ca. 1900 photo. The log structure on the left side of the stack may be a remnant of the casting house.
Courtesy RHS/SC, WLU

Above: Red Mill, Natural Bridge vicinity.
Photo by Michael Pulice, courtesy DHR

Top: The Campbell-Lyle Mill near Timber Ridge. Photo by Michael Pulice, courtesy DHR

Immediately above: A millstone hangs from its crane in the Campbell-Lyle Mill. Photo (1974) by Edward Chappell, courtesy DHR

a horizontal set of millstones. Tubmills were ideal for farmers who could not afford, or did not need, more complex mills, and they also made excellent "starter mills." Such seems to have been the case at Jordan's Point where John Jordan and his associates built a tubmill between 1801 and 1806 (probably ca. 1804) which they replaced in 1808 with a more substantial "merchant" mill, a mill for supplying the commercial trade.[1]

The Mutual Assurance Society records provide a snapshot of the county's milling industry at the beginning of the nineteenth century. Like houses of the era, mills were typically built of wood or stone, sometimes both in combination as in Joseph Paxton's large and valuable (over $5,000) gristmill, apparently known as Fork Mill, which featured a stone first story with two wooden stories above at the time of Paxton's first policy in 1803. The records mention a number of stone mills with "gavel [gable] ends of wood." This may simply mean that the gables were wood rather than stone, an important distinction for an insurance agent because of the greater fire hazard. Or it means the gable-end walls from the foundation to the roof were of wooden construction. Some masonry mills had framed walls or gaps in the masonry that may have facilitated repairs to the hurst (or husk) frame, the heavy timber framework that supported the machinery inside.[2]

The insurance declarations occasionally described mill equipage. Joseph Walker's two-story Mount Pleasant Mill, built of stone and insured in 1803, had "one pair Burhs & one pair Counter Stones 4 Bolting Cloathes &c." The "Burhs" were burrstones, millstones made from a granular type of limestone good for milling, and the term may indicate they were of French make. The counter stones were presumably the stones "counter" to the burrstones on which the grain was ground.

Bolting cloth was a fine cloth used in sifting flour, and the information suggests the cloths were fixed to machinery that performed the task automatically. The declaration gives the impression Walker's mill was a relatively advanced facility based on the improvements introduced to milling by American inventor Oliver Evans beginning in the late 1700s. Evans introduced greater automation to milling by using waterpower to operate a system of "chain of pots" elevators for moving product vertically through the building. The height of some of the county's mills in the early 1800s, two-and-a-half or three stories tall, is a strong indication they employed the Evans system. Other, smaller mills may have used more labor-intensive methods dating back to the medieval period.[3]

A sawmill extends from the side of Red Mill, Natural Bridge vicinity.
Courtesy of the Library of Virginia

Wade's Mill (Kennedy-Wade Mill), exterior and interior views taken by Edward Chappell and Dell Upton in 1977. Through stenciled manufacturer names and other labels, machinery in the mill can be traced to the Salem [Virginia] Machine Works, the Prinz and Rau Manufacturing Company of Milwaukee, and the S. Howes Company of Silver Creek, New York. Courtesy DHR

Sawmills were sometimes operated in conjunction with gristmills, powered by the same waterwheel. In historic photographs they are typically low-slung, open-sided linear structures, and the insurance declarations suggest the same layout was in use by the early 1800s. William Harper's sawmill, 40 by 16 feet, recorded in 1805, and James McCampbell's, 52 by 13 feet, recorded in 1816, were linear in form. These early sawmills sawed wood with an up-and-down motion. Modern circular saws probably came into local use in the antebellum period.[4]

Most of the county's surviving historic mills belong to later periods, although tax records and architectural features suggest one, Hays Creek Mill at the location known as McClung Mill west of Brownsburg, dates in part to ca. 1819. Hays Creek Mill was erected for William Steele Jr. and appears in the 1820 census of industries with two pairs of millstones for the grinding of wheat, rye, and corn into flour and meal. By 1838, when Steele sold out to his son Robert G. Steele, the operations included a sawmill. The McClung family acquired the mill in 1870, hence its alternate name McClung Mill, and it was likely the McClungs who enlarged the building to its present size and appearance. A wooden overshot wheel was replaced in the early twentieth century by a Fitz Water Wheel Company metal wheel (Fitz was a major supplier of waterwheels in the region). Much of the interior machinery has been removed with the exception of a flour dresser and some of the chute-like wood-cased elevators that moved product vertically through the mill's two and a half stories. An interesting feature, one seen in other old mills, is the presence of shims at the tops of the interior support posts that could be adjusted to counteract shifting of the structure caused by machinery vibrations. Hays Creek Mill also preserves a room with built-in cabinets that probably served as the mill office or counting room.[5]

The Kennedy-Wade Mill on Otts Creek near Raphine, better known as Wade's Mill, was largely rebuilt in the 1870s after a fire destroyed an earlier mill. A mill may have stood on or near the site in 1797 and some of the present mill's stone foundation may date to the early 1800s, a period during which the operation included a sawmill (one account suggests a late 1700s date for the foundation). In 1846 the Kennedy family sold the mill to Henry B. Jones at which time it was described as being "very much out of repair." Over the following years Jones made improvements which are detailed in his surviving diary. By

June 1846 he had installed a new waterwheel and by July 1847 he had the partially refurbished mill up and running and was grinding wheat. In 1848 burrstones were brought over the mountain from Scottsville in Albemarle County (presumably the millstones were shipped on the James River and Kanawha Canal), and a millwright named "Major Hutton" was at work making more repairs. William Lucas acquired the mill in 1877 and in 1882 rented it to James F. Wade (or Waid) who bought the mill outright in 1888.[6]

Wade's Mill's rebuilding and subsequent improvements occurred at a time of change in the milling industry. The mill's burrstones, used to grind corn and buckwheat, illustrate the old technology but in the early twentieth century belt-driven roller mills were installed to handle most of the work. Roller milling, which ground grain between metal rolls, improved efficiency and product quality and is associated with the alternative power sources that freed millers from fickle and often destructive water sources. At Wade's Mill at least three dams were washed out and rebuilt in the twentieth century alone, and a gasoline engine was installed to get the mill through periods of low water. Portable steam engines were good in a pinch. A drought curtailed operations at Sterrett's Mill near Timber Ridge in October 1895. "Owing to the dry weather the water is too low to run the mills," reported the *Rockbridge County News*. Mill owner T. A. Sterrett rented a steam engine to get him through. The following February, "on account of the recent rains which have replenished our creeks," he switched back to water power, "thereby saving $4.00 per day running expenses."[7]

Other traditional industrial buildings used water as a power source. By 1751 John Hays had added a water-powered fulling mill to his milling operations, following only a few years after Solen Hays established a fulling mill on Moffett's Creek between 1747 and 1749. Fulling, a process for improving the quality and durability of cloth, involved beating the cloth with wooden mallets in a water-filled trough. Evidence suggests a stone building on Alexander Beggs's Vineyard Hill property near Buffalo Forge is the same building as a fulling mill described in Beggs's 1786 will. The building features large interlocking corner stones, a wide front entry, and a specialized niche or infilled opening that appears to have faced the race or ditch that provided water to power the equipment. A possible upper wooden level is now missing.[8]

The Hays and Beggs fulling mills attest to the existence of a nascent woolen industry. Most textile production during the era of

Large quoin (corner) stones are among the features of the building believed to be the Vineyard Hill fulling mill. Photo by Dan Pezzoni

A 1937 photo by William Hoyt shows two textile-related buildings at Jordan's Point. The large gabled building on the left was built as a "cotton factory" in the 1850s. The smaller gabled building between it and the mansard-roofed mill may have incorporated part of the Jordan and Moorhead fulling mill. In the foreground is the C&O railroad trestle and to the right is the end of the antebellum covered bridge at the Point. VMI is in the background.
Courtesy SC, WLU

"homespun" occurred in the home or on the farm. In 1805 the farm of John McKee had what is described in the Mutual Assurance Society records as a "Weving Shop." A follow-up declaration in 1817 refers to the building as a "Spining house" and notes that it was a one-story wooden structure measuring 26 by 22 feet. Some farms had outbuildings known as loom houses.[9]

Numerous water-powered carding machines operated during the period. At least two stood on Mill Creek in Panther Gap in 1837, including Baer's Carding Machine, and were depicted in a Board of Public Works canal survey along the Maury River and its tributaries. Whistle Creek was a particular focus of the industry. James McFarland is said to have erected his carding mill there in 1813. The mill, described as a two-story stone building of about 30 by 40 feet with a

large attic-story space, was inherited by McFarland's grandson John Patterson who in the mid-1800s outfitted it as a woolen mill for the manufacture of yarn, cloth, and blankets. According to one account, the "machinery consisted of a picker, a set of carding machines, a spinning machine of 192 spindles, four looms, a fulling mill, a chiring machine and a machine to double and twist stockings of yarn." Though the function of some of the machinery may be obscure, it is clear from the description that Patterson's mill was well-equipped. According to the 1850 census of industries the mill employed two hands in the conversion of 10,000 pounds of wool into 9,300 rolls of cloth valued at over $3,000.[10]

Patterson's mill, known variously as the Monmouth Woolen Mill and the Rockbridge Woolen Factory, was acquired by R. H. Brown in 1856 and afterward operated by his son F. M. Brown until it closed in 1902. An 1850s description enumerated in addition to the stone mill a "large frame cloth house, a wool house, three good dwelling houses, and necessary out houses." In 1856 R. H. Brown and an associate advertised their need for wool and announced they would provide customers "all kinds of Coloring [including] silk or woolen dresses, shawls, &c." The mill produced uniforms during the Civil War. In 1862 the mill manager petitioned the governor to return to him five workers who had been called to active service, noting that the mill was "the only factory of its kind in the county." At full capacity the mill employed eight to ten hands during the period. According to tradition a detachment from Hunter's Union raiding force paid a visit in 1864 and though most of the goods had been loaded in wagons and driven off to hiding places in the mountains, the soldiers "did considerable damage, shooting out windows, breaking the machinery and destroying material." The Rockbridge Woolen Factory anticipated the twentieth-century textile industry that was an important source of employment in such communities as Glasgow and Goshen.[11]

The James River Cement Company, established at Balcony Falls in 1848 according to census reports, was one of the county's most important industries during the second half of the nineteenth century owing to the scale of the operation, the size of its work force, and its unusual product. Charles Hess Locher built the plant to make hydraulic cement for the construction of the James River and Kanawha Canal, which passed beside the plant through the Balcony Falls lock. According to some accounts, a deposit of natural cement (argillaceous

limestone suitable for processing into cement and mortar) was discovered upstream on the James at Tunnel Hill, dug and hauled to the nearby river in carts, and transported by barge to the cement mill. The Locher plant operated during a period of experimentation in the manufacture of cement and was likely one of the nation's largest processors of natural cement at the time. In 1872 the plant employed approximately sixty men and featured in addition to kilns a blacksmith shop, a cooper shop, and a store which according to a period newspaper account did "a fine business." In the early 1870s the plant was reported to produce fifty barrels of cement a day.[12]

Photographs, one taken in 1879 or 1880 by Michael Miley, show a two-and-a-half-story building of conventional gable-roofed mill form with weatherboard siding and windows fitted with what appear to have been board shutters. The plant is said to have straddled the canal; it does not appear to do so in the Miley view but a later photo shows a frame building bridging the Balcony Falls lock which likely housed the turbine described in an 1879 census report. That year the canal was still the plant's principal mode of shipping its finished product, most of which was marketed in the cities of Richmond and Lynchburg and the state of Tennessee. The company used hand drills and horse-drawn conveyances to mine the cement and transport it to the river.[13]

The demise of the James River Cement Company in the early twentieth century is credited to the widespread adoption of Portland cement, an artificial cement, though Oren Morton blames a destructive flood for the plant's closing. Buildings come and go in photographs so perhaps a flood did sweep some away. The Locher family went on to found the Locher and Company brickworks at Glasgow, later operated by General Shale, and the cement mill site was redeveloped for hydroelectric power generation in the early twentieth century.[14]

Distilling was one of the most wide-spread of traditional Rockbridge industries. Estate inventories often mention whiskey-making equipment and the distilleries or stillhouses that housed the equipment appear among the declarations of the Mutual Assurance Society. Whiskey was the quintessential value-added product of the frontier and many farmers engaged in converting a portion of their grain harvests into more readily transportable spirits. The resourceful Christopher Clyce, wagon maker and lodging house operator, also operated a distillery which appears in his insurance declarations of 1803, 1805, and 1816. In 1803 the Clyce distillery was a one-story wood building containing a single still and apparently served by a chimney. By 1805 it had been extended on one end and raised to one and a half stories. Fairfield resident Samuel Moore had in 1803 two stills in his one-story wooden stillhouse, which measured 22 feet square. Two years later Moore had made substantial improvements, adding a half story to the building and increasing its value from $300 to $1,100.[15]

An extraordinarily detailed description of a period distillery is contained in the John Robinson papers. Robinson was an Irish-born entrepreneur known as "Jockey John" for his skills in horse trading. He made successful investments in military land certificates after the Revolutionary War and in 1790 purchased a 400-acre plantation at Hart's Bottom, a rich bottomland along the Maury River that a century later was developed as the city of Buena Vista. In 1802 Robinson opened an account with builder George Edgar to construct a complex of domestic, farm, and industrial buildings at the plantation. The complex included a stillhouse which from materials lists appears to have been a log building approximately 30 feet square with three doors, glazed windows (including two small ones that may have gone in a gable to light a loft), and a "porch platform & steps." A notation for "94 feet of spouts for eve" may refer to wooden gutters and downspouts. The interior was furnished with wooden equipment for converting grain into spirits; the still itself, which would have been copper, was not included in the lists, suggesting Robinson contracted for it with another party. The stillhouse had a "vat for pot ale" and a "warmer for still beer" with a step ladder to reach its top. Water was conveyed to the distillery from a springhouse through over two hundred feet of wooden pipes. These appear to have been square in section, hewn on four sides and bored through the center. The grain was stored in four garners or bins. Edgar's workmen also made mashing shovels, a painted cupboard and table, and a "scullary & trough for waste water." Robinson owned three stills in 1826 and his whiskey was said to have "the reputation of being the very finest that a 'gentleman could buy.'" That reputation extended regionally, for in 1826 a Lynchburg merchant requested of Robinson "a boat load of your common whiskey." Robinson complied by shipping the merchant forty-two forty-gallon barrels.[16]

By the eve of the Civil War the sixteen county distilleries enumerated in the census of 1860 produced 97,000 gallons of whiskey. The more advanced operations, like the "stone distillery, newly re-fitted" in 1859 at Bolivar Mills on Buffalo Creek, boasted mechanized production. Evidence suggests whiskey may have been consumed at stillhouses. In the 1820s or 1830s a drunken Bath Iron Works employee drowned "on his return from the Stillhouse," leaving "a widow with a parcel of children." Tragedies like this fueled temperance sentiment that led to local prohibition in 1900 and national prohibition two decades later, but the industry had begun to experience trouble earlier, in the late 1860s, when government excise taxes and regulations squeezed small producers. Some went underground to become the moonshine stills of mountain lore.[17]

The 1880 industrial census may have caught the transition in progress. In addition to big distilleries like that of Adam Zollman on the waters of Buffalo Creek, capitalized at $6,000 with a production of $10,000 in spirits, the census listed smaller outfits like Joseph Crawford's distillery, capitalized at $50, and Edward Herring's, capitalized at $35. The Crawford and Herring distilleries produced spirits the year the statistics were gathered (1879) but several other small stills were described as "not in operation during year," either a temporary shutdown or the beginning of the end. The census also enumerated the "fruit" distilleries of W. T. Womeldorf and David A. Hemp, relatively small operations that presumably made apple brandy. Though it is possible some nineteenth-century distilleries operated in nondescript buildings that survive on county farms, most are apparently gone. Fire was an essential part of the distilling process and likely contributed to the loss of many stillhouses. Jack Campbell's distillery in the South

The stillhouse at
Willson Farm (Tuckaway).
Courtesy RHS/SC, WLU

River area was one such casualty, burned along with thirty barrels of
whiskey in 1885.[18]

One of the few historic distilleries in the county to be documented photographically was a stone stillhouse ruin surveyed by Pam
Simpson on the Lexington-area Willson Farm (Tuckaway) in 1978.
A photographer captured it in more intact condition in the 1930s
at which time it was a story-and-a-half building with a storage loft. A
door to the loft had a pulley boom for lifting heavy items like grain
sacks from wagons parked below. Despite the costliness implied by
its stone construction, the Willson distillery is elusive in the records.
Samuel Willson, an early owner of the farm, possessed two stills, miscellaneous distillery equipment, and sixty-five gallons of apple brandy
at the time of his death in 1808. He and his son Robert insured what
was presumably the same property with the Mutual Assurance Society in 1805, although the declaration does not appear to include a
stillhouse. Robert Willson acquired the farm and in 1812 erected the
handsome Federal style brick house that stands there today. He may
have been the one to build the distillery that Hoyt and Simpson documented although it has not been identified in the 1850 or 1860 federal censuses (an omission that may have a number of explanations).
Two other Willsons—John, who lived on nearby Whistle Creek, and
James—worked as distillers in 1820. It may be that one or both operated the distillery for Robert Willson.[19]

A sense of the craft industries that were once common in the county's villages can be had in Brownsburg. According to Joseph Martin's *Gazetteer*, in 1835 Brownsburg and its vicinity boasted three wheelwrights, two blacksmith shops, a cabinet-maker, a carpenter, a gristmill, and a merchant mill. There were also a tanyard and manufactories for the making of leather goods such as a saddler, a hatter, and two shoe factories (the latter perhaps more on the order of cobbler shops). The saddler may have been John Alexander who insured his two-story wood dwelling and saddle shop with the Mutual Assurance Society in 1845. The 1860 federal census adds other trades: cooper, wagon-maker, millwright, potter, plasterer, brickmasons, stonemasons, and distiller. The principal survival from this cohort of industries is a one-story brick blacksmith shop dated to the 1820s which adjoins the log dwelling known as the Kerr House. (The two buildings were joined in recent years.) The blacksmithy stands on the village main street, a former turnpike, convenient to travelers and townsfolk.

From a later period is the William Dunaway shoe shop, a small gabled frame building dated ca. 1880. When railroads bypassed Brownsburg in the late nineteenth century its industrial component faded away—with an important exception: a saddle factory where the Wilburn Saddle (a saddle type reminiscent of a cavalry saddle) was produced.[20]

Blacksmith shops like the one in Brownsburg make their appearance in the Mutual Assurance Society declarations. William S. Douglas, "residing at the Bent of Buffalo," insured a one-story brick "smith shop" in 1817. According to the declaration for the building, "This shop has in it a tilt hammer worked with water, upon each fireplace there is a chimney." A tilt hammer was a water-powered device for hammering iron on an anvil and a common sight in the county's forges.[21]

Another small-scale industry of the era was pottery making. At the end of the eighteenth century Benjamin Darst established a pottery in the section of Lexington later known as Mudtown. Darst's pottery would have included a pugmill for processing the clay and a kiln for firing the wares. From

Tompkins Mill, a log mill from the early days.
Photo (ca. 1900) courtesy RHS/SC, WLU

pottery making it was a short step to brickmaking, which Darst profitably followed beginning in the 1790s. Others established potteries in the nineteenth century, and a good deal is known about their setups as the result of excavations by Washington and Lee archaeologists led by pottery specialist Kurt Russ. The Rockbridge Baths Pottery, established ca. 1840 across the Maury River from the resort community by the same name, had a circular updraft kiln, a "Potter shop" mentioned in an 1857 reference, and a small clay processing and storage area. The Firebaugh Pottery at Bustleburg featured an oval kiln of complex construction with brick arches, fireboxes, and flues. It appears to have been operated by John Firebaugh, a Pennsylvania native who moved to Rockbridge around 1820 and established the pottery in conjunction with another potter, John Morgan, probably in the 1820s. An indication of the products of the Firebaugh Pottery is given by items sold from Firebaugh's estate in 1867 including a "pipe mold" and "pitcher molds."[22]

Potteries, blacksmith shops, distilleries, and mills were relatively standard fare in the region. More unusual was an industrial use conceived for Natural Bridge during the War of 1812. In 1814 Lexington entrepreneur William Caruthers Sr. traveled to Monticello to propose a lease arrangement with then-owner Thomas Jefferson for the making of lead shot at the Bridge, a process that involved dropping molten lead from a height. Through a misunderstanding Jefferson instead leased the Bridge to Dr. Philip Thornton of Richmond, but Jefferson subsequently facilitated a mutual undertaking by the two men. Thornton acquired the lead for the undertaking at the lead mines in Wythe County, not far from the famous ca. 1807 Shot Tower on the New River which presumably inspired the scheme Thornton and Caruthers developed.[23]

An 1872 Lexington newspaper article picks up the story. Caruthers and Thornton constructed a frame housing that overhung the edge of the Bridge. An opening in the floor connected to an "immense tube of tow linen with ribs or hoops of wood inside to keep it fully open, extending from the Bridge to the creek [Cedar Creek] below." Workers dripped molten lead into the tube, the drops forming into spherical shot by the time they hit the water which provided a (relatively) soft landing.[24]

In February 1815 Caruthers wrote to Jefferson that peace between the United States and Britain ("the late pleasant change in our National affairs") had forced him and Thornton to rethink their plans.

"It may be necessary to add some other branches of the plumbery business," Caruthers wrote. He concluded his letter with a promise: "Soon as I get the Shot Making a little more perfected I will send you a sample to amuse yourself with." Between Caruthers's February letter and one in March a "part of the fix" burned and Caruthers suggested to Jefferson that if he wanted the shot factory to continue he would need to consider selling the Bridge to Caruthers and his partners (a Mr. Brown of Richmond was also involved) because they did not plan to make the necessary repairs and improvements on leased property. "I have no idea of selling the land," Jefferson replied. "I view it in some degree as a public trust." Jefferson's decision appears to have ended the Natural Bridge Shot Factory, but Caruthers had other metal industries to keep him busy. He operated an ironworks at the location of the future Buena Vista Furnace and a workshop with a forge and tilt hammer at Irish Creek where cannon carriages were said to have been produced for the government during the War of 1812. He also manufactured nails, although according to the author of the 1872 article Caruthers "did not succeed well . . . whether because of a want of sufficient market here, or its remoteness from city markets and cost of transportation, we know not."[25]

Another specialized industrial activity occurred at Natural Bridge, or more specifically at Saltpeter Cave located on the property. The shallow shelter-type cave takes its name from saltpeter, a naturally occurring form of potassium nitrate that forms in bat guano and is an essential ingredient of gunpowder. Saltpeter was mined on the property by at least 1809, as described in a letter from William Caruthers to Thomas Jefferson in which Caruthers reported $90 in proceeds "arising from the sale of Salt petre got for rent of a little Cave on the N Bridge Tract of land." Caruthers noted that the operation was not without problems. The proceeds "ought to have been more But two of the fellows ran off and I have never been able to collect from them what they owed you."[26]

Saltpeter was again mined on the property during the Civil War. Hoppers, kettles, and a hearth with a flue for processing the saltpeter stood across Cedar Creek from the cave mouth. Associated with the works was a water main of four-foot-long sections of narrow-bore concrete piping. Geologist Chester A. Reeds, who studied the Bridge and associated caves in the 1920s, believed the pipes were laid to deliver water to the 1812 workings, and it appears the manner of their

The Buffalo Forge mill was an integral part of William Weaver's antebellum industrial enterprises. Photo (1935) by William Hoyt, courtesy SC, WLU

manufacture was described to him because he wrote, "A pole of green wood, slightly tapered and greased, was used as an inner form for laying the cement. After the mortar about the pole had hardened, the pole was withdrawn for the next section."[27]

Reeds was likely off on his date for the concrete pipes, which more likely dated to the Civil War saltpeter manufactory, though his interest in the subject was warranted. Concrete use during the nineteenth century was experimental and Rockbridge County appears to have been at the forefront of innovation. In the 1850s Fancy Hill farmers T. B. and W. F. Poague patented a *"new mode* of making Hydraulic Cement Piping." A correspondent to the *Southern Planter* reported on the Poagues' invention in 1854, noting that a "good specimen of this piping can be seen at the old Hotel at Natural Bridge, where the water is conveyed some 600 yards, by a two inch pipe, crossing Cedar Creek twice." The pipes were also installed "at the Hotel of Mr. N. G. Moore, ten miles south of Lexington" (possibly the Fancy Hill vicinity). Concrete tile pipe thought to date to the antebellum period is reported at Buffalo Forge where three-foot-long sections with two-inch bores conducted water from a spring to William Weaver's house. The *Southern Planter* correspondent touted the affordability of cement and suggested readers purchase it from "Locker's [Locher's] Cement Works . . . at 37½ cents a bushel." The Natural Bridge Hotel preserves a specimen of old water pipe in its collections although it is apparently wood instead of cement, perhaps a relic of an earlier waterworks. Another vestige of the saltpeter workings, a log ruin from the Civil War era, survived long enough to be pictured in 1880s Natural Bridge promotional materials. The ruins may have belonged to a "leaching device" though they appear larger and cruder than saltpeter hoppers that survive in Organ Cave in West Virginia, the region's (and perhaps the nation's) largest collection of such hoppers.[28]

Industries sometimes clustered at locations with good waterpower or access to materials and transport. The leading industrial complex

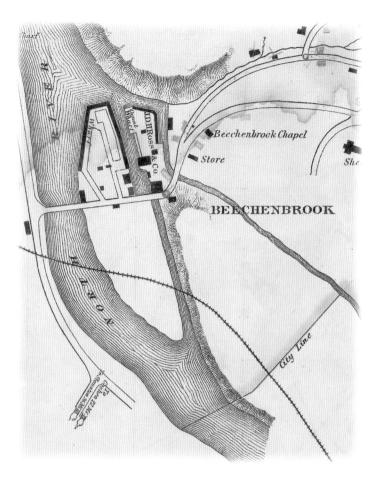

Detail of "Gray's New Map of Lexington" (1877) showing Jordan's Point.
Courtesy SC, WLU

prior to the era of urbanization was Jordan's Point, developed on the low-lying point of land at the confluence of the North (later Maury) River and Woods Creek, also the location where the Great Road crossed the river. In 1778 William Alexander opened a store at a ford at the Point (he also sold a little unlicensed liquor on the side, for which he was fined), but the location takes its name from later owner John Jordan who in 1818 built the house now known as Stono on the commanding heights above the river. In 1837 an engineer with the state Board of Public Works passed through on a river navigations survey and sketched facilities including as many as four water-powered industries, among them Jordan's Mill, a cotton factory, and a small tilt hammer. A structure spanning the river was labeled "Jordans Mill Dam & Bridge" and is shown with what appears to be a sluice used by batteaux to get through the dam. An 1839 description makes reference to a Lexington Mills and Smithery. In 1854, after John Jordan's death, development at the Point included two dwellings, a slaughterhouse, and a stable, and in 1859 a mill, foundry, and factory also stood there.[29]

The North River Navigation company located the terminus of its canal at Jordan's Point and the first canal packet is said to have docked there in November 1860. The Point's new status as a head of canal navigation for the James-Maury river system touched off an industrial and commercial boomlet. Architectural historian Catharine Gilliam lists in her study of the Point some of the buildings standing in 1863: a mill and miller's house, sawmill, foundry and forge, factory, shops, public wharf, gauge dock, and dwellings including a tollhouse/dwelling for a second, covered bridge built across the Maury River in the antebellum period.[30]

Photographs of the Point in later decades show a density of development that was urban in feel. The complex functioned almost as an independent community, a commercial-industrial satellite of Lexington. Today, except for the Miller's House on the northern periphery of the complex, the Point has lost most of its above-ground historic resources, though an echo of its former importance as a magnet for development, and the importance of the associated river crossing, is seen in the nineteenth-century buildings that trail along US Route 11 below VMI and the development in East Lexington. Extensive stonework retaining walls, foundation remnants, and bridge abutments also survive at the Point.

The industrial heart of Jordan's Point in the late 1800s. The forward wing of the Beechenbrook Foundry and Machine Works, probably the factory office, has chevron-pattern Stick style wood siding. Courtesy SC, WLU

An 1862 advertisement described the factory at Jordan's Point as "a large building originally designed for a Cotton Factory," also the term used in the 1837 river survey. Rockbridge was not a cotton-growing area; perhaps the plan was to process cotton shipped by canal from the Piedmont. A later reference noted that the building stood four stories in height and was used as a "Storing House," by which was presumably meant a warehouse. It and other buildings were burned in Hunter's Raid in 1864 but the Point was rebuilt after the war. Interest in textile manufacturing revived in the early 1880s with a proposal to use a four-story building (probably the old factory) for a woolen mill, although the project did not come to pass. The Loyall, Lilly, and Gilmore sash and blind factory opened in the 1890s, offering a range of building supplies to the Lexington public. In the early twentieth century the Lexington Roller Mills used a water-powered turbine to produce flour in a mansarded brick building that may have been the remodeled mill from earlier. The roller mill and other buildings were served by a spur of the Chesapeake and Ohio line, the successor to the Richmond and Alleghany line which in the 1880s had built its tracks on the tow path of the James River and Kanawha Canal along the James River through the southern part of the county.[31]

The C&O line downstream from Jordan's Point. The modern Chessie Trail follows its course.
Courtesy of Jeremy Leadbetter

A park and playing fields now occupy Jordan's Point. The City of Lexington, with the guidance of preservationists, has restored the Miller's House, a two-story stone and brick dwelling of side-gabled form, and archaeologists are investigating remnants of the Point's industrial heritage. The Point's transportation heritage lives on in the Chessie Trail, a rails-to-trails conversion that follows the Maury River between Lexington and Buena Vista and is a vantage for observing canal locks and railroad trestle abutments from the days of the packet boats and steam locomotives.

Ironworking activities at Jordan's Point were supplied by iron produced at county furnaces. One of the best preserved is Glenwood Furnace, a charcoal-fired blast furnace erected in 1849 for ironmasters Francis T. Anderson and David Shanks at a location in Arnold's Valley (also known as Arnold or Arnolds Valley) about a mile from the James River. The truncated pyramidal stone structure retains a number of features associated with its former use. Its tuyere arch, a cavelike opening spanned by massive lintel stones, received the spouts of water-powered tub bellows that fed oxygen to the fire inside.[32]

When the furnace was "in blast," molten iron dripped down through a layer cake of iron ore, charcoal, and limestone flux in the core of the furnace (the bosh chamber), collected in a crucible, and ran out through a tap arch into grooves dug into the sand floor of the casting house. The main grooves were known as sows and the subsidiary ones as pigs for the resemblance of the whole to a sow with nursing piglets (hence the term "pig iron"). Workers loaded the furnace from a charging bridge that formerly connected the top of the stack to a bank behind. With its sharply defined stonework, traces of the race through which water flowed to turn the bellows wheel, and evidence of an 1874 refurbishing, Glenwood Furnace illustrates important aspects of ironmaking during the period, and its stone stack is the best preserved in the county, though it lacks the many essential ancillary buildings and structures that once crowded around it.[33]

Glenwood Furnace.
Photo by Michael Pulice,
courtesy DHR

The county's first ironworks may have been Grant's Furnace, located on Irish Creek and believed by some to have been in operation by about 1760. This may have been the same furnace as the Irish Creek Furnace which historian D. E. Brady Jr. prudently noted was "variously dated" 1760 to 1779. Also on Irish Creek stood the Dougherty Forge, later known as the Rockbridge Foundry. In 1854 new owners of the foundry, J. M. and T. B. Taylor, stated in the Lexington paper that "Our Machinists and Casters are very superior workmen — skilled and possessing a thorough and accurate knowledge of their business in its minutest details." Taylor and Taylor's Rockbridge Foundry manufactured "one, two, four and six-horse Axles, together with Plows, Corn-crushers, Plaster Crushers, Corn Shellers, and Cooking Ranges, &c., &c." Their wagon axletrees were made from "Rockbridge *hammered* iron," the ironmasters stressed, not Northern rolled iron. "Any man who tries these hammered iron Axle-trees," they boasted, "will never again resort to the rolled or the wooden ones." The foundry also manufactured Cardwell's Horse-Powers and Threshers, "the best, safest, and in the end the cheapest" farm machinery of its type. (By "horse powers" the advertisers may have meant horse-powered power-trains.) Mill gearing and waterwheel components were among the foundry's products, and the owners noted that "old castings [are] taken in trade," presumably to be melted down and recast as new ironware.[34]

Buena Vista Furnace and commissary. The furnace was also known as Jordan Furnace.
Photos (1968) by Isley, courtesy DHR

Irish Creek flows into South River, an area D. E. Brady Jr. dubbed "Iron Valley" for its iron ore deposits and the ironworks they supported. Vesuvius Furnace was built in 1828 in the community that bears its name, and its operators scoured surrounding mountainsides for timber to make the charcoal used for fuel. According to accounts the Vesuvius Furnace colliers "would clean off a place for a hearth, burn all the wood close around, then move on somewhere else, and do the same thing." Down South River, near its confluence with the Maury River, the Buena Vista Furnace was built in 1848 and christened for the famous Mexican War battle that took place the year before. (The name was later chosen for the scenically-situated nearby boomtown of Buena Vista, presumably in part due to its meaning, "good view.") A period photograph shows the Buena Vista ironworks to have been an extensive complex. At the center stood the truncated pyramid of the furnace which had a pointed, corbelled tuyere arch instead of the square-headed type seen at Glenwood. On top of the furnace perched what may have been a gabled bridge house, the terminus of the charging bridge. Furnace bridge houses were "liable to burn," wrote a nineteenth century insurance underwriter, "as the blaze from the stack when being charged will often strike the roof and fire the building."[35]

In a row near the Buena Vista Furnace stood the superintendent's house and the company store or commissary. The house was a standard two-story side-gabled dwelling of brick construction. The one-story store was also brick but, unlike the gable-fronted stores common in the nineteenth century Rockbridge countryside, it had a side-gable form entered on the non-gable side. A two-story stone mill was erected in the 1830s (evidence suggests ironworking at the location long preceded the construction of the 1848 furnace). According to tradition, before the furnace was disabled in Hunter's Raid in 1864 the ironworks transported its product to canal boats on the Maury River via a tramway.[36]

Ironmaking attracted men who were willing to gamble for a shot at fortune. In 1834 Robert McCormick and his son Cyrus H. McCormick tried their luck in the trade, purchasing the Cotopaxi Furnace on the South River, but the venture failed. More promising were their activities in the blacksmith shop at their farm Walnut Grove, located on the Rockbridge-Augusta line between Steeles Tavern and Raphine. Robert tinkered with a design for a mechanical reaper, a machine that would automate the ancient chore of reaping and gathering grain. He was unable to perfect the device but in 1831 Cyrus successfully demonstrated an improvement in a neighbor's oat field and went into production. Local demand was limited for the McCormick Reaper, manufactured by Cyrus, other family members, and their slaves in the farm's log blacksmith shop (located on the Augusta side of the county line), but Cyrus found eager customers in the Midwest. He left Virginia for Chicago and with two brothers founded the McCormick Manufacturing Company. The company's machines contributed to a revolution in American agriculture and farming practices abroad. The blacksmithy/workshop where it all began has been preserved, as has the Walnut Grove house, a well-appointed Federal style brick residence with attached dependencies which stands partly in Rockbridge County.[37]

Though the county's early iron industry centered on the Blue Ridge, in the nineteenth century outliers developed in other parts of the county. The Mount Hope and California furnaces operated on Brattons Run near Rockbridge Alum Springs, an area of abundant mountain forest lands for making charcoal. In the valley at the head of Goshen Pass stood Lydia Furnace, purchased by William Weaver in 1825 and renamed Bath Furnace in honor of the Rockbridge Baths resort below the Pass. Weaver arrived in Rockbridge from his native Pennsylvania in 1814 to take up ownership of Union Forge on lower Buffalo Creek, which he renamed Buffalo Forge. His partner in the

The Caroline Iron Ore Mine in the Blue Ridge Mountains near Buena Vista. Photo (ca. 1890) courtesy RHS/SC, WLU

venture was Thomas Mayburry, scion of a Pennsylvania ironmaking family, and the two acquired the forge and two furnaces in Botetourt County from William Wilson. The partners entered the business at a profitable time—the War of 1812 and a British blockade had raised prices for bar iron—but ironmaking was still a risky undertaking. "Iron makers had to balance a variety of components," notes historian Charles Bodie. In addition to the technical aspects an ironmaster needed to assemble and supervise a work force and had to anticipate and react to shifting markets. Fires, floods, and cash-flow problems were constant headaches. Ironmaking, writes Bodie, "was not for the weak-hearted."[38]

At first Weaver and Mayburry used a mixed force of free and slave furnace hands carried over from Wilson's operation. Weaver subsequently moved toward work forces composed chiefly of slave workers, a story told by historian Charles Dew in *Bond of Iron*. The partners may also have acquired a preexisting ironmaster's or overseer's house at the forge. The oldest section of Mount Pleasant is a two-story frame dwelling with beaded weatherboards (visible in the attic) attached with wrought-headed nails, features that suggest the house was built before Weaver and Mayburry came into ownership in 1814, though the date is early enough in the transition from wrought to cut-nail technology that it is possible the partners manufactured the nails and had the house built.[39]

Mount Pleasant, the ironmaster's mansion at Buffalo Forge.
Photo by Dan Pezzoni

Wilson's forge building was located on or near Buffalo Creek since forges on the scale of his operation typically had water-powered tilt hammers for beating raw pig iron castings into more finished product. Further working produced the "merchant bar" iron prized by industrialists and village blacksmiths and shipped down the James River to markets in Lynchburg and Richmond. In Weaver's day the stone building that contained the forge stood directly on the creek below a dam and was accompanied by a sawmill and a coal house for storing charcoal. Further downstream stood a blacksmith shop and gristmill, the latter located on a millrace that fed water to the complex from another source and powered a flour mill higher up. The flour mill, now a precarious stone ruin, stood two and a half stories on a tall basement story and was likely among the larger milling operations of its day in the county. It appears prominently in an 1860 ambrotype photo of the forge property and another photo from about the same time; images also show Weaver's mansion (minus the Gothic Revival dormers his heir Daniel C. E. Brady added to the roof), the mansion's detached stone kitchen and adjacent guest house, Weaver's office, stables, a harness shop, and a store. The mansion and two slave houses behind it, as well as the mill ruins and extensive stone terraces, survive at Buffalo Forge, which was listed in the national and state registers in 2004 owing to its architectural richness and the wealth of its historical associations.[40]

A portion of the extensive Buffalo Forge complex is shown in this sketch from the late 1800s.
Courtesy RHS/SC, WLU

Weaver had dissolved his partnership with Mayburry by the time he acquired Bath Furnace in 1825. The furnace was located on the opposite side of the county from his forge on Buffalo Creek and was also separated from it by Goshen Pass through which threaded a treacherous, albeit scenic, wagon road. To process a portion of the Bath Furnace castings into more transportable bar iron, Weaver had Bath Forge erected downstream in 1827–28, at the head of the Pass and just below the confluence of the Big and Little Calfpasture rivers which form the Maury. Water power was an important consideration in siting the new forge. (The older forge on Buffalo Creek operated at capacity during the period and could not expand owing to insufficient water to run additional machinery.) The product of Bath Forge was freighted through the Pass and loaded onto batteaux at Cedar Grove, the head of navigation on the Maury River.[41]

The case brought against Weaver by Jordan, Davis and Company in the late 1830s and the subsequent appeal detail the physical features of buildings and structures at Bath Iron Works. Jordan, Davis and Company's stonemasons rebuilt the furnace in 1830 at an expense of over $3,000. Unlike most of the county's furnaces the rebuilt Bath Furnace was conical in form and appears to have had three levels: a base, a 36–foot-tall main stack, and what may have been a 30-foot-high conical stone chimney that tapered from nine feet across at the base to one and a half feet at the top. Iron sows, each weighing 1,600 pounds, served as lintels over the furnace openings. A bellows wheel stood close by the stack, the water to power it delivered by race from a dam across the Big Calfpasture River. The dam was built of hewn log

Wooden crib dams for canal works and industrial waterpower were once a common site on the Maury River (the location of this example) and lesser streams.

cribbing, filled with stone and planked on the upstream side, and it measured nearly 200 feet across its breast. Also at the furnace stood a warehouse, a shop with a turning lathe and carpentry and smith tools, a "sleeping room" (perhaps a shelter for the workers to rest when the furnace was in blast), a stable and associated sheds, a bark mill, a kitchen and smokehouses, and a privy. The exhaustively detailed inventories in the *Weaver* case enumerated tools, listed work horses by name (Charley, Ned, "Dare-devel" and others), and even affixed a $33.33 value to "all the turnips, potatoes, beets, &c., in [the] garden."[42]

The forge at Bath Forge had multiple "hammer wheels." One was built by millwright William Clark in 1833 and stood eleven and a half feet high. The forge complex included dwellings, a kitchen, saw and gristmills, a coal house, a log blacksmith shop with a board roof, a stable, and a springhouse containing "crout jars." There were also miscellaneous bridges, necessary to cross the races that ran through the site (and which are visible today along with the stone foundations and chimney falls of the forge buildings). The coal house was built of logs and measured about thirty feet square. This was apparently small by

Industries

the standards of the nineteenth century when iron-works coal houses could measure 150 by 60 feet in dimension and 20 feet high, but the constant supply of charcoal from surrounding forests probably obviated the need for long-term storage and a larger structure. Charcoal production was one of the more destructive aspects of period ironmaking; a single blast furnace could consume as much as 250 to 300 acres of hardwood forest annually.[43]

Bath Iron Works was a community as much as it was an industrial complex and in that respect it was similar to industrial communities based on other types of activities that coalesced in the county during the antebellum period. Mechanicsville, a diffuse aggregation of workshops and dwellings, developed along Mill Creek near its confluence with the Maury River below Buena Vista. In February 1838 the hydraulic cement mill of David Edmondson that stood near the mouth of the creek was described in detail in a Lexington newspaper:

> The works consist of three permanent kilns for burning the limestone, and a mill with two pair of [mill] stones, for reducing the burnt stone to a fine powder. The stone after burning, is crushed in common plaster mills, from which it falls into the hoppers of the pulverizing mills. The Cement is put up in barrels of five bushels each, and is shipped from the door to its place of destination.

"Shipped from the door" meant by batteau since the North River Canal had not yet been built, though construction of the James River and Kanawha Canal was the impetus for Edmondson and his partner, a Mr. Graham of Lexington, to produce cement. The newspaper noted that the canal's contract for the firm's cement "will bring into our county nearly $20,000–$12,500 for the Cement and $5,000 for the barrels, for which the [canal] pays 50 cents each. If to this the freight be added, the amount will not be far short of $30,000." The Edmondson Cement Mill predated the Locher cement works at Balcony Falls by about ten years; presumably it was an impetus for Locher to establish the larger works downstream.[44]

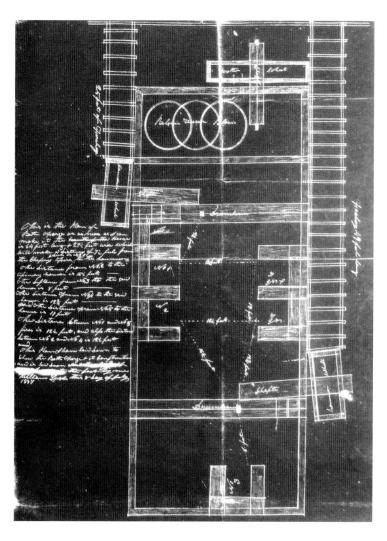

Bath Forge plan drawn by William Lusk in 1837 showing forebays, waterwheels, bellows, and drumbeams. Blueprint copy courtesy SC, WLU

The Edmondson mill stood in the midst of other industries. Hartsook's blacksmith shop operated near the Forge Road crossing of Mill Creek. Somewhere in the vicinity stood the wheat fan factory of Henry and Joseph Amole, in operation by 1823. Wheat fans, also known as fanning mills, were hand-cranked machines used to separate wheat from chaff. According to an 1880s account of the Amoles' manufactory, its wheat fans were the "first made in this part of the country," and in period advertisements the Amoles claimed their machines were "warranted first rate and have Cast Iron Cog Wheels." In an 1835 "Notice to Blacksmiths" which Henry Amole ran in the Lexington paper, he stated, "I wish to employ two first rate Blacksmiths on the shares, a man of family would be preferred. A person of steady, industrious habits, would do well at this place." In addition to wheat fans and other items, batteaux were apparently made at Mechanicsville; in 1823 the Amoles described their factory as being "near the Boat Yard Mills." An 1837 river navigation survey shows this to have been a name for the mill at the mouth of Buffalo Creek.[45]

Balcony Falls on the James River across from Glasgow was another early industrial community although originally its transportation component appears to have been uppermost. The Blue Ridge Canal came through in the 1820s to bypass the falls and Charles Locher established his cement plant at the location in 1848. The community extended upstream on the Maury River to the farm of Edward Echols where iron ore was mined in the 1850s. In 1859 Echols wrote to his son that the iron manufacturing firm of Jordan Winn and Company were:

> Starting a large furnace near Richmond and expect to get the most of their iron from here. They are now running two heavy tunnels into the mountain, above the schoolhouse, for the purpose of reaching the vein of ore and when they do so they will commence a very heavy work here. They now have employed at this point 16 hands and have authorized me to employ 6 or 8 more. All the houses on my little place are pretty well filled at present and they are erecting more for their miners.

In addition to the schoolhouse and miner houses mentioned in the letter, buildings on the Echols property formerly included a canal warehouse, a slave cabin (built ca. 1855), and, by the early twentieth century, a church.[46]

Mechanicsville, Balcony Falls, and the county's other pre-boom industrial communities were generally small affairs. In the twentieth century they mostly faded away — Mechanicsville, for example, is now virtually indistinguishable from the rural landscape that surrounds it — but quite a different fate awaited the community of Green Forest. The village was established in the 1880s at the north end of Hart's Bottom near the junction of two important regional rail lines, the Shenandoah Valley and the Richmond and Alleghany. The principal landowner, Benjamin C. Moomaw, was probably inspired by the explosive growth of Roanoke on the Shenandoah Valley line (a predecessor of Norfolk Southern) to lay out a town, which he named Green Forest, near the confluence of Chalk Mine Run and the Maury River (Moomaw's nearby house was named Green Forest). In 1882 Moomaw attracted a sizable industrial plant, the Appold Tannery, to the village. When a reporter visited the tannery in 1886, thousands of cords of tanbark were stacked on the grounds, the harvest of surrounding forests and the source of the tannins used to process the four hundred hides that weekly went into the making of leather for footwear, saddles, and harnesses. Photographs show long one- and two-story tannery buildings and the iron stack of the boiler that powered the machinery. In terms of physical size the Appold Tannery may have been the largest industrial plant of its day in the county.[47]

But it was not enough for the boosterish Moomaw. "A flourishing village preceded Buena Vista by several years," he wrote in 1909, and "it was the rapid growth of this village which suggested to the writer the possibility of a much larger development. In addition to the tannery I had secured a canning factory, planing mill, pulp mill, and was reaching out after some other industries, but it soon became clear that unless large capital and good executive ability could be enlisted in the enterprise I would at best only have a village, with a few industries and a store or two." Moomaw teamed with T. E. McCorkle, Alexander T. Barclay, and others to form the Buena Vista Company, chartered in 1887. Two years later the company laid out the town and soon-to-be city of Buena Vista. What would come to be known as the Boom was on in Rockbridge County.[48]

This 1890 photo of Buena Vista shows Green Forest-related development including the Appold Tannery in the distance.
Courtesy SC, WLU

Goshen Depot.

EIGHT

Cities

"BOOM IT TO THE CLOUDS." That's what Thomas Grasty promised he would do for the infant city of Buena Vista. The Washington and Lee alumnus, a correspondent with the *Manufacturers' Record* journal which promoted city development "booms" across the South, made the offer in a January 1890 letter to his friend Frank Glasgow, one of the directors of the Buena Vista Company. Grasty was in North Carolina after reporting on urbanization initiatives in Alabama. "Strictly *entre nous*," he wrote Glasgow, "I am greatly disgusted with some of these Southern schemes. I believe Virginia is to be the coming state [if] properly managed. Those Florence [Alabama] fellows have seriously shaken my confidence by their apparent reckless disregard for their *word*. There is an old saying that a man who will lie will steal." A few years later, in the midst of the economic depression of the mid-1890s, there would be investors in Rockbridge County boom towns who felt, if not lied to and robbed, greatly disgusted with the investments they made.[1]

But at Buena Vista in 1889–1890 the present was too exciting for people to worry about the future. A lot survey in February 1889 resulted in the laying out of an extensive grid across low-lying Harts Bottom — prone to flooding from the Maury River, but no one worried about that either — and up onto the flanks of the Blue Ridge. According to one account, the development company "strung up thousands of light bulbs over fields plotted out as neighborhoods" to help prospective lot purchasers locate streets and lots. The grid of lights

Facing page: Goshen Railroad Station. Photo (early 1900s) courtesy of the Library of Virginia

Above: Goshen Land Company Bridge ornamental cresting. The bridge was built in 1890 at the height of Goshen's boom. Photo by Dan Pezzoni

175

must have dazzled visitors — Edison's incandescent light bulb was just over a decade old and largely a big city luxury at the time — and would have contributed a carnival atmosphere to the proceedings. The bright mirage of the future metropolis, quipped a visitor, was the only place in Virginia "where you could hunt bull frogs by electric light."[2]

Meanwhile, at the south end of the county, another boom was getting under way. "Wednesday, March 5th, 1890, was the opening day of our new city, GLASGOW," wrote a correspondent to the *Lexington Gazette*. "All day the clouds hung low but the rain and snow failed to dampen the enthusiasm of the men who have started this enterprise, and of the seekers for the best lots. The future prosperity of Glasgow shone like a ray of sunlight through the gloom, and the hearts of the real estate agents beat high with hope, for every train brought an addition to the crowd, and they all wanted — LOTS."[3]

A series of panoramic photographs of Glasgow's town site taken from surrounding mountainsides depicts a lot sale from the period. Out amid the streets and blocks carved into the flat bottomland at the confluence of the James and Maury rivers a crowd of people mills around a false-fronted frame building, presumably the development company office. The building stands at the middle of a block; to its north, at the corner, is what appears to be a tent with a drift of smoke issuing from it, maybe a concession stand to provide warming snacks to the gathering throngs. On the south corner of the block stands a larger tent, probably the location of the lot sale itself. Perhaps appropriately, the second tent has the oval form and drooping roof of a circus tent. The photographs show a dreary winter day: not, however, evidence of "the worst March snow storm we have been in since the war" described in the newspaper account of the initial sale. At that event "about 200 people waded through the slush from early morning till late in the evening in search of lots. The real estate agents, although half frozen, did a good business, and sold over two hundred thousand dollars worth of lots."[4]

While the rabble braved the cold and slush, the stockholders drew their Glasgow town lots in the comfort of the Natural Bridge Hotel. They included Governor Philip W. McKinney and a former governor, Fitzhugh Lee, a nephew of R. E. Lee and president of Glasgow's development company, the Rockbridge Company. The stockholder drawing took place "under the management of Mr. C. M. Figgat, cashier of the Bank of Lexington." That was Charles M. Figgat, a trusted member

The site of Glasgow during an 1890 lot sale. Courtesy of Dan Pezzoni

of the community who in 1895, after the development boom went bust, departed the Lexington train station with two heavy valises. As Charles Bodie tells the story, a bystander who assisted Figgat joked that the bags were heavy enough to contain gold. He was not far off; they held $180,000 in stolen deposits. Figgat eluded capture for four years, dying, apparently by his own hand, in Colorado in 1899. The investigations into his affairs revealed he had been embezzling for years—and spending some of the proceeds on bad boom town lots.[5]

Another account of the Glasgow boom—and its eventual bust—comes from the memoir of Sally Sadler Cleveland, who arrived in Glasgow with her husband, Dr. John Cleveland, at the height of the Boom in 1890 or 1891. "The Duke and Duchess of Marlborough were touring the Southern States," at the time of a Glasgow lot sale, Cleveland recalled. "They stopped for a few days in Natural Bridge and were invited to attend the [land] auction sale at Glasgow . . . Even these dignified Britishers caught the bidding infection, bought a lot and paid half cash as the terms required. That added good fuel to the fire and many lots were sold that day in the prospective town."[6]

Before the Clevelands moved to Glasgow, the doctor visited the town site with investor John Williams. Cleveland bought a lot and built a house and drugstore. Williams established a large sash and blind factory for the manufacture of wooden building components. "There were contracts for fifty five-room houses to be built in sixty days," Sally Cleveland recalled:

A large force of carpenters [was] brought in. Their hammers made music early and late. A large brick Masonic Temple was built. Several large homes were built and occupied. Several large industries were established; a rolling mill, a stove factory, and a tile mantle factory. Two hotels opened, a saw mill, several small business houses, meat shops and cake and candy shops.

"For several months all went merrily as a wedding bell," Cleveland summed up. But it was not to last. The development company had made "too large purchases of industrial plants with too liberal terms to the owners . . . All the industrial plants were in full blast for a few months, then the sad fact became known that the funds were exhausted. Everything came to a standstill by December 25 [1891]. So when the carpenters and all the employees went home for the holidays, they never came back to resume their jobs."[7]

"Build it and they will come" failed as a development model for Glasgow. The value of the town's building stock in 1892, over $50,000, had dropped to $16,425 by 1896. Factories idled when the Boom went bust were scavenged for building materials. St. John's Episcopal Church (ca. 1900; 1002 Blue Ridge Drive) is said to have been built with brick from an abandoned factory. But the fact of the church's construction was an indication of the town's reviving health at the turn of the century. Though some "paper towns" in the region failed to materialize or shriveled after a brief life, Glasgow survived.[8]

Several large buildings were built in Glasgow during the Boom, and these experienced varied fates in the following decades. The Rockbridge Hotel (1892), which was apparently shuttered before it opened as a hotel, served various functions including an African American school until it passed from the scene in the mid-twentieth century. The Masonic Temple described by Cleveland was the Baldwin-Echols Building (1890), an impressive three-story brick commercial block with Romanesque Revival arched windows, pressed metal globe finials and other façade ornament, and a pyramidal roof at its corner. Carl August Ruehrmund, a German-born and trained architect based in Richmond, designed the building, which housed a store on the first floor, the Rockbridge Tobacco Company on the second floor, and the Masonic meeting hall at the top. The building caught fire in 1940 and mostly collapsed though a one-story remnant survives. Comparable to the Baldwin-Echols Building in size and quality of detail was the Blue Ridge Building (ca. 1890), which stood on Blue Ridge Drive until its recent demolition. The three-story brick block featured ornamental metal cornices and window heads and "Queen Anne" windows and transoms edged with stained glass panes. A succession of cafes occupied

Early Glasgow churches: First Baptist Church, now Union Baptist Church *(top)*, and St. John's Episcopal Church *(bottom).* Photos by Don Hasfurther

Goshen Land and Improvement Company Office. The two-story building is identified as the Goodloe Hotel. Photo (ca. 1890) courtesy RHS/SC, WLU

the ground floor including, in 1937, the Blue Ridge Tea Room. Later than these boom-period buildings, but with a brighter future, is the former Glasgow Elementary School (1939; 800 block Fitzlee Street), a one-story brick building of understated Colonial Revival character designed by Waynesboro architects Fleming R. Hurt and C. D. Hurt Jr. The school closed in 1982 but in the mid-1990s was rehabilitated as housing for the elderly.[9]

Buena Vista's boom proved more robust than Glasgow's, although development during the first year (1889) failed to meet expectations. The editor of the *Buena Vista Advocate* blamed the poor showing on speculation which short-circuited the development feedback loop town promoters tried to foster. "Build! Build!!" the editor urged readers in January 1890. "Stop this everlasting speculation and go to building. A naked lot won't bring any rent, and has no real value except as the possible site of a building which would command a revenue."[10]

Two projects remedied Buena Vista's speculation problem. One was the construction of a handsome railroad station, the Union Depot, beginning in the summer of 1889. (The depot no longer stands.)

Railroad stations as a building type are closely associated with the boom era. The stations built by the Richmond and Alleghany line beginning in the 1880s were generally linear in form, with multiple entries opening onto a platform along the tracks and others on the opposite side to receive passengers and goods. The Balcony Falls Station across the river from Glasgow was representative: a one-story gabled building of board-and-batten frame construction with decorative Stick style bracing in the gable ends and more functional braces in the projecting side eaves. The station had a canted bay projection on the track side which gave the station master views up and down the line. At least two generations of coaling towers stood beside the station: the older (before 1935) with a square plan and shed roof, the later one cylindrical and constructed of concrete. The Richmond and Alleghany station at Gilmore Mills was similar but with simplified gable bracing.[11]

The other project that gave staying power to Buena Vista's boom was construction of the Buena Vista Company headquarters (2110 Magnolia Avenue) at the town's main intersection, 21st and Magnolia, on axis with the Union Depot. In October 1889 the company announced plans for a "handsome brick building three stories high." The mansard-roofed Second Empire style building, completed in early 1890, features a center tower (also mansarded), decorative slate shingle roofing, and pedimented dormers with molded trim. In 1892 the development company sold the building to the newly incorporated City of Buena Vista which moved in its administrative and court functions. A telephone exchange occupied a room on the second floor. When the city built its present courthouse in 1971, the old courthouse was slated for demolition, but city residents called for its preservation and it was listed in the National Register in 1979. The Buena Vista Company Building now houses the Buena Vista branch of the Rockbridge Regional Library.[12]

In 1890, early in Buena Vista's boom, the town council considered guiding architectural development by requiring builders to submit plans and receive building permits. Council member B. C. Moomaw, the town's main promoter in the 1880s, moved to declare a "fire limit" that would encompass lots in the core commercial area along 21st Street, Magnolia, and Sycamore. Moomaw's proposed ordinance required all construction in the area be of brick, stone, or metal and be roofed with metal or slate. The durable, fire-resistant construction

Buena Vista Company Building.
Photo by Dan Pezzoni

Buena Vista Paper Company
(later Bontex). Courtesy of
Jeremy Leadbetter

would also create an appearance of greater quality and permanence, an architectural declaration that Buena Vista was not a fly-by-night get-rich-quick scheme (though it was to some). It is unclear whether Moomaw's motion was adopted, although few frame structures were in fact built in the downtown and those that were were typically "iron clad," that is, sided with fire-resistant sheet iron.[13]

Rockbridge experienced an industrial transformation in conjunction with the rapid urbanization of the Boom. A synergy developed: industry generated a demand for workers who formed the populations that sustained the economic life of the new towns. Local developments mirrored changes that had occurred earlier in other parts of

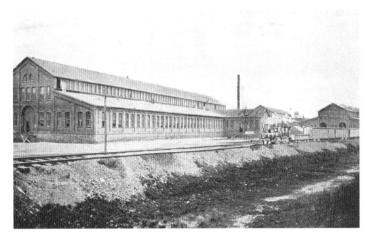

The Alexander K. Rarig machine shops (exterior) and the Buena Vista Cassimere Mills (interior). The train in the Rarig image is painted in.

the county, the transformation of community life and physical form wrought by the Industrial Revolution. Most of the new industries sprang up in Buena Vista, and a well-preserved representative is the Buena Vista Paper Company (1890). Located on the Maury River upstream from the town, and operated until recent years as Bontex, the facility consists of large processing and machinery buildings wafered between the railroad tracks and the river, the plant's water source and (formerly) sewer. The gable-roofed brick buildings have monitors along their ridges for light and ventilation, and they feature pier-reinforced walls with corbeling at the eaves, windows and entries with segmental and round-arched heads, and largely decorative circular gable windows, the latter a satisfying recapitulation of the ultimately Roman arched-brick structural grammar. A tall brick smokestack, the emblem of nineteenth-century industrialization, punctuates the complex. The plant changed names through the years: the Columbia Paper Company (1897), Mead Paper, Piedmont Paper, and finally Georgia Bonded Fibers in 1954, later known as Bontex.[14]

A rival of the Buena Vista Paper Company in size was the Alexander K. Rarig Company (1891), which made boilers, engines, and furnaces from iron produced in Buena Vista. The company's main production hall, located near the railroad tracks, was an immense building of brick with a shed-gable-shed profile created by a second-story popup that ran the length of the structure. Like the paper plant, the Rarig building used wall piers and round and segmental arches in its construction. The Rarig Company was short-lived, a victim of the depression of the 1890s, and its colossal factory building no longer stands. The Buena Vista Stationery Manufacturing Company, which formerly stood at the intersection of US Route 60 and Beech Avenue, was the city's main employer of women at the turn of the twentieth century. The company operated out of a simple gabled factory building adjoined by a boiler house, all in all a relatively modest facility by boom-time standards but as large as the larger industrial plants of the era before the Boom.[15]

Glasgow's boom industries mostly closed with the bust but the community received an economic windfall at an unlikely time: the Great Depression. In 1933–34 the Philadelphia-area textile manufacturer James Lees and Sons chose Glasgow as the site for a modern carpet plant, a choice that recognized the community's good rail and road connections and access to water from the rivers. James Lees and Sons established a training program in the Blue Ridge Building to teach local workers the operation of the machinery, and in 1935 the first section of the plant was completed: a one-story brick building enclosing over two acres of floor space and illuminated by ranks of shed monitors that give a distinctive sawtooth profile to the roofline. During World War II the plant converted to the production of cotton duck cloth for the armed forces. By the early 1950s the Lees Carpets plant occupied nearly twenty acres of level river terrace on the northeast side of town. Huge carpet looms lined its production floors. The complex included a "completely equipped industrial waste plant [built] to neutralize and purify the acid dye waste and alkaline scouring waste before emptying into the beautiful Maury River." In the 1950s Lees employed approximately 2,300 workers, necessitating another important feature: a parking lot. Employees who had walked to work in the pedestrian-scaled communities of the nineteenth century now often drove. Burlington Industries acquired the carpet plant in 1960 and it is now a division of Mohawk Industries.[16]

Industrial development was heaviest in the cities of the era but also occurred in rural areas. According to the caption for this 1952 photo by W. Edwin Hemphill, the antebellum Vesuvius Plow Company burned in 1913 and was replaced by this building. *Courtesy of the Library of Virginia*

Boom-era industrialization at Goshen included Victoria Furnace in the flats along the Calfpasture River south of town. The furnace smokestack appears prominently in the etching and in the middle distance in the photo. The photo also shows worker housing (the rows of dots in the middle distance) and, in the foreground, the silica plant at the location of the present Stella-Jones wood treating facility. *Courtesy of Anne Drake McClung*

Top: Historic windows at 19 West Nelson Street in Lexington. Large-dimension plate glass became increasingly available and affordable as the 19th century progressed and is a character-defining feature of boom-period commercial buildings. Photo by Dan Pezzoni

Directly above: The decorative brick parapet of the Coiner Building (ca. 1905) at 2122 Magnolia Avenue in Buena Vista. Photo by Dan Pezzoni

Industry was central to the economies of Buena Vista and the county's other boom communities, but commercial activity buoyed the downtowns. In Buena Vista, Glasgow, and Lexington the larger commercial buildings were of brick construction with street-level storefronts dominated by large plate glass display windows that enticed shoppers with glimpses of the goods to be had inside. The windows typically angled inward toward the entrance, another architectural feature which subtly lured prospective purchasers. Long transoms of plate glass or the little squares of textured glass sometimes referred to as prism glass ran across the top of the display windows and pumped more light into the salesroom, usually a long shoebox-shaped space with barred windows and a freight entry at the rear. Above the transom might be a decorative wood or metal cornice, a miniature version of the cornice that ornamented the top of the façade. Upper floors contained professional offices, apartments, and sometimes meeting space for the fraternal organizations that were a mainstay of male socialization during the era.

The Southern Inn Building (1886; 37 South Main Street) in Lexington is representative of the era's downtown commercial buildings. Hardware merchant Henry H. Myers had the building erected for his store, though he sold half of it to Louis G. Jahnke, a German born jeweler, soon after completion. The two-story brick building is distinguished by a pressed metal cornice with large floral-ornamented brackets at the two ends. Floral motifs also appear in galvanized iron lintels over the second-story windows. In 1932 restaurateur George Macheras opened the Southern Inn on the first floor and lived with his wife, Florence, and their children in the second-floor apartment. The Macheras family converted the salesroom to a diner, adding Arts and Crafts and Tudor-inspired features such as wooden booths and a ceiling of white panels trimmed with dark battens. The Southern Inn's best-known feature is its sign, a large vertical composition of metal and neon that identifies the restaurant and informs diners of "parking in rear." The Southern Inn burned after it was struck by lightning in 2010 but was faithfully rehabilitated and remains a college-town institution.[17]

Like the Macheras family, most downtown business owners advertised with signage, a practice that began early in the county's history. "We breakfasted at the sign of the General Washington," wrote an English visitor to Lexington in 1790, the tavern "kept by Humphreys Ellis, a civil Irishman." The Brownsburg Museum preserves one such historic signboard, a yellow and black sign for "Miley & Son Furniture & Undertaking" (the cabinet-makers were related to celebrated local photographer Michael Miley). Late nineteenth century photographs of Lexington's Main Street show a range of signage forms: freestanding on posts, hung on rods and wires and brackets, affixed to the façade, and painted on walls, in banners over storefronts, and in splashes of fancy gilt lettering on display windows.[18]

Extravagant painted signage, partially legible though fading, survives on the three-story Myers and Gilkeson Building (1890; 227 West 21st Street) in Buena Vista. Words squeezed in between and around the upper-story front windows hawk the goods that were sold in the hardware store that formerly occupied the ground floor. Sash, doors, blinds, and building supplies appear (or appeared) in the third-story painting; roofing, fencing, plows, iron pipe, glass, nails, and razors are or were enumerated on the second story. The sign painter used black, white, yellow, and possibly green paint for the lettering and embellished it with underlines and other flourishes. Painting on the sides of the building advertises Coca-Cola, Bull Durham tobacco, and H. L. Gilkeson Sporting Goods. The building originally housed the Buena Vista branch of Henry H. Myers' Lexington hardware business, which also had a branch in Roanoke, and it occupies what at the time was a choice location next to the former Union Depot. Myers' deed for the lot required him to build a three-story brick building with a "handsome front," another instance of period architectural guidelines. That front features ornamental cast iron detail in the pilasters that flank the storefront and in the cornice that spans it.[19]

With urbanization came a new approach to domestic architecture epitomized by the Queen Anne style. The style grew out of the Gothic Revival style and shared with it an enthusiasm for medieval architecture, although transitional medieval/Renaissance English architecture of the Elizabethan and Jacobean eras was the favorite source of

Downtown commercial buildings had their rural counterparts in the ubiquitous country stores of the era. This Effinger-vicinity building, possibly for the storage of bulk items associated with the adjacent Clemmer Store, has the common gable-fronted country store form. Photo by Dan Pezzoni; information from Stewart Bennington

inspiration. Like many trends in American architecture, the Queen Anne style was an English import, appearing on this side of the Atlantic in the 1870s and spreading to become the nation's leading Victorian-era house style by the 1880s.[20]

The William G. McDowell House (1891; 108 Preston Street) in Lexington is one of the county's most fully realized Queen Anne houses. The two-and-a-half-story brick house features a multiple-gabled roof which corresponds to an irregular multi-winged plan below, both characteristics of the Queen Anne style and a nod to the Gothic Revival style and its asymmetrical possibilities. A one-story porch wraps around three sides of the house — wraparound porches are another common Queen Anne feature — and the supports for the porch, fancifully turned wooden posts in groups of two and three on stone plinths, relate to the style's propensity to mix materials, forms, and finishes. The visual complexity carries through to the brickwork, which is elaborately corbelled in the prominent off-center chimney, and the gables, which are sheathed with wood shingles in a variety of rounded and angular shapes.[21]

Not surprisingly, the McDowell House was built by and for an architect. William George McDowell, an 1872 Washington and Lee civil engineering graduate, no doubt intended his house to serve as an advertisement of his skills. McDowell later designed the former Rockbridge County Courthouse (1896–97), which along with alterations to the Lexington-area house Mulberry Hill in the first decade of the twentieth century demonstrated his abilities in the classical idiom as well. Later phases of the Queen Anne style absorbed classical forms such as fluted Doric, Ionic, and Corinthian porch columns and mantels with classically-derived ornament.[22]

From about 1880 to 1920, Queen Anne houses filled the residential areas of Buena Vista and the new neighborhoods that extended east and west from Lexington. The style was also popular in the smaller boom communities of Glasgow and Goshen and it was occasionally used for farmhouses, though it is primarily identified with boom-era urbanization and was relatively rare in rural areas. Other styles made their appearance during the same period. The Stick style, a close cousin to the Queen Anne style, makes a rare local appearance in the gable ornament of certain Buena Vista houses. More common — but still rare in comparison with the Queen Anne style — was the Second Empire style, seen in Lexington houses like 303 Jackson Avenue (1884) and the Davidson-Tucker House (1888; 10 East Washington Street). The Second Empire style was relatively rare though not insignificant, as the 1890 Buena Vista Company Building demonstrates. In addition to these examples with their clearly defined styles, hundreds of houses were built during the period that make only passing reference to style. These "Victorian" houses might share sawn porch post brackets and other gingerbread ornament with fully realized Queen Anne houses, but in their use of simple plan forms such as the center-passage plan they belong more to the regional vernacular.[23]

One such relatively modest dwelling has the distinction of being Buena Vista's "first" house. The honor was conferred on the 1889 house by Buena Vista historian Francis Lynn and means the house was the first to be built outside the bounds of the preexisting 1880s village of Green Forest as part of the Buena Vista development boom. The house was built on Seminary Ridge by building contractor William N. Seay for his own residence (the first of two he built on the hill) and is a two-story frame house with a decorative center gable on the side-gable roof, a one-story porch on turned posts with simple sawn brackets, and two canted front bay windows. The house illustrates the simplified Gothic Revival-derived features and technomorphic

The second William N. Seay House.
Photo by Dan Pezzoni

detailing characteristic of hundreds of other "Victorian" houses built in the county.[24]

Though much simpler than the McDowell House, the first William N. Seay House shares with the Lexington house an important trait: it was built by and for an individual involved in the building trades. William N. Seay moved to Green Forest from Amherst County in 1886 at the invitation of Benjamin Moomaw and once in the village opened a planing mill and established himself as a building contractor. He was poised to profit from the Buena Vista boom and in fact the initial exponential growth of the city encouraged him to build another, finer residence next door to his first house, into which he and his family moved in January 1890. The second William N. Seay House, listed in the National Register in 2007, also features two canted front bay windows, but they are two stories in height rather than one and they are offset, one on an off-center front wing, the other set back and partially sheltered by a one-story porch. The decorative millwork on the porch and in the Italianate bracketed cornice is more elaborate than the sparse ornamentation of the first house. The second house includes such interesting interior features as a front entry transom with an unusual mosaic pattern of polygonal and circular glass panes in shades of yellow, blue, and red; and turned and scrolled stair elements that are holdovers from earlier styles but period in execution.[25]

The second William N. Seay House shows more connection to the Queen Anne style than the first but there are others in town that are closer to the Queen Anne ideal. The Charles F. Jordan House (ca. 1890; 2252 Maple Avenue) bristles with gables, one- and two-story porches, a gabled dormer, and a one-story canted bay window with a concave roof. The paint scheme by present owners Pat and Keith Gibson honors the polychromatic effects of the late Victorian era, a period when advances in industrial chemistry unleashed a wave of new colors on the American architectural landscape.[26]

Queen Anne-period homebuilders were fond of a two-story canted bay window form with a gable roof that overhangs the two cutaway corners of the bay. The detail is seen on the former Buena Vista Presbyterian Manse (1890; 807 24th Street), also known as Gospel Hill, where the overhang is supported by triangular brackets and the gable has a Stick style-inspired design of vertical battens and a center lozenge with a pierced vent, and on the house at 2154 Chestnut Avenue, where the overhang brackets have a more conventional curved form. Beaded tongue-and-groove panels under the windows and a small decorative porch gable in line with the front entry are other features of this house which, like the Charles F. Jordan House, has a spirited polychromatic paint scheme.[27]

Multi-gabled roofs and the asymmetrical hip-and-gable form were favored for their eye-catching rooflines, water-shedding functionality, and relative ease of construction, but some Queen Anne homebuilders experimented with other forms. The John M. Henkle House (547 25th Street), the residence of an early Buena Vista mayor, features a turret with a convex beehive roof, and the turret-like two-story bay window on the former Buena Vista Baptist Parsonage (2514 Maple Avenue) has a polygonal peaked roof with a finial spike. Similar in some ways to these Queen Anne houses but built later is the ca. 1903 Jordan House (2068 Chestnut Avenue). A hip-and-gable roof and two-story canted bay window/turret identify the house as Queen Anne, though the curving wraparound porch with its fluted Corinthian columns and unusual stacked and decoratively wood-shingled entablature is a Classical Revival feature.[28]

Queen Anne houses were also built in Glasgow during its brief boom beginning in 1890. Among them is the Alden House (1890; 905 Anderson Street), a two-story frame residence distinguished by a three-story square-plan turret. A three-story turret also graces the E. T. Robinson House (1890; 10th and McCullough streets). A photo from the late 1890s shows the Robinson House with decorative bracing and diamond-shaped vents in the tower and front gable. The Robinson House is also notable for its resplendent mantel of carved slate adorned with glazed green tiles that depict Roman gladiators and other classical figures and motifs. The tiles may be associated with the tile mantel factory said to have operated in Glasgow during the 1890s boom.[29]

The Charles F. Jordan House ca. 1891 and in 2013. Historic photo courtesy RHS/SC, WLU; modern photo by H. E. Ravenhorst

Buena Vista Queen Anne/
Classical Revival: a house
constructed of rockfaced
concrete block *(top)* and the
Jordan House *(immediately above)*.
Photos by H. E. Ravenhorst
and Dan Pezzoni

Another boom-period Glasgow house, the Walter A. Plecker House (10th and Fitzlee streets), is known from newspaper accounts to have originally received a dark red paint scheme. In Goshen, aside from the outstanding example of the Queen Anne style represented by the Alleghany Hotel, there was the Rockbridge Inn (1904), a two-and-a-half-story building with a wraparound two-tier veranda, multiple gabled dormers on its hipped roof, and a Queen Anne-inspired four-story tower with a polygonal peaked roof. The Rockbridge Inn stood near the train station and connected to it by way of a boardwalk along the tracks.[30]

One of the county's most interesting Queen Anne residences, and also one of its best documented, was Stonewall Lodge (1892–93) at Natural Bridge. The story-and-a-half stone house was built for Norfolk businessman Leroy H. Shields and his wife, Mary Orra Novella Love Shields. In 1892 Orra Shields purchased a "villa" site, laid out as part of a prospective resort community that overlooked the complex of hotels at the Bridge and perished in the ensuing depression, and by 1893 she and her husband had erected what is described in deeds as a "cottage residence." The builders were I. H. Adams Jr. and H. P. Woodson of the Lynchburg contracting firm Adams and Woodson, whose involvement is known from a detailed mechanic's lien recorded at the county courthouse. The lien enumerates pressed brick, stained glass, and a copper pantry sink among the home's many original refinements. A spreading hip roof with large gabled dormers and a peaked polygonal corner element projected to engage a wraparound porch supported by paired columns on stone pedestals. Historic interior photos show a cantilevered stair with elaborately turned newels and balusters and a large brick fireplace with a stepped stack and a stone plaque inscribed with verses from *The Faerie Queene* by the Elizabethan poet Edmund Spenser. Ada P. Polly (or Polley) acquired the property in 1940 and operated it as a tourist home known as Stonewall Lodge until selling it to the Natural Bridge company in 1954. When the Natural Bridge Hotel burned in 1963 the Lodge was pressed into service as guest rooms and afterwards is said to have been used as an "artist's lodge." Stonewall Lodge was destroyed by fire in 2012, leaving only stone ruins.[31]

What may be the county's earliest representative of the Queen Anne style is not a residence but a train station. In 1883, after over a decade of fits and starts, the Valley Railroad completed its line southward through the Valley of Virginia as far as Lexington and built a brick passenger and freight station in the Woods Creek valley west of town. In its linear form and deep overhanging eaves, supported on the track side by turned brackets, the 1883 Lexington Train Station (224 McLaughlin Street) was typical of rail stations of the era, but in its Queen Anne design it was cutting-edge. The style is most evident in the building's prominent cross gable which mixes wood sheathing treatments: paneling in the upper part, which also incorporates the building date in artistic letters, and wood shingles in the lower part. Bands of corbelled brickwork that link the tops and bottoms of the segmental-arched entries and windows are also characteristic of the style. Washington and Lee University acquired the station and rehabilitated it in the 1970s. In 2005 the university moved the building to its present nearby location to make way for the construction of the Lenfest Center for the Arts. Currently the station houses the national headquarters of the Omicron Delta Kappa fraternity.[32]

Development companies and their architects favored the Queen Anne style for the hotels they erected in the county's boom communities. The most sophisticated of these was the Alleghany Hotel in Goshen, designed by Philadelphia architects Albert Yarnell and William Goforth in 1890. Yarnell and Goforth were rising stars in the Philadelphia architectural firmament at the time: young (Goforth was twenty-four), educated (Yarnell attended the Franklin Institute,

Stonewall Lodge during its tourist home era.
Postcard view courtesy SC, WLU

Alleghany Hotel exterior and lobby.
Courtesy of Anne Drake McClung and Arthur Bartenstein

Goforth the University of Pennsylvania), and well versed in the precepts of the Queen Anne style, as demonstrated by their design for the mammoth Goshen hotel.[33]

The salient feature of the Alleghany Hotel was a stone veranda that undulated with the twists and turns of the rounded and polygonal façade elements behind it. At the main entry the veranda projected as a porte cochere, a drive-through shelter for carriages, and at its two ends its buttressed pillars and arches resolved into slender stone piers that were almost modernist in their simplicity. A promotional brochure printed for the hotel's 1893 opening touted such up-to-date amenities as rooms with baths, steam heat, and a telegraph office, but there was nothing modern about the building's style, its turrets and finials and crazy-quilt half-timbering calculated to evoke the old-money luxury of an English manor house. The lobby centered on a grand fireplace with Gothic carving and featured archways to other public rooms and hallways and a ceiling of patterned and varnished woodwork. The ballroom had Stick style paneled walls and fanciful roof trusses of a slenderness that suggests they were made of cast iron. The Alleghany Hotel burned in 1923, a sad loss to Goshen and the county.[34]

The architectural sensibilities of the late nineteenth century permitted, even encouraged, a wide range of expression, and a house known as New Alsace pushed the possibilities to their limits. The Weiss family, headed by John H. Weiss Sr. (d. ca. 1883), emigrated

New Alsace (detail).
Courtesy RHS/SC, WLU, and the Virginia Historical Society

from Alsace-Lorraine on the French-German border and in 1876 purchased thirty-three acres on Brushy Hill west of Lexington where the family established a vineyard. Tax records suggest the family lived at first in a small dwelling that may have been enlarged during the mid-1880s.[35]

John Weiss is said to have claimed that his home "successfully reproduced a bit of the old country, amid scenery suggestive of the Alps," which, if so, suggests at least a part of his architectural vision was realized before his death. The frame house was divided into two parts: a story-and-a-half wing clad in board-and-batten and fringed with Gothic vergeboards, and a two-story section that appears to have been sided with flush boards painted to suggest masonry. Billboard-sized cut-out letters proclaimed "New Alsace" from the roof balustrade of the two-story section below a gable ornament in the form of an upturned horseshoe, presumably for good luck. In the gable of the lower wing a balcony projected like bric-a-brac on a cuckoo clock. Mrs. Weiss trained ivy to grow on the walls and clipped the tendrils into emblems of love and piety such as a cross, an anchor, and a heart. There may have been a commercial aspect to it all; historian Henry Boley notes the "big-hearted" Weisses operated a nightclub on the premises.[36]

The Queen Anne style and gingerbread ornament fell from favor in the 1910s, the result of a growing interest in classical architecture inspired by the 1893 opening of the World's Columbian Exposition in Chicago. "The exposition's planners mandated a classical theme," write architectural historians Virginia and Lee McAlester, and gleaming white exhibition halls—triumphal confections of columns, arches, and domes—rose beside the fair's reflecting pool and amid its landscaped grounds. "The exposition was widely photographed, reported, and attended," the McAlesters write, and soon its "neoclassical models became the latest fashion throughout the country." As the Queen Anne style belatedly waned in Rockbridge County in the 1910s, the Neoclassical or Classical Revival style took its place, but there was no simple replacement as in some earlier stylistic turnovers. Just as the exposition fairgrounds in Chicago thronged with state and international pavilions in a babel of styles, including a Virginia pavilion modeled on Mount Vernon, the architectural landscape of twentieth century Rockbridge County would prove to be an eclectic place.[37]

NINE

Automobile Age

THE GALA OPENING of Lexington's Robert E. Lee Hotel in November 1926 afforded Lexingtonians an occasion to reminisce about their fabled past and gaze ahead to an equally bright future. The six-story hotel's classically-derived Colonial Revival style, replete with cornices and arches and balusters, referenced a bygone Virginia culture that in the 1920s was glorified to the point of mythology, a culture evoked by the paragon of Southern gallantry for whom the hotel was named. Richmond architect Marcellus E. Wright Sr., who in the 1920s cultivated a specialty in large downtown hotels, channeled the community's historicist imagination in his design for the hotel, expertly melding classical features with modern conveniences like an elevator and individual guest room bathrooms. The six-story Robert E. Lee Hotel remains the tallest building in the county, a monument to 1920s optimism.[1]

In his remarks to the gala attendees, local businessman Hugh White, representing the hotel corporation and stockholders, celebrated the recent completion of Lee Highway (US 11), the Interstate 81 of its day, and anticipated the imminent completion of present US Route 60, "the last link in the Midland Trail from Lexington to West Virginia and the Middle West, the Plains states, and the Pacific." White described, presciently as it turned out, a "not distant future" in which homes would be built "even beyond the borders of the town on our grass grown or wooded hills, out to the mountain coves."[2]

Facing page: R. E. Lee Hotel.
Postcard view courtesy RHS/SC, WLU

Above: Southern Inn sign.
Photo by Dan Pezzoni

195

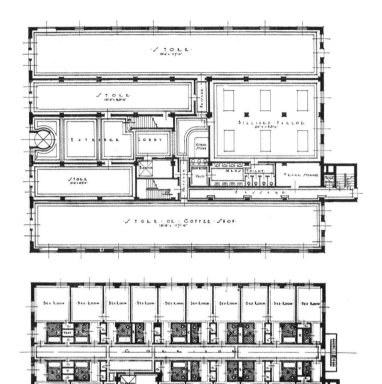

R. E. Lee Hotel plans, ground floor and typical room floor. Courtesy RHS/SC, WLU

The wondrous agent of White's vision of highways and suburbs was the automobile, which, more than any other factor, transformed Rockbridge County's architectural landscape during the early and mid-twentieth century. No better illustration was there of the inauguration of the automobile age than the Robert E. Lee Hotel itself, conceived with the motoring public in mind. The hotel's prospectus assured stockholders that guests would have at their disposal not one but two fireproof garages behind the hotel. Local residents needed garages for their cars too, and filling stations to feed them fuel, repair shops to fix them when they broke, and paved roads to drive them on. A quarter century after Hugh White's comments, the quintessential icon of the automobile age — a drive-in movie theater — opened in the county. The car had unquestionably arrived.[3]

Long before automobiles, trucks, and paved highways, Rockbridge residents understood the importance of transportation to economic vitality. Boatmen braved the rapids of the James River Gorge to transport local goods and manufactures to downstream markets. Canals improved the safety of river transport in the 1800s: first the Blue Ridge Canal in the 1820s to bypass the worst of the James River falls; then the James River and Kanawha Canal, completed to Buchanan upstream from the county in 1851; and the North River Navigation Company canal, completed up the Maury River from Balcony Falls (Glasgow) to Jordan's Point (Lexington) by the eve of the Civil War.

Settlers hacked rudimentary roads from the wilderness in the eighteenth century. In the nineteenth century, profit-minded consortiums formed to construct turnpikes, for-pay roads that were kept in better repair than the county-maintained system. One of these was the Lexington and Covington Turnpike, incorporated in 1829 to link Lexington and Covington, the county seat of Alleghany County forty-one miles to the west. In 1834 the turnpike company erected toll houses as collection points for tolls and residences for its toll "gatherers," including a tollhouse at the junction of the present Lime Kiln and

Enfield roads just west of Lexington. The original ca. 1834 section of the Lexington and Covington Turnpike Toll House is a two-room brick dwelling of typically compact toll house form, and despite its small size it has refinements such as a Flemish bond front elevation and a molded brick cornice.[4]

John F. Tompkins, the father of historian E. Pendleton Tompkins, acquired the house in 1864 and a year or two later added a board-and-batten ell to the rear. Tompkins the son tells an interesting story about the construction of the ell. While his father was building the foundation and had mixed a batch of mortar for the stonework, "Gen. Lee rode by on Traveller, he recognized Father and stopped for a chat. They discussed for one thing the bed of mortar; many years after I heard the incident from my father I read that General Lee as an army engineer, was always looked upon as an authority, on the mixing of various mortars." Another notable feature of the house is a series of plank or "boxed" additions dating to the late nineteenth century. Boxed construction largely dispensed with vertical framing members, relying instead on vertical sheathing boards to provide both enclosure and structure. The method relates to forms of plank construction dating back to colonial times, but its more immediate source was the abundance of cheap sawn lumber produced by the

Lexington and Covington Turnpike Toll House. Photo by Dan Pezzoni

A Buena Vista garage from the early 20th century. Photo by Dan Pezzoni

Spanish influence in local architecture: 11 Sellers Avenue in Lexington and the ca. 1923 Brownsburg High School vocational-agricultural building. Photos by Dan Pezzoni

region's postbellum wood products industry. Close investigation of the county's tenant houses and late-period mountain dwellings would likely reveal that many are boxed.[5]

In Rockbridge, as elsewhere, the automobile was at first a novelty, the noisy, smoking "horseless buggy" that panicked horses on county roads, but through the efforts of Henry Ford and his affordable and wildly popular Model T automobiles reached the masses. A host of new building types catered to the burgeoning fleet of cars. Stables and carriage houses had long been a fixture of farms and town lots, and they could be retrofitted to house automobiles, but by the 1920s many householders constructed purpose-built garages. Early examples of the type, identified by their small and narrow profiles scaled to the Model T and its contemporaries, pepper the alleyways of Buena Vista and Lexington.

Filling stations appeared, some of extravagant and whimsical design intended to catch the attention of motorists and lure them to the pumps. Quite a few of the county's stations referenced the Spanish Mission style, typically through the use of terra-cotta or simulated terra-cotta roof tiles. One is the ca. 1930 Whiting Oil Company Service Station at the foot of the Main Street hill in Lexington, now converted to offices. The Mission style evoked travel to sunny destinations, to carefree California and auto tours of its celebrated

The Colonial Service Station, also known as the Pure Oil Station. This rear view shows the repair garage underneath. The First Baptist Church steeple rises behind. *Courtesy of Jeremy Leadbetter*

colonial-era missions, but few local homebuilders opted for the style. A rare example is a Sears, Roebuck and Company you-build-it kit house at 11 Sellers Avenue in Lexington. The two-story stucco-finish house with its Baroque-inspired rounded parapets is an example of *The Alhambra* model illustrated in Sears' mail-order kit house catalogs from 1919 to 1929. Sears, one of several kit house manufacturers during the era, published its first kit house catalog in 1908 and acquired lumber plants in Louisiana, Illinois, and Ohio to manufacture components, which were shipped to customers by rail along with plans and instructions for assembly. By 1929 the company had manufactured approximately 49,000 kit houses. The firm of Ruble and Hutcheson Building Supplies in Lexington helped customers order and assemble Sears, Roebuck houses, of which approximately twenty are thought to have been built in Lexington. Robert Steele Hutcheson was a partner in the firm and a house he built at 607 Stonewall Street is a Sears, Roebuck house.[6]

Other styles appealed to local filling station owners. At least two stations were built to cottage designs provided by the Pure Oil Company,

Banks in Brownsburg, Raphine, and Fairfield. Photos by Dan Pezzoni

one on US Route 60 heading into Buena Vista from Lexington, the other at 107 North Main Street in Lexington. The latter, originally known as the Colonial Service Station, was built in 1937 by contractor W. W. (Walton Wilmouth) Coffey, one of the era's leading builders. The brick building (now a restaurant) with its characteristic steep blue-tiled gables is best described stylistically as an example of the Period Cottage style, an eclectic blend of the Colonial and Tudor revival styles and other influences. The originator of the design, Pure Oil Company architect C. A. Peterson, is said to have modeled it on English cottages in the Cotswold Hills. Other gas stations are Tudor in inspiration. One, at 1973 Magnolia Avenue at the edge of Buena Vista's downtown in the 1930s, features a front gas-pump drive-through originally crowned by large urns or globe light fixtures. The sprightly little station was run by Dan Glass in 1956 and today houses the Blue Ridge Auto Center.[7]

A block away from the Magnolia Street filling station stands the Robey Garage (2019 Forest Avenue), a large repair garage and filling station that expanded to accommodate auto sales. The Robey business began as the W. T. Robey and Brother livery stable "established in 1890 with four horses," as W. T. Robey later put it. The business was well situated to provide mounts and conveyances to guests at the adjacent Palace (later Marlbrook) Hotel. In 1916 Robey began the transition from horse and buggy to automobile with demolition of the frame livery stable and construction of the original brick section of the present building, which housed a repair shop and a garage with a capacity of thirty cars. The business added "cars for hire" by 1928 and auto sales by the mid-1940s when a brick-faced cinder block addition was constructed along Forest Avenue. The addition's large plate glass windows encouraged car-shoppers to peer inside. Other windows are glass block, a popular mid-century material.[8]

Downtown Lexington also has large automobile-oriented buildings from the era. The two-story Rockbridge Motor Company at the corner of Main and Preston was an automobile dealership that originally featured large display windows, gas pumps, and a repair department. A Colonial Revival remodeling made when the building was converted to office use masked but did not erase the building's decorative Craftsman-inspired brickwork. The present Rockbridge Regional Library (138 South Main Street) was created out of the former Woody Chevrolet Dealership, a brick building built by contractor W. W. Coffey with castle-like corner towers pierced by tall lancet-arched windows. Press reports on the occasion of the dealership's grand opening in March 1938 emphasized the hydraulic jacks, frame aligners, and other modern equipment in the repair garage rather than the building's medieval style. When the Lexington town council approved owner D. D. Woody's building permit in 1937 it stipulated that he "conform to such architectural style with reference to the front of the proposed building as might be required by a committee composed of the mayor, the Town Attorney, and the Superintendent of Public Works."[9]

The trend toward functional specialization exemplified by filling stations and car dealerships produced other notable downtown building types. Financial institutions were present by the end of the antebellum period: Brownsburg had a Savings Institute chartered in 1854 and the Bank of Rockbridge opened in Lexington in 1857. In the early twentieth century the Bank of Raphine erected a two-story building of brick crowned by a bracketed pressed-metal cornice with the institution's name embossed on the frieze. The Bank of Brownsburg operated from a roughcast stuccoed building which shares with its sister in Raphine a slender, two-story, parapeted shed-roofed form. The bank formed in 1913 but did not build the stucco building until 1920 or 1921. Lexington builder H. A. Donald, proud owner of a concrete block machine, built the Bank of Fairfield out of rockfaced block in 1923. The block lends an appearance of impregnability to an otherwise modest building but the choice of material apparently raised eyebrows. Local versifier Ernest Sale offered a wry tribute on the occasion of the bank's dedication:

> Now for the building, shall it be frame or brick?
> We want something we can build right quick;
> Don't mind the expense, we can sell more stock,
> Then they decided to build it of concrete block![10]

The Peoples Bank of Buena Vista (128 West 21st Street) erected one of Buena Vista's finest bank buildings in 1907 with the construction of a two-story Classical Revival building of red and blond brick. Three elliptical archways with cast stone voussoirs grace the first story. Like other bank buildings of the era, the Peoples Bank housed additional functions: the Buena Vista post office for a time, the offices of dentist Dr. R. W. Williams and lawyers R. H. Willis and A. W. Robertson, and a millinery shop. In 2009 an unsympathetic 1960s front was removed to reveal the original façade as part of the building's rehabilitation for the Buena Vista branch of Community Bank, an improvement that earned the bank a Founder's Award from HLF. In Lexington the Rockbridge National Bank occupied a handsome stone-faced building on the north corner of Main and Nelson streets in the early twentieth century. The Classical Revival building had standard features intended to project an aura of financial integrity, such as monumental Ionic columns in antis to symbolically guard the front entry and a modillion cornice that formed a pediment with carving in the tympanum.[11]

The present Lexington and Buena Vista post offices are highly accomplished works of Classical Revival architecture. Monumental fluted Doric columns march across the front of Lexington's 1911–13 building. The columns are limestone, as is the entablature they support, ornamented with triglyphs and classical motifs like the caduceus, the emblem of swift-footed Mercury appropriate for the carrier of the mails. Washington and Lee graduate Benjamin C. Flournoy designed the Lexington Post Office during a brief (1910–13) tenure in the Office of the Supervising Architect of the U.S. Treasury. He also designed many classically inspired buildings on the Washington and Lee campus during the first three decades of the century, including the Doremus Memorial Gymnasium (1914–15; in conjunction with Park P. Flournoy Jr.). Like the post office the Doremus Gym features a Doric colonnade, in this instance flanked by triumphal arches of brick. One of Flournoy's successors at the Office of the Supervising Architect, James A. Wetmore, is credited with the design of the Buena Vista Post Office (1930), a more delicately proportioned building than Lexington's post office, fronted by a portico with Corinthian columns and tendril and lozenge carving in the entablature. The building's classical treatment extends down to the level of details such as the urn finials on the iron front step railings.[12]

Theaters, like banks and post offices, also used architecture to produce an effect, in their case excitement and gaiety instead of civic sobriety. The Lexington Motion Pictures Corporation, chartered in 1919, erected the New Theatre on West Nelson Street, a two-story building with Spanish features

State Theatre.
Photo by Dan Pezzoni

that gave it an exotic flare. When the New Theatre burned in early 1937, then-owner Warner Brothers engaged New York architect John Eberson to design a replacement, the State Theatre. Eberson, a Romanian who studied technical engineering at the University of Vienna, was an apostle of modern styles like Art Deco and Moderne which he used in his 1936 remodeling of the interior of Staunton's Dixie Theater. Some Lexingtonians, presumably aware of Eberson's work in Staunton, worried what the architect might do in their town and made a preemptive strike, lobbying for a more contextual design. In July 1937 theater-owner Warner Brothers announced it was "happy to comply with the request of the citizens of Lexington [that] the State be planned in the colonial tradition of architecture so characteristic of Lexington." Eberson gave the 1937 building a Flemish bond Colonial Revival façade ornamented with arches, pilasters, and oculus windows under a modillion cornice and pediment. The architect took greater liberties on the interior where he detailed certain secondary spaces in the Moderne style. An event of cinematic interest occurred at the State in 1938 when the movie *Brother Rat*, filmed at VMI with Ronald Reagan as one of the leads, premiered in the theater. In its early decades the State Theatre operated during the era of segregation and though black patrons were allowed in they were required to sit in a specially designated section of the balcony.[13]

The romance of the silver screen found parallels in the domestic architecture of the first half of the twentieth century, especially the period from the 1910s to World War II. Of the many styles that competed for the affections of homebuilders, one of the most popular locally was the Colonial Revival style. The style was closely related to and initially contemporaneous with the Classical Revival style, though its chief source of inspiration was colonial and early national American interpretations of classicism. The Colonial Revival style was generally less grandiose than the Classical Revival style with its penchant for monumental columns, on houses as well as banks and city halls. Instead, domestic versions of the Colonial Revival style typically featured simply massed, side-gabled, hipped, and gambrel-roofed house forms clad in traditional materials like brick and wood weatherboards, with

Buena Vista Post Office.
Photo by Dan Pezzoni

relatively understated but often historically faithful classical details like entry surrounds with pilasters and pediments, gabled dormers, and mantels with Georgian or Federal forms and detail. The style is also known as the Georgian Revival style, although that name implies greater fidelity to Georgian prototypes, whereas Colonial Revival houses could be more free-wheeling. The Colonial Revival dominated home construction in the county's established neighborhoods and new suburbs during the 1920s and 1930s. It lost market share to the Ranch style after World War II but rebounded later in the century and remains popular today.

Lexingtonians were especially enamored of the Colonial Revival style which resonated with the community's conservative cultural values through its explicit celebration of the past, as premiere buildings such as the Robert E. Lee Hotel and State Theatre demonstrate. In the 1930s the style's local popularity coincided with the first stirrings of interest in historic preservation, and Colonial Revival construction from that period and later featured the red brickwork and contrasting white trim that were hallmarks of the style in Virginia. Buildings that strayed into other styles were sometimes brought back into the fold with Colonial Revival makeovers. Such was the case with the Grand Furniture Building (ca. 1950; 1 South Main Street), an originally modernist building which in the 1980s was given an arcaded brick façade meant to fit in with the downtown's predominantly brick architecture. Colonial Revival houses thronged newly developed suburbs in Lexington and the county's other communities and the style remains popular today. Of the many Colonial Revival houses built in Lexington, several are complemented by garden designs of Charles Gillette, a Richmond landscape architect popular among well-heeled Southern clients from the 1910s on.[14]

Owners of large rural houses who wished to expand and upgrade them usually selected the Colonial Revival style as their idiom. Col Alto (1827), the home of Congressman Henry St. George Tucker at the turn of the twentieth century, passed to Tucker's daughter Rosa Tucker Mason in 1932. Mason quickly set about beautifying and modernizing the estate, hiring nationally prominent New York architect William Lawrence Bottomly, a specialist in the design of Virginia great houses, to help her achieve her vision. Bottomly designed the "Palladian" porch on the north elevation, a graceful loggia-like composition of round brick columns, arches, and circular openings in the spandrels

between the arches. For the front elevation he created a new entry porch with concave quarter-round corners by reusing fluted Ionic columns from the nineteenth century porch. Rosa Mason also hired Rose Greely, a graduate of Harvard's school of landscape architecture, who laid out a new maple-lined axial driveway to connect the front of the house to present Spotswood Drive. Greely also designed a boxwood "maze" and other landscape elements. Though the grounds are now partly occupied by the Col Alto Hampton Inn, Mason and Greely's 1930s landscape scheme remains much in evidence and adds to the aesthetic appeal of Lexington's eastern entry corridor.[15]

The grandest of the country house makeovers was Forest Oaks, also known as Vine Forest, which stands near the Botetourt County line. The two-story brick house, dated to ca. 1806, was enlarged and remodeled later in the 1800s before it was acquired in 1916 by Lily Walton, a wealthy Englishwoman residing in Cleveland. Walton and her adoptive son, Curtis Walton, an architect trained at Case Western Reserve University, transformed the house along the lines of an English country estate. They encased it in brick made to look intentionally antique, a popular Colonial Revival conceit, extended it with brick and weatherboard-frame additions on each end, and gave it a monumental Mount Vernon-type portico on the elevation facing the Blue Ridge Mountains and, on the north front, a smaller but architecturally sophisticated demi-octagonal reception porch with arched niches, octagonal columns, and Greek triglyphs. The highpoint of the interior is a lofty two-story center passage spanned by a triumphal arch of varnished wood. (The two-story configuration is thought to predate the

Mayflower Hotel.

Mayflower Hotel - Lexington, Va.   3-D-46

Franklin Colored Tourist Home.

Walton period and a vaulted ceiling is said to survive above the present flat ceiling.) The carpenters adorned the interior with decorative paneling, arcaded balusters, and arched doorways with paneled and fluted surrounds—Jacobean (early English Renaissance) treatments that mixed with vestiges of the original Federal interior. "Preventor" automatic fire extinguishers, glass cylinders filled with fire-repressing carbon tetrachloride fluid designed to burst when heated by fire, survive in secondary spaces, and the back stair retains a call button indicator board used to summon the servants to the library, the "Japanese Room," and other rooms. The main hall boasts a resplendent two-story canvas wall hanging painted with a Renaissance scene of plumed knights and caparisoned horses.[16]

Curtis Walton and his wife, Martha Paxton Walton, operated Forest Oaks as a country inn beginning in 1929, constructing three guest houses as lodgings for travelers on US Route 11, which passes in front. In 1931 the Waltons sold the property to John Clothier, a former manager of the Natural Bridge Hotel, who operated it as the Forest Tavern. The 1920s and 1930s were the heyday of such genteel "tourist home" type accommodations. Another well-preserved example is the Colonial Revival style Mayflower Hotel on Main Street in Lexington, built in 1929 by contractor W. W. Coffey. The Mayflower was converted to a retirement home in 1983 but it retains its spacious Doric portico (an early addition) where residents enjoy the sun and socialize with neighbors. A multi-windowed dining room extends to the side and a basement-level parking garage opens to the rear.[17]

During the era of Jim Crow, African American visitors to Lexington were barred from lodging at white-owned establishments. Instead they stayed at the Franklin Colored Tourist Home (9 Tucker Street) in the Green Hill neighborhood, operated by Zach and Arlena Franklin in the early twentieth century. The tourist home, which appeared in the Green Book, the first travel guide intended for African Americans, is a two-story frame house with classical elements such as Doric porch columns and dentil moldings in the eaves and in a pediment-like front gable, features which may date to a 1920s remodeling. Neighbors recall limousines parked out front, driven to Lexington by the chauffeurs of white guests staying at the R. E. Lee Hotel. Harry and Eliza Walker, owners of the antebellum house Blandome on the same street, also operated lodgings for blacks, both at Blandome and in a cluster of cottages at the Garden Grill, a 1930s restaurant and

The Natural Bridge Hotel was a popular conference venue. An unidentified group poses in front of the hotel in 1957. Photo courtesy of the Library of Virginia

dance hall located on US Route 60 east of Col Alto. Nearby stood Eliza Walker's Lexington Old Folks Home and Orphanage. The Garden Grill and the Old Folks Home are gone but Evergreen Cemetery, Lexington's African American cemetery, survives in the neighborhood. Route 60's commercial character is a legacy of the Garden Grill, one of the first automobile-oriented businesses on the stretch of road.[18]

The Natural Bridge resort, located on US Route 11, was able to capitalize on the motor traffic that streamed through its grounds, unlike the county's more remote nineteenth century resorts. Photographs of the Bridge property from the 1930s and 1940s show various phases of beautification focused on the highway. After World War II a motel was added to the complex, as were a collection of guest cottages with names honoring Southern state capital cities such as Austin and Tallahassee. Bridge management was always on the lookout for promotional opportunities. May 21, 1927, marked the "formal opening of the electrical illumination" of the Bridge with Governor Harry Byrd and hundreds of others in attendance. New York lighting contractor Phinehas V. Stephens, whose credits included work at Niagara Falls and Endless Caverns, engineered the floodlight system. (The Bridge and grounds were illuminated twice weekly, perhaps by lantern, in the late nineteenth century.) In 1931 music was piped to loudspeakers under the Bridge. Interest in Natural Bridge Caverns (Buck Hill Cave) as a potential scenic annex dates back to the end of the nineteenth century but in 1949 resort president J. Lee Davis wrote that there had never been a serious effort to develop the cave as a tourist attraction. That came in 1977 when Natural Bridge Caverns opened to the public.[19]

In April 1963 a fire destroyed large sections of the Natural Bridge Hotel. Within weeks management announced plans to erect a replacement "of Jeffersonian design," and on August 20, 1964, the first guests checked in to the new hotel, a grand three-story building fronted by a full-façade arcade and a center portico. The *Lexington News-Gazette* claimed the style conveyed "an elegance inspired by the Virginia mansions of Thomas Jefferson's day." Among the building's interior features were a lobby with brass chandeliers and a floor "of black and white terraza [terrazzo] in a diamond pattern" and guest rooms with blue and green draperies, "soft blue carpeting and matching vinyl wall covering," and that indispensable appliance of the 1960s, television sets.[20]

Views of Camp Okahahwis.
Courtesy RHS/SC, WLU

County woodlands attracted rustic camps. Among the first was Camp Okahahwis, established in 1918 at Wilson Springs but soon relocated across the Maury River to the Rockbridge Baths side. At its second location the camp centered on a Rustic style lodge of boxed construction with a front porch on log posts with railings constructed of crisscrossed tree limbs. The Rustic style, which developed out of the great Adirondack camps of the nineteenth century and other sources, emphasized natural materials and pioneer construction techniques and was meant to harmonize with natural settings. Camp Okahahwis was owned and operated by Ellie Frayser Chesterman, "Mrs. Chess," from 1918 to 1953, and by Janet Johnson "J. J." Stern from 1953 until its closing in 1966. Campers hiked at nearby Jump Mountain and Castle Rock, played sports, swam in the camp pool, and competed in song contests. A photograph album from 1924–25 shows the main building labeled "Cradle Lodge" accompanied by buildings known as the Nursery and the Mess Hall and an assortment of cabins.[21]

Downstream from Camp Okahahwis, adjacent to the Rockbridge Baths resort, the Ned Graham Memorial Camp operated out of a ca. 1940 two-story bunkhouse and multi-purpose building with wrap-around screen porches. The camp management developed a park with benches, walkways, and a bathing beach on the Maury River. Camp Kiwanis, a Girl Scout camp, operated on the Zollman Farm in the Buffalo Creek area. In or near Arnold's Valley the Roanoke city Boy Scout troops opened a camp at Poteet's (or Petite's) Gap, located on the Rockbridge-Bedford line, and the state YMCA organization ran Camp Kent. The Arnold's Valley camps existed in close proximity to the Blue Ridge Parkway, a major tourism and landscape development of the era which threads in and out of the county along the crest of the Blue Ridge.[22]

Arnold's Valley was a focus of federal conservation efforts during the Great Depression and early 1940s. The valley's forested mountain sides, which today constitute parts of the James River Face and Thunder Ridge wilderness areas, were absorbed into the George Washington National Forest earlier in the century and were prime candidates for attention from the Civilian Conservation Corps (CCC), a New Deal "alphabet soup" agency tasked with putting unemployed men to work in reclamation and development projects. The quasi-military CCC housed enrollees in camps composed

Natural Bridge Camp. Photo by Michael Pulice, courtesy DHR

The Rustic style was also popular for early roadside architectures as shown in this unidentified area motor court, apparently located on US Route 11. Courtesy of the Library of Virginia

primarily of simple barracks-like wooden buildings. CCC camps were established near Vesuvius and on Old Buena Vista Road and a third, Natural Bridge Camp, was established in Arnold's Valley in 1933.[23]

Natural Bridge Camp survives today as one of the most intact CCC camps in the nation. In its present form the camp consists of approximately twenty buildings dating from the 1930s and later. A quadrangular grouping of three dormitories and an office and classroom building forms the camp's core. A dining hall retains exposed roof trusses and a brick and stone fireplace likely from the CCC era. According to a recent evaluation by the Virginia Department of Historic Resources, the Natural Bridge Camp (which is currently closed) is "rare if not unique."[24]

The second CCC company to occupy the Natural Bridge Camp, Company 2345, made up of World War I veterans instead of the teenagers and young men who predominated as CCC enrollees, built the Cave Mountain Lake dam and artificial lake in 1936 and constructed buildings and a campground at the lake in 1937–38. The thirty-five-foot-high dam was built between rock ledges that form natural buttresses along Back Run. The Rustic style picnic shelter makes both structural and decorative use of logs in its construction. The walls and roof trusses are log as are the cruck-like brackets that frame the wide window openings, the railings under the windows, and a crisscross detail over the building's stone fireplace. The shelter retains what appear to be original trestle tables and benches of pegged construction. Not only did Company 2345 build the Cave Mountain Lake facility, but CCC men served as lifeguards at the swimming beach and kept the campfire sites stocked with cut wood. The "resort," so described in 1939, was "a most attractive spot; for on Sundays and holidays people from twenty miles around flock here for swimming and water sports, or to have picnic dinners in the woods." The facility is operated by the US Forest Service as Cave Mountain Lake Recreation Area.[25]

After the dissolution of the CCC at the beginning of World War II the Natural Bridge Camp served briefly in a military capacity before being converted to an "experimental" federal juvenile correction and rehabilitation center which local news reports claimed was the only facility of its kind in the nation. The federal center closed in 1963 but reopened the following year as a state correctional institution for juvenile offenders, by which date the camp was described as having buildings of simple composition shingle-sided frame and cinder block construction. The camp is currently closed but well maintained.[26]

Cave Mountain Lake picnic shelter exterior and interior views.
Photos by Dan Pezzoni

The Rustic style that was a staple of the county's summer camps and CCC construction shared affinities with another style popular in Rockbridge and the nation during the period, the Craftsman style. The style was in large part the creation of two brothers, Charles and Henry Greene, who practiced architecture in Pasadena, California, at the beginning of the twentieth century. Greene and Greene pioneered a house form known as the bungalow, which in its later iterations was a relatively informal dwelling of one or one-and-a-half stories characterized by spreading low-pitched roofs and non-historical detail. Although the bungalow name was borrowed from British Colonial houses in India, important stylistic inspiration came from Japanese architecture which was admired for its simplicity and naturalistic

Craftsman bungalows: a stuccoed house in Fairfield and the stone Nathaniel and Agnes Massie House in Glasgow. Photos by Dan Pezzoni

treatment of materials, not major themes in the western stylistic tradition. Also important was the influence of the Arts and Crafts and Shingle styles, the former a craft-focused British movement, the latter a relative of Queen Anne.[27]

Greene and Greene's beautifully crafted Pasadena bungalows and others like them appealed to the editors of magazines like *House Beautiful* and *Good Housekeeping* who disseminated the bungalow form nationwide during the first two decades of the century. An early local example of the form is the house at 507 Jackson Avenue in Lexington, built in 1913 for John W. H. Pollard. Another is the Quist House (2230 Walnut Avenue) in Buena Vista, built in 1917–18 for the town photographer and his family. The story-and-a-half frame house features a wraparound porch engaged under the main hip roof (not separately roofed as was typical in the Queen Anne style) and large side dormers sheathed with staggered square-edged wood shingles. Glasgow has several interesting bungalows. The Nathaniel and Agnes Massie House (1924; 919 Anderson Street) is constructed of limestone; original owner Nathaniel Clayton Manson Massie was an employee of the Lone Jack Limestone company. The Charles and Dorothy Locher House (ca. 1925; 929 Anderson Street) is modeled on a design featured in the Common Brick Manufacturers' Association of America publication *Brick: How to Build and Estimate*. The house is constructed using a rowlock system, superficially similar to Flemish bond, that resulted in thick walls with interior cavities spanned by bricks that appear as headers on the exterior. Charles Locher was associated with the Locher family concrete and brick business. Another house type often detailed in the Craftsman style was the Foursquare, a roughly cubical form, often hip-roofed, with a four-square interior plan that featured a front parlor and adjoining entry/stair hall. Foursquares were built in most of the county's towns and villages during the 1910s and 1920s.[28]

If the Craftsman style could be said to have a contemporary opposite it might be the Tudor Revival style, a twentieth-century continuation

Belfield exterior and interior views.
Photos by Sally Mann

of the medievalist impulse in American domestic architecture. A prominent local example of the style, one that illustrates a number of Tudor characteristics, is Belfield (1928), a sprawling brick mansion built across Woods Creek from the Washington and Lee campus to a design by Lynchburg architect Pendleton Scott Clark and surrounded by extensive gardens. The house exhibits complex irregular massing with steep slate-shingled hip roofs, casement windows with diamond-pattern muntins, and chimneys with clustered stacks and elaborate flared corbeling. A wall dormer features false half-timbering: applied wooden strips, straight and curved, meant to evoke the half-timber construction of traditional English houses.[29]

The Tudor Revival style, like the Colonial Revival, embodied interest in the past, but as the success of the Craftsman style in the county demonstrated, some local citizens and their builders were comfortable with a house style that largely ignored the traditional historical styles (for example, the nearly unbroken line from the Renaissance to the Colonial Revival style). In that sense the Craftsman style paved the way for the modern styles that followed. Generally speaking, modernist architecture eschewed historical reference for an emphasis on innovative materials like concrete, glass, and metal, and it rejected ornament in favor of simple forms and finishes. An exception was the lavishly decorative Art Deco style, a modernist style most popular regionally during the second quarter of the twentieth century, which typically featured stylized geometric and vegetal ornament. The Art Deco style was employed for the brick and concrete Lexington Water Tower on the west side of town, a New York skyscraper in miniature constructed with funds from the New Deal-era Public Works Administration. Modernism's luminaries included such architects as Frank Lloyd Wright, Le Corbusier, and Mies van der Rohe who helped establish the movement internationally during the first half of the twentieth century. In America, the dislocations of the Great Depression and World War II encouraged a break with tradition and helped prepare the ground for modernism's acceptance in the postwar era.

Enderly Heights School.
Photo by Sally Mann

Boxerwood (1951–52), built as the home of Robert and Elizabeth Munger in the countryside near Lexington, is a notable early example of modernist domestic design in the county. The one-story house, characterized by a simple low-pitched shed profile, window walls, and a stone and redwood exterior, was designed by the Roanoke architectural firm of Wells and Meagher and built by local contractors W. W. Coffey and Son. As architectural historian Leslie Giles writes in a report on the house, its "compact, low-impact design reflects a passive solar, organic approach to Modernism, akin to the Usonian House ideal promoted by architect Frank Lloyd Wright." Interior features include a central stone fireplace, radiant underfloor heating, and a multipurpose room (added ca. 1956) with a pattern of Japanese tatami mats in the floor. Boxerwood is also notable for its extensive gardens, developed by Robert Munger beginning in the 1950s and eventually growing to include ponds, walkways, abstract sculptures, and over 7,000 trees and shrubs attributable to Munger's planting campaign. One specimen, a Sicilian fir planted in 1974, is one of only twenty to thirty mature trees of the species thought to survive in the world. Boxerwood is currently operated by the not-for-profit Boxerwood Education Association as a nature education and special events center. Another early modernist house is the Williams House at 614 Stonewall Street (ca. 1953), built to a design by architect Hugh Stebbins

Stonewall Jackson
Memorial Hospital 1952–54
building: aerial and detail views.
Courtesy SC, WLU

who was associated with the internationally recognized modernist architect Walter Gropius. The same model was built elsewhere in the country and in 1955 was the *Better Homes and Gardens* "Idea Home of the Year."[30]

Within a decade of the end of World War II, modernism supplanted other styles as the standard mode for civic architecture and most new commercial construction. Schools, of which many were needed to accommodate the Baby Boom generation, were built to modernist precepts. Enderly Heights Elementary School (101 Woodland Avenue) in Buena Vista is an inspired example among the new crop of postwar modernist school buildings. The construction itself is fairly straightforward for the era—long two-story classroom blocks with flat roofs and recessed window walls—but the arrangement of the blocks takes advantage of the sloping site, with one block behind and upslope from the other so that when viewed from the front the complex reads as a series of terraces. Enderly Heights and its postwar kin were anticipated to a certain degree by developments just before the war. The two-story brick building constructed for the Natural Bridge High School about 1940 has an underlying classical symmetry but its relative lack of ornamentation is modernist in spirit.[31]

Stonewall Jackson Memorial Hospital (1952–54) in Lexington was perhaps the most prominent modernist building in the county when constructed. Its predecessor opened on a full-time basis in 1911 in the

Lee Hi Truck Stop, when US Route 11 was the county's major north-south highway before the construction of Interstate 81. Courtesy SC, WLU

Automobile Age

Hull's Drive-In Movie Theatre.
Photo by Carol M. Highsmith,
courtesy of the Library of Congress

former home of Thomas and Mary Anna Jackson, which had been purchased by the Mary Custis Lee Chapter of the United Daughters of the Confederacy and enlarged and renovated for hospital use. In 1949 the community began to explore options for a new facility and the following year Aaron N. Kiff, head of the New York architectural firm of York and Sawyer, presented preliminary sketches. As built on its spacious "Hospital Hill" site overlooking town, the new hospital exemplified the International Style, an austere version of modernism characterized by unornamented planar forms and an interplay of solids and voids. The building's entry portico featured a slab-like roof supported by slender metal poles and broken by light wells that cast sunlight into the lobby through a wraparound window wall. Lynchburg contractor J. P. Pettyjohn and Sons built the hospital and Board member and one time Blue Ridge Garden Club president Louise Gilliam is said to have

The Coffee Pot. Photo by Michael Pulice, courtesy DHR

designed the landscaping for the twenty-acre site, with involvement from other Blue Ridge Garden Club members and members of the Lexington Garden Club. The 1952–54 front wing of the hospital was torn down when the hospital was expanded in recent years.[32]

Commercial development of the postwar era was also modernist in character and gravitated toward the "strip," the highway frontages leading into and out of Lexington, Buena Vista, and other Rockbridge communities. Strip development was typified by simplified construction using period materials and techniques such as the light-weight cinder-aggregate concrete block known as cinder block, built-up asphalt flat roofs, and aluminum-framed plate glass display windows. Business owners erected large neon signage masts that beckoned to motorists day and night. In the century's final third, Interstate 81 intensified strip development, leading to the growth of commercial/service nodes adjacent to Fairfield, Lexington, and Raphine.

Hulls Drive-in Movie Theatre on US Route 11 near Timber Ridge epitomizes postwar car culture. W. C. Atkins opened the theater in 1950 with a showing of *The Wake of the Red Witch* (1948) starring John Wayne and Gail Russell. The outfit was basic: a screen, a cinder block projection and concessions bunker, and radiator-grill cast aluminum speakers. Sebert W. Hull purchased the business in 1957 and operated the theater until his death in 1998. Hull's Drive-In entered a brief period of uncertainty which ended with its rescue by Hull's Angels, the nation's first non-profit drive-in theater operator.[33]

Another beloved product of the era is the Coffee Pot on US Route 60 between Buena Vista and Lexington. According to interviews by Washington and Lee architectural history student Aaron Michalove, the cylindrical metal-sided building in the form of a coffee pot with handle and spout was built by brothers Thomas, Kenneth, and M. Wills in 1961. "They used no plans or blueprints," Michalove reports. "When they ran into a problem . . . they simply sat on a stump and thought about what to do next until a reasonable solution came to them." The Wills brothers bent plywood to form the curved interior walls and they painted the concrete walkway around the building red to suggest a hot plate. A restaurant with thirteen soda shop stools originally occupied the first floor. An apartment occupied the second story and a gas pump stood out front. The Coffee Pot's roadside location put it in the path of traffic mishaps—a runaway truck tire once damaged the front door—and the Maury River on the other side

The Lexington US Route 11 bypass under construction. The view also shows the nascent US Route 60 West commercial strip, Evergreen Cemetery, and Col Alto and its grounds. Courtesy of Jeremy Leadbetter

of the highway flooded it during Hurricane Camille in 1969, yet it survived to accommodate a variety of uses, including a river outfitter business and a fish market in recent decades, and stands ready for its next tenant.[34]

Rockbridge County's downtowns at first benefited from the prosperity of the postwar period, but as the age of the automobile peaked and investment and vitality shifted to the commercial strips, the town cores began to suffer. In the soul-searching that followed, community leaders discovered an important revitalization tool in historic preservation.

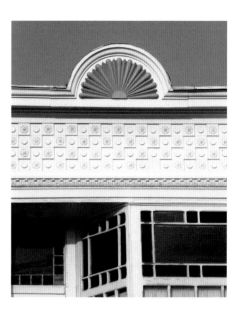

TEN

Preservation

I N 1939 AN "uncared-for and forlorn" house on Lexington's Main Street came under imminent threat of demolition. The Nannie Jordan House, also known at the time as the James R. Jordan House, had come to the attention of the community four years earlier when historic architect A. G. Lambert studied it while on an inspection tour of Public Works Administration activities at VMI. Lambert offered a glowing report to the community. "Lexington should prize and preserve this fine example of early American architecture. It is certainly one of the best examples of small two-story eighteenth century frame houses standing in Virginia today." Lambert admired the house's "superb" modillion cornice, its beaded weatherboards attached by wrought nails "with no attempt to conceal the heads, as we do in modern work," and a Flemish bond chimney with an unusual decorative detail: vertical lines of glazed headers which followed "both sides of the chimneys to the 'haunches' [shoulders]."[1]

The threatened house, which was believed to date to within a few years of the town's establishment in 1778, galvanized interest in historic preservation. Among those whose interest was piqued was Ruth Anderson McCulloch, who was "fired [with] an impulse to try to band together in this community, those interested in preserving its historical landmarks." McCulloch discussed her idea of a history and preservation society with friends at a Fourth of July party at her home Wee Dornoch (her name for the Willson House or Tuckaway, misspelled in recent years as Wee Darnock), and by the end of the year

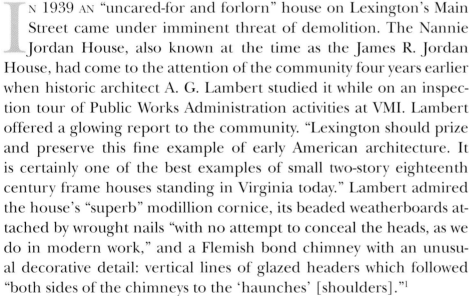

Facing page: The Nannie Jordan House in Lexington, flanked by the Wilson-Walker House (left) and a corner of the Troubadour Building (right) in a 1930s photo snapped shortly before the house was demolished. Courtesy RHS/SC, WLU

Above: Detail of the Arcade Building, Buena Vista. Photo by Dan Pezzoni

221

The Miller's House, Jordan's Point, during an HLF function.
Photo by Don Hasfurther

the Rockbridge Historical Society (RHS) formed with twenty-nine founding members.[2]

RHS failed to save the Jordan House, but it moved on, publishing the first volume of its long-running *Proceedings of the Rockbridge Historical Society* in 1941 and saving for posterity the eighteenth century stone house in Lexington known as The Castle (6 South Randolph Street). Though committed to preservation of the old, RHS was not averse to using modern technology to get the word out on preservation. In December 1941, shortly after the attack on Pearl Harbor, the Roanoke radio station WDBJ broadcast an address on the society read by McCulloch's nephew, Charles McNulty. "In this time of strain and uncertainty," McNulty told listeners, "there comes a feeling of security in turning to the things of the past—the things and people who have made what is best of our present day." Today Rockbridge Historical Society, the oldest of the community's organizations devoted to historic preservation, owns a total of three historic properties. These include the Campbell House Museum (1844–45), a Greek Revival brick house which is one of the first historic buildings to greet visitors to Lexington as they emerge from the visitor center on East Washington Street; the Sloan House, an antebellum brick house next door to the Campbell House; and the aforementioned Castle.[3]

Other events inspired preservation action in Lexington during the 1930s. Concern about the design of the reconstructed State Theatre was one; another was the proposed construction, in 1936, of a service station at the east corner of Main and Nelson streets in the heart of the downtown. The station was built, but the controversy surrounding it opened a debate about traffic, parking, and automobile infrastructure that continues to the present day. Power lines, chain stores, and neon signage were other hot-button topics of the era. In 1937, Matthew W. Paxton Sr., well positioned to influence public opinion as publisher of the *Rockbridge County News*, urged that care be taken so that new construction in downtown Lexington would enhance rather than detract from the town's historic character.[4]

Preservation extended to rural areas of the county. Fancy Hill (ca. 1821) is a case in point. The old mansion fell on hard times in the early twentieth century and when Elmer Knick acquired the property in 1934 he planned to demolish the house and salvage its materials for the construction of a Cape Cod (Colonial Revival) residence. E. Pendleton Tompkins, a local historian and strong proponent of preservation, convinced Knick to rehabilitate instead. The work, which began in 1936, preserved the essential character of the house though a kitchen that was considered too deteriorated to save was demolished and an attached garage with upstairs apartment built in its stead. Historic detached and semi-detached kitchens seem to have been a frequent casualty of early rehabilitation work in the county; the one at Forest Oaks was also taken down during that home's ca. 1916 renovation, as was a possible kitchen and

Campbell House.
Courtesy RHS

slave dwelling that stood behind the McCampbell Inn in Lexington. Kitchens were presumably in worse condition than the residences they served when rehabilitation commenced and hence were more likely to be sacrificed. In recent decades property owners have come to appreciate the rustic charm of these once essential buildings, but historic outbuildings in general, in the words of Michael Pulice,

Fancy Hill. Photo by Don Hasfurther

A Brownsburg street scene with the Brownsburg Museum at center. Photo by Dan Pezzoni

"continue to be under-appreciated, misinterpreted, and demolished without ample consideration."[5]

Fancy Hill belongs to a group of pre-Civil War houses known as the Seven Hills of Rockbridge. The others are Fruit Hill, Herring Hall (earlier known as Clover Hill), Hickory Hill, Liberty Hill, Marlbrook (earlier known as Cherry Hill), and Rose Hill. The concept of grouping and calling attention to the seven houses may have been the brainchild of J. Lee Davis, an enthusiastic promoter of the county's historic and scenic resources. Davis and co-author Edmund P. Tompkins wrote in *The Natural Bridge and its Historical Surroundings* (1939), "The ancient city of Rome boasted its seven hills; it might be suggested that Rockbridge County has a counterpart in the seven 'Hills' of the Welch-Grigsby-Greenlee clan." Though the appellation has limited use as an architectural classification, it did catch on with the public and helped boost appreciation for the seven honored houses and, by extension, historic county houses in general.[6]

Since the birth of modern preservation in the county in the 1930s, historic houses have received most of the attention from

Lexington's Knights of Pythias Building during its 2014 move to make way for VMI construction. The building awaits rehabilitation at its new location on North Main Street. Photo by Kit Huffman, courtesy of the *News-Gazette*

Lexington Presbyterian Church, gutted by fire in 2000,
was rebuilt within the historic walls and a replica steeple
installed. Photo above by Patrick Hinely, Work/Play®;
photos at right courtesy of the *News-Gazette*

preservationists and homeowners. Many historic houses continue to serve as single-family dwellings but some have been repurposed in interesting ways. A two-story frame house on Brownsburg's Main Street, ornamented with an Italianate bracketed cornice that suggests construction or remodeling in the late 1800s, was converted to the Brownsburg Museum in 2009, replete with professionally designed exhibits which present the village's rich Civil War history and other subjects. Donated to the community by former owner Mollie Sue Whipple, the house is thought to have served as a saddlery and the Bank of Brownsburg at various times.[7]

The popularity of bed and breakfast accommodations in recent decades has proved a boon for historic residences in Lexington and the county's smaller communities and rural areas. The Hummingbird Inn in Goshen occupies the Teter House, a textbook Gothic Revival residence which appears to date to the third quarter of the nineteenth century, though it may incorporate earlier fabric. The house was rescued by Frank Miller in the 1970s and converted to an inn by Jeremy and Diana Robinson in the 1990s. The barn that stands behind the house on Mill Creek served as Goshen's town livery stable before it was moved to its present location. Other conversions include the Bed and Breakfast at Oak Spring Farm, which operates in a Raphine-area house dated to 1826; Stoneridge Inn near Lexington in a Federal style brick house dated to 1829; the Frog Hollow Bed and Breakfast in a nineteenth century farmhouse near the Virginia Horse Center; and the Herring Hall Bed and Breakfast located in the Federal style house by the same name, the main part of which may date to ca. 1832 as suggested by tax records, and which was used as a country inn in 1926. The Walter and Irene Searson House, occupied by the Steeles Tavern Manor Bed and Breakfast in Steeles Tavern, is more recent than most, dating only to 1916, but its symmetrical five-bay façade and portico on square Mount Vernon type columns gives it the same air of gracious hospitality. Walter Searson managed the McCormick Farm at the turn of the twentieth century, and

The Peoples Bank of Buena Vista building now houses the Buena Vista branch of City National Bank.
Photo by Dan Pezzoni

The Georges Inn (McCampbell Inn).
Photo by Don Hasfurther

Hummingbird Inn.
Photo by Dan Pezzoni

with his wife, Irene, a member of the Steele family, operated the 1916 house as a tourist accommodation as well as a private home. Maple Hall is another prominent historic bed and breakfast, and work is under way to convert Forest Oaks into one as well.[8]

State and federal rehabilitation tax credit programs have assisted owners of historic properties with high-quality rehabilitations. Properties qualify through historic listing or (in some instances) eligibility, and the rehabilitations must be certified as meeting the Secretary of the Interior's Standards for Rehabilitation. Property owners in Lexington (compared to those in the county at large) have been the principal beneficiaries of the program to date, in large part because of the long-term existence of the Lexington Historic District, which was listed in the Virginia Landmarks Register and the National Register of Historic Places in 1971 and 1972, and because of the community's commitment to maintaining its historic character. The Lexington rehabilitations include conventional single-family dwellings and commercial buildings and more unusual properties like the Lexington and Covington Turnpike Toll House, the Troubadour

Maury River Middle School.
Photo by Dan Pezzoni

Building (an antebellum Odd Fellows hall), and the Hileman-Hamric Tombstone Workshop.

Major tax credit rehabilitations that were in progress in Lexington in 2014–15 included the Alexander-Withrow Building and the McCampbell Inn. The two buildings were also early Historic Lexington Foundation success stories. HLF acquired the Alexander-Withrow Building in the 1960s and retained Charlottesville preservation architect Thomas Craven to advise on its rehabilitation. Work on the McCampbell Inn, also known as the Central Hotel, began in 1971 and was completed with assistance from the rehabilitation tax credit program. After the passage of several decades the two buildings were again in need of rehabilitation, this time to be reborn as The Georges Inn. The Lexington city government assisted downtown revitalization efforts in the late twentieth century through infrastructure projects and the establishment of a local historic ordinance.[9]

Tax credit rehabilitations in the county outside Lexington, though fewer in number, include such important initiatives as the Glasgow Elementary School, rehabilitated as housing for the elderly and approved in 1996, and the rehabilitation of the Peoples Bank of Buena

Barclay House (Beaumont).
Photo by Dan Pezzoni

Vista, approved in 2010. In order for the two buildings to qualify for the credits it was necessary to include them in newly created historic districts, the
Glasgow Historic District and the Buena Vista Downtown Historic District, a consequence being that
other property owners in the two districts can explore tax credit rehabilitation as an option for their
historic buildings. Brownsburg also has a state- and
nationally-designated historic district, the Brownsburg Historic District. Another county building
to benefit from the credits is Wade's Mill (Kennedy-Wade Mill), rehabilitated as a working flour mill
in 1993. Wade's Mill, a popular heritage tourism
destination in the countryside near Raphine, houses
a store that sells products ground in the mill as well
as Virginia-made specialty foods.[10]

As important as building preservation to the
health of historic cultural landscapes is the stewardship of the land itself, and this has been aided
through the work of the Rockbridge Area Conservation Council (RAAC), founded in 1976, and the
Valley Conservation Council, based in Staunton,
which assists property owners with conservation
easements. RACC's accomplishments include the
creation of the Chessie Trail and the protection of the top of House
Mountain. RACC and the Valley Conservation Council recently joined
forces to form Friends of Natural Bridge, a group that has successfully
promoted the conservation of Natural Bridge. A recent addition to
the roster of local organizations with an interest in rural preservation
is the Mountain Valley Preservation Alliance based in Lexington and
serving Rockbridge and surrounding counties.[11]

The county's historic schools represent a special class of rehabilitation. School-to-housing rehabilitation, though common elsewhere
in the nation, has only occurred once with the rehabilitation of the
Glasgow Elementary School—not counting the reuse of the Ann
Smith School in Lexington as a fraternity and early frame schools that
may survive disguised as houses. Continued use as schools is more
common, and a successful recent example is the rehabilitation and
enlargement of Maury River Middle School in Lexington. Built as the

Architect Thomas U. Walter's
Rockbridge County Jail (ca. 1839)
on Lexington's Courthouse Square
was rehabilitated in recent decades.
Photo by Dan Pezzoni

The timber frame Lyle Shelter in Goshen Pass, shown under construction, memorializes Royster Lyle and his contributions to conservation and preservation efforts in Rockbridge County.
Photo by Anne Drake McClung

Lexington High School in 1960, the building was transferred to the county school system which in 2011 decided to consolidate all its middle school programs at the location and hired the Roanoke architectural firm Spectrum Design to design an expansion. The modernist brick-veneered 1960 building, characterized by a slab-like flat-roofed form and ribbon classroom windows, was retained and a new gymnasium, cafeteria, and other facilities added, the additions modernist in design in keeping with the original aesthetic. A striking feature is the cafeteria window wall with a translucent photomural of Goshen Pass by photographer Anne Drake McClung. The predecessor Lexington High School, a Classical Revival building built in 1927 and later used as Harrington Waddell Elementary School, has not fared as well. In 2014 it was torn down to make way for a new school on the same site.[12]

For over a quarter century the Rockbridge Historical Society was the principal local organization dedicated to preservation. In 1966 it was joined by Historic Lexington Foundation (HLF), which grew out of the Ruth Anderson McCulloch Branch of the Association for the Preservation of Virginia Antiquities (the statewide preservation organization that subsequently evolved to become Preservation Virginia). Concerned citizens formed and reformed a local branch of the APVA twice, in the 1890s and 1930s, to work for the preservation of the remains of Old Monmouth Church and the covered bridge at East Lexington. Each effort petered out but a third attempt in the mid-1960s, inspired by the threatened demolition of the 1820s Barclay

House (Beaumont) on Lee Avenue in Lexington, resulted in the formation of HLF with D. B. Clayton Jr. as the first president and Royster Lyle Jr. on the first board of directors. The story of HLF's founding and early successes is well told by Royster Lyle and Pam Simpson in *The Architecture of Historic Lexington*, a book that was itself one of the organization's chief early accomplishments.[13]

Recent rehabilitations completed by or with major input from HLF include the Miller's House at Jordan's Point, which houses exhibits on the transportation and industrial heritage of East Lexington; the Roberson-Phalen House, rehabilitated by former HLF president Jean Dunbar and her husband, Peter Sils; and the Rebecca and Hayden Holmes House in the Green Hill neighborhood, one of Lexington's oldest documented African American houses, saved through the leadership of former HLF president Pam Simpson and former HLF director Leslie Giles. The Roberson-Phalen and Holmes houses were the latest properties to be purchased and rehabilitated by the HLF revolving fund.

HLF has always concerned itself with the county as a whole, a commitment reaffirmed and strengthened in 2013 by adding explicit mention of the county's historical heritage and fabric to the organization's mission statement. *The Architecture of Historic Rockbridge* is one of the first fruits of this renewed emphasis, and HLF hopes the book will inspire and assist present and future generations in their stewardship of the county's irreplaceable architectural heritage.[14]

Pam Simpson with a new generation of preservationists at an HLF event on Lexington's Hopkins Green.
Photo by Leslie Giles

Glossary

A granary on the Muse Farm near Timber Ridge advertised patent medicine to motorists on US Route 11. A vestige of the painted ad is still visible on the building. Photo (ca. 1970s) by Royster Lyle, courtesy RHS/SC, WLU

ACADEMIC   A design or building that follows rules of proportion and detail generated by the architectural profession or the scholarly community. See also POPULAR, VERNACULAR.

ACANTHUS   A Mediterranean plant used as a model for the foliated ornament in the capital of a Corinthian capital.

ANTHEMION   A classical ornament derived from the form of honeysuckle leaves or palmettes.

APRON   The space under a window, often paneled, or a panel between a window and the floor.

APSE   The semicircular or polygonal projection from the back wall of a church.

ARCADE/ARCADING/ARCADED   A series of arches.

ARCH   A curved structural element that spans an opening. Masonry arches often have a specialized keystone at the top. A keyblock refers to a decorative element, usually of wood, that is similar in appearance to and occupies the same place as a keystone. An impost block or springer sometimes appears at the foot of the arch on both sides, and the blocks between the imposts and keystone may be referred to as voussoir blocks. A flat arch or jack arch is flat and may be supported by a concealed lintel. A round arch is semicircular. A segmental arch

Wade's Mill interior.
Photo by Dell Upton,
courtesy DHR

consists of a curved segment that is less than a semi-circle. A lancet arch, characteristic of the Gothic Revival style, is composed of two curved sections that meet at a point. A Tudor arch, characteristic of the Tudor Revival style, is a flattened lancet arch.

ARCHITRAVE   A division of a classical entablature. May also refer to the molded surround or frame of a door, window, or fireplace.

ART DECO STYLE   A modernist style appearing locally in the 1930s and 1940s, characterized by stylized geometric ornament. See MODERNISM.

BALUSTER/BALUSTRADE   A turned, rectangular-section, or sawn support for a stair, porch, or roof deck railing. A railing consisting of balusters is a balustrade. A roof deck with a railing is often called a widow's walk.

BARGEBOARD   A board, usually decorative, in a roof eave or the rakes (diagonals) of a gable roof. Barge-boards are common in Gothic Revival architecture and also appear in Queen Anne architecture. Also referred to as a vergeboard.

BARREL VAULT   A vault that is semi-circular or nearly semi-circular in section.

BATTEN DOOR/SHUTTER   A door or shutter constructed of horizontal boards called battens fastened across vertical boards.

BAY   A division of a building elevation usually corresponding to window and door placement. A window/door/window elevation would be a three-bay elevation.

BAY WINDOW   See WINDOW.

BEAD   A narrow rounded molding that may be cut into the lower edge of a weatherboard, ceiling joist, trim piece (like a chair rail or door frame), or the edges and face of a tongue-and-groove board.

BED MOLDING   See MOLDING.

BELFRY   An enclosure for a bell in a tower or set on a roof.

BELT COURSE   A projecting horizontal band of brick, stone, or wood that usually corresponds with a floor level change.

BOND   See BRICK.

BOSS   A projecting ornament.

BOARD-AND-BATTEN   Vertical board cladding with narrow vertical strips of wood (battens) over the gaps between boards.

BOXED STAIR   A stair with a board enclosure and often a door. Also known as an enclosed stair.

BRACKET   A supporting member that projects from a wall or post or under projecting elements of a mantel. A bracket may be truly supporting or merely decorative. A tread bracket is the applied ornamental piece under the lip at the end of a stair tread.

BREEZEWAY   A short open-air passageway connecting a house to a dependency, usually a kitchen. Also known as a dog trot when it separates the two parts of a dog trot house.

BRICK   A clay, clay-loam, or processed shale masonry unit formed in a mold and fired until hard. When laid in a wall so that its long side is visible, referred to as a stretcher (brick). When laid so that its short end is visible, referred to as a header (brick). The coursing or pattern of bricks in a wall is referred to as the bond and the divisions between bricks and courses are referred to as mortar joints. Stretcher bond is composed of stretcher bricks exclusively. Flemish bond is composed of alternating stretcher and header bricks and is associated with early and Colonial Revival brickwork. Flemish variant bond may double the headers or otherwise modify standard Flemish bond. English bond is composed of courses of stretcher bricks alternating with courses of header bricks. Common bond has two or more courses of stretcher bricks alternating with header bricks. A molded brick has a decorative end or profile as seen in the molded brick cornices popular in Rockbridge County before the Civil War. Paving or paved refers to bricks used like paving bricks to cover sloped chimney shoulders or buttress weatherings.

BROKEN PEDIMENT   See PEDIMENT.

BUNGALOW   An early twentieth century house form characteristic of the Craftsman style. A bungalow is characterized by one- or story-and-a-half height and often has such Craftsman features as triangular gable brackets, an engaged front porch, tapered square wood porch posts on brick pedestals, and vertically divided upper window sashes.

BUTTRESS   A vertical mass that projects from a wall to provide structural reinforcement. Common in Gothic-inspired church architecture.

CA.   See CIRCA.

CAPITAL   The top, usually decorated or molded, of a column or pilaster.

CASEMENT WINDOW   See WINDOW.

CENTER PASSAGE PLAN   A plan in which a narrow passage or hall extends through the center of a house and is flanked by two or more rooms.

CHAIR RAIL   A molding on a wall around a room at or about the height of the back of a chair. Often runs at the top of a wainscot.

CHAMFER A beveled corner.

CHANCEL   The altar end of a church interior, usually distinguished from the nave by an arch or some other feature.

CHINKING   See LOG CONSTRUCTION.

CIRCA or CA.   The Latin term for "about" or "approximate" usually used to indicate the estimated date or period of construction for a building or to indicate uncertainty in dating.

CIRCULAR-SAWN   Sawn with a mechanical circular saw. Circular sawing creates telltale curved saw or "chatter" marks.

CLAPBOARDS   Split boards used for siding or roofing.

CLASSICAL   Embodying or inspired by classical Greek and Roman architecture, particularly the classical orders.

CLASSICAL REVIVAL STYLE   An early twentieth century style inspired by classical architecture from the ancient period through the nineteenth century. In domestic architecture characterized by monumental columned porches or porticos.

CLERESTORY   A high roof or wall window.

COLLAR BEAM   A horizontal beam that ties rafter pairs together and prevents them from spreading.

COLONIAL REVIVAL STYLE   A classically-inspired style, conceived in the late nineteenth century and still popular, based on American colonial architecture and, to a lesser extent, the Federal style. Some examples are referred to as Georgian Revival.

COLONNETTE   A small column generally employed as a decorative feature in mantels and overmantels.

COMMON BOND   See BRICK.

CONSOLE   A scroll-shaped bracket or corbel.

CORBEL   An outward stepping individual support or band of masonry that may be structural and/or decorative.

CORINTHIAN ORDER   See ORDER.

CORNCRIB   A generally small outbuilding for storing corn, often with provision for ample ventilation such as unchinked log construction.

CORNICE   A decorative crowning element for a wall or opening. Many pre-Civil War brick buildings in Rockbridge County have cornices constructed of molded bricks.

COVE   A concave interior corner.

CRAFTSMAN STYLE An architectural style popular in Rockbridge County from the 1910s to the 1930s. The bungalow and Foursquare house forms are associated with the style. A Craftsman porch is usually supported by tapered wood columns on brick bases. See also BUNGALOW, FOURSQUARE.

CRESTING An ornamental feature along a roof ridge or parapet.

CROWN MOLDING The upper molding of a cornice.

CUPOLA A structure, typically for light or ventilation and often decorative, built on a roof.

DAUBING See LOG CONSTRUCTION.

DENTILS Small, tooth-like, closely-spaced blocks in a classical entablature. Used to ornament cornices, mantels, and other classically derived features.

DORIC ORDER See ORDER.

DORMER See ROOF.

DOVETAIL NOTCHING See LOG CONSTRUCTION.

ECLECTIC/ECLECTICISM Elements or influence from diverse stylistic sources.

ELEVATION An exterior wall or vertical face of a building or structure. An elevation drawing is a drawing of the side of a building.

ELL A perpendicular rear wing of a house.

ENCLOSED STAIR See BOXED STAIR.

ENGAGED COLUMN A column partly attached to a wall rather than free standing.

ENGAGED PORCH A porch contained under the principal roof of the building.

ENGLISH BOND See BRICK.

ENTABLATURE A horizontal band or structural element typically consisting of an architrave, frieze, and cornice.

FAÇADE The front or principal elevation of a building.

FALSE HALF-TIMBERING   A Tudor Revival surface treatment consisting of decorative (false) timbers and an infilling of stucco, brick, or other material. True or structural half-timbering is a hallmark of early modern northern European domestic architecture including that constructed in England during the reigns of the Tudor monarchs (Henry VIII, Elizabeth I, and so forth).

FANLIGHT   An arched transom window above an entry or in a gable or pediment.

FASCIA   A flat, usually unornamented, horizontal band of a classical cornice; most commonly, the fascia is the uppermost flat face of a wooden cornice, to which the crown mold is applied.

FEDERAL STYLE   A classically-inspired style dominant in Rockbridge County from about 1800 through the 1830s and occurring less frequently later. The style is characterized by the delicate use of classical ornament and is sometimes referred to as the Adam or Adamesque style.

FINIAL   A pointed or decorative element at the peak of a roof or other feature.

FLAT ARCH   See ARCH.

FLEMISH BOND/FLEMISH VARIANT BOND   See BRICK.

FLUTING   Vertical concave channeling or grooving on the surface of a column, pilaster, or other classically-inspired feature.

FOLIATED   Decorated with leaf-like or vegetal ornament.

FOURSQUARE   An early twentieth century house form characterized by boxy, cubic massing and a four-room (foursquare) plan, often with a hip roof and Craftsman or Colonial Revival detail. See also CRAFTSMAN STYLE.

FRIEZE   A division of a classical entablature. Used to describe the horizontal part of a mantel that spans the fireplace opening. May also refer to any relatively wide horizontal band.

FULL DOVETAIL NOTCHING   See LOG CONSTRUCTION.

GABLE ROOF   See ROOF.

A transitional Federal/Greek Revival mantel in Liberty Hill. The label on the original ca. 1940 photo reads "very fine carving presumably by Pole." The reference may be to Lexington builder John Gwynne Pole Sr.
Courtesy RHS/SC, WLU

GABLE END   The side of a building under the triangular gable of a gable roof.

GAMBREL ROOF   See ROOF.

GARRET   An upper half story or habitable attic space.

GEORGIAN STYLE   The dominant classically-inspired architectural style of the 1700s in Great Britain and Virginia. Georgian influence extended into the early 1800s in Rockbridge County.

GEORGIAN REVIVAL STYLE   See COLONIAL REVIVAL STYLE.

GLAZED/GLAZING   A glossy vitrified surface on a brick, or glass in a window sash.

GOTHIC REVIVAL STYLE   The mid-nineteenth century revival of medieval Gothic architecture, characterized by the lancet (pointed) arch. The style remained popular for churches and academic buildings into the twentieth century, after it had fallen out of use for domestic architecture.

GOUGEWORK   Ornament made by a carver's gouge in the form of small grooves reminiscent of fluting. Common in Federal style woodwork.

GRAINING   The painted simulation of wood grain. Also known as false or faux wood grain or graining.

GREEK REVIVAL STYLE   The mid-nineteenth century revival of ancient Greek architecture. Popular in Rockbridge County from about 1840 to the Civil War and more rarely after.

HALF DOVETAIL NOTCHING   See LOG CONSTRUCTION.

HALL-PARLOR PLAN   A traditional vernacular house plan consisting of two principal rooms: a larger "hall" and smaller "parlor." Two-story examples often replicate the plan on the second floor.

HIP   An inclined ridge or angle formed by the meeting of two sloping roof surfaces.

HIPPED ROOF   See ROOF.

HISTORICISM   Interest in or use of historical styles. See MODERNISM.

HL HINGE   An early, typically wrought, hinge type composed of iron shapes resembling the letters H and L side by side. Also known as an H-L, H&L, or H-and-L hinge. Machine-made reproductions are common in Colonial Revival architecture.

HYPHEN   A connecting element between two sections of a building.

IMPOST   See ARCH.

IN ANTIS   Columns in front of a recess and freestanding between pilasters or sections of wall.

IONIC ORDER   See ORDER.

ITALIANATE STYLE   A nineteenth century revival style inspired by the villa and farmhouse architecture of Italy. Bracketed cornices and arched window and door openings are characteristic of the style which was used in Rockbridge County from the 1850s through the 1880s.

JACK ARCH   See ARCH.

JOIST   One of a series of parallel horizontal timbers or beams, usually set on edge, which span a room from wall to wall to support a floor or ceiling.

KEYBLOCK   See ARCH.

KEYSTONE   See ARCH.

LABEL MOLDING   A molding that appears to drape over the top of an opening but does not extend all the way down the sides; a hood molding. Common in Gothic Revival and Italianate architecture.

LANCET ARCH   See ARCH.

LATH   A thin strip or strips of wood used as a support and base for a plaster finish.

LINTEL   A wood, stone, or metal beam that spans an opening, or a decorative spanning element over an opening.

LOG CONSTRUCTION   A traditional construction technique in which logs are stacked horizontally to form a wall. Notching is the technique by which the logs are joined together at the ends. Saddle notching is the simplest, with crudely scalloped notches. In half dovetail notching the top of the end of the log is sloped and the bottom is squared. In dovetail or full dovetail notching both the top and bottom of the end of the log are sloped. In v-notching the top of the end of the log is given an inverted V form. The filling between the logs is known as chinking and daubing.

LOZENGE   A diamond shape; a rhomb.

LUNETTE   See WINDOW.

MANSARD/MANSARDED ROOF   See ROOF.

MANTEL   The often decorative surround of a fireplace. Usually wooden but occasionally stone and/or brick. Mantel form and detail are closely related to architectural style.

MARBLING, MARBLEIZING   Painted to simulate marble or other stone.

MEDALLION   A plaque-like ornament, generally rounded.

MISSION STYLE   A style derived from the Spanish Mission architecture of California and, more generally, a range of Mediterranean sources. Defining features include shaped parapets (ultimately Baroque in inspiration), real or imitation Spanish tile roofing, and smooth (often stucco) wall finishes. The style was used infrequently in Rockbridge County in the early twentieth century.

MODERNISM/MODERNIST   A broad twentieth century architectural movement that rejected historicism. The Art Deco and Moderne are modernist styles. See HISTORICISM.

MODILLION   A diminutive console or scrolled bracket. A modillion cornice has multiple modillions.

MOLDING   A trim piece with a generally decorative profile, either curved or rectilinear. A bed molding is a molding under another element such as a mantel shelf.

MONITOR   A raised section of roof with clerestory or skylight windows or vents.

MONUMENTAL   Two stories or more in height. Used to describe columns and porticoes.

MORTAR JOINT   See BRICK.

The Buena Vista Paper Company (Bontex) appears in this mid-20th century photo of the Maury River, Buena Vista, and the Blue Ridge Mountains.
Courtesy of Jeremy Leadbetter

A ceiling border and other decorative finishes appear in this late 1800s view of poet Margaret Junkin Preston's parlor in Lexington. Preston wrote the poem "Beechenbrook" for which Beechenbrook Chapel was named.
Courtesy RHS/SC, WLU

MORTISE-AND-TENON CONSTRUCTION A traditional construction technique in which wooden framing members are joined together with projecting tenons and slot-like mortises, often held together with wooden pegs. Mortise-and-tenon heavy frame construction eventually gave way to light nailed frame construction.

MUNTIN See WINDOW.

NATIONAL REGISTER OF HISTORIC PLACES   A federal roster of historic buildings, districts, and other resources of archaeological, architectural, and/or historical significance. The report used to designate such properties is typically referred to as a National Register nomination.

NAVE   The main interior space of a church, generally rectangular in floor plan.

NECKING   A molding or ornamental band below or at the base of a capital.

NEWEL   A post used to rigidify a stair railing or balustrade.

NOGGING   Hidden infill, usually bricks, stacked between the studs of a frame wall for the purpose of insulation and/or pest deterrence.

ORDER   A classical system of design and construction. There are three Greek orders: Doric, Ionic, and Corinthian, each with distinctive details and in academic examples governed by strict rules of proportion. The Doric order is characterized by columns with simply molded capitals and bases (although the bases may be omitted) and in academic versions may feature triglyphs and other distinguishing ornaments in the entablature. The Ionic order is characterized by capitals with pronounced spiral scrolls known as volutes. The Corinthian order is characterized by capitals with acanthus leaf ornament. (Two Roman orders, the Tuscan and Composite, are not discussed in the text.)

ORIEL WINDOW   See WINDOW.

OUTBUILDING   An auxiliary building in a domestic or agricultural complex.

OVERMANTEL   The section of a mantel over the mantel shelf. Georgian and Colonial Revival overmantels are often composed of panels. Queen Anne and Classical Revival overmantels often feature mirrors, colonnettes, or spindle ornament.

PALLADIAN WINDOW   See WINDOW.

PANEL   A portion of a flat surface set off by moldings or by being raised or indented.

PARAPET   An extension of a wall above a roofline.

PATERA   A small, relatively flat circular, oval, or elliptical ornament. In Federal style mantels often carved with a fanfold or sunburst pattern. Also a term for the circular carving on turned corner blocks. Plural: paterae.

PAVILION   A portion of a building's facade that projects forward slightly from the main face.

PLAN   The arrangement of the interior of a building or a drawing of such an arrangement. A site plan depicts the arrangement of buildings, landscape features, and such on a site.

PEDESTAL   A block-like support for a column or pilaster.

PEDIMENT   The well-defined triangular end of a gable roof in classical and classically-inspired architecture. In Greek temples like the Parthenon the pediment was a setting for sculpture. Pediments often appear over porticos or projecting façade pavilions. The tympanum is the often recessed triangular surface separate from the cornices that define the pediment. A broken pediment has a gap at the top instead of a peak, sometimes occupied by an ornament.

PENCILING   In brickwork, the application of fine lines of pigment on the mortar joints using a straight edge and a thin brush called a pencil.

PENDANT   Hanging, as in an ornament at the bottom end of a structural or decorative element.

PIT-SAWN   Manually sawn by two sawyers in an up and down manner. Pit sawing leaves telltale irregular vertical or slightly inclined saw or "chatter" marks.

PIER   A pillar-like masonry support, either free standing or engaged in a wall surface.

PILASTER   A shallow column-like element engaged in a wall surface or a vertical supporting elements on the side of a fireplace.

PINNACLE   A pointed crowning element on a buttress or parapet indicative of the Gothic Revival style.

PLATE   In traditional frame construction the horizontal timber at the top of a wall. Also the top log, usually fully squared, in log construction.

PLINTH   A base for a column, porch support, or door surround.

POLYCHROMATIC/POLYCHROME   Multicolored.

POPULAR   Refers to architecture of standardized character, often disseminated by the media and predominant in the twentieth century. See also ACADEMIC, VERNACULAR.

PORTE COCHÈRE   A projecting porch or drive-thru that provides shelter for a vehicle and people getting into or out of the vehicle. A common feature of the early twentieth century Classical Revival, Colonial Revival, and Craftsman styles.

PORTICO   In classically-inspired buildings, a columned porch, typically with a pediment.

PYRAMIDAL ROOF   See ROOF.

QUARRY-FACED   Stonework chiseled with a rough surface meant to look natural.

QUATREFOIL   A form having four lobes, in cloverleaf fashion, common in Gothic Revival architecture. The trefoil and cinquefoil are three- and five-lobed forms.

QUEEN ANNE STYLE   An architectural style popular in the late nineteenth and early twentieth century inspired by medieval prototypes and characterized in domestic architecture by irregular plans and roof massing, intricate milled detail, and varied and textural exterior wall finishes. The style is sometimes referred to as Victorian although that term is broader and implies a less distinctive or fully realized version of the style.

QUEEN ANNE WINDOW   A window edged with small rectangular panes, often of colored glass.

RAKE   The slope or pitch of a roof.

REEDING   Decoration consisting of multiple fine parallel convex moldings that create a corrugated appearance. Common in Federal style woodwork.

In the 1970s Ed Dooley wrote and illustrated the "Restoration Notes" series which ran in the *Main Street Magazine*, edited by Dooley and his wife, Louise Dooley. Courtesy of Ed Dooley and SC, WLU

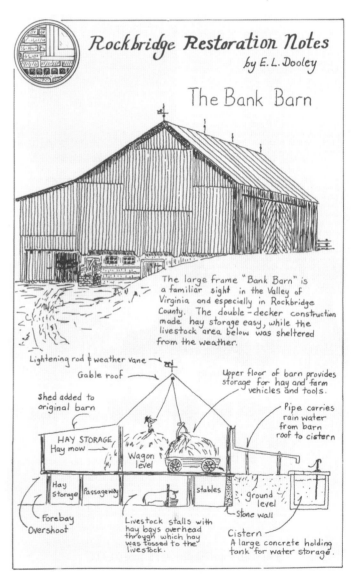

RETICULATED   Netlike. Used to describe asterisk-like muntin or grill patterns in window and vent openings in classically-inspired architecture.

RISER   The vertical board under a step, perpendicular to the tread.

ROCKFACED   Describes concrete block with a molded quarry-faced surface.

ROMANESQUE/ROMANESQUE REVIVAL STYLE   A late nineteenth century revival of pre-Gothic architecture characterized by round arches rather than Gothic lancet arches.

ROOF   The cover of a building.   A shed roof is a single-sloped roof. A gable roof is a double-sloped roof with a triangular or A-shaped section. A gambrel roof is a double-sloped roof typical of dairy barns and some Colonial Revival buildings. A hip or hipped roof has four slopes; a pyramidal roof is a hipped roof where the slopes meet at a single point. A mansard (or mansarded) roof is similar to a truncated pyramid in form, occasionally with concave or convex sides. The roofs of Craftsman and Colonial Revival houses often feature dormers, windows or ventilation features that project from the slope of the roof and that can have gabled, pedimented, shed, or hipped roofs.

SADDLE NOTCHING   See LOG CONSTRUCTION.

SCARF JOINT   An interlocking joint that splices together two pieces into a single piece or beam.

Thorn Hill.
Courtesy RHS/SC, WLU

Glossary

SECOND EMPIRE STYLE   A nineteenth century style inspired by the architecture of the French Second Empire of Napoleon III (1852–1870) characterized by the French mansard roof form.

SHED ROOF   See ROOF.

SHOULDER   The point at which a chimney narrows, typically stepped or sloped.

SIDE PASSAGE PLAN   A house plan with an off-center passage, typically with the exterior wall on one side and a room or rooms on the other.

SIDELIGHT   A narrow vertical window on the side of an entry usually treated as a part of the entry surround.

SILL   A heavy horizontal timber at the bottom of a frame wall.

SMOKEHOUSE   An outbuilding for curing and storing meat.

SOFFIT   The exposed underside of an architectural element.

SPANDREL   The triangular section of wall under a flight of steps or between the curves of two adjacent arches and an entablature or roof above.

SPINDLE   A small turned piece of wood, one of the technomorphic elements of Queen Anne ornament.

STICK STYLE   A nineteenth century style akin to the Queen Anne style identifiable by the use of patterned stick-like wooden claddings and strut-like ornament.

STRETCHER, STRETCHER BOND   See BRICK.

STUD   In frame construction, a vertical supporting member in a wall.

STYLE   A fashion or mode of architecture.

SURROUND   The border or casing of a window or door opening or a fireplace.

TABLET   A projecting panel, either plain or ornamented and typically rectangular, in the frieze of a mantel or surround.

TECHNOMORPHIC   A descriptor for the form of an architectural element that is characterized by the technology that made it, for example turned and scroll-sawn Queen Anne ornament.

TERRAZZO   A decorative polished paving material made from marble chips in a cement matrix.

TONGUE-AND-GROOVE   The projecting tongues and indented grooves used to join the edges of boards for a tight fit. Beaded tongue-and-groove sheathing consists of narrow boards decorated with one or more rows of beading.

TRABEATED   Characterized by post and lintel (or post and beam) construction or appearance.

TRACERY   See WINDOW.

TRADITIONAL   Historical or customary architecture or building practice. See VERNACULAR.

TRANSOM   A window, typically narrow and horizontal, above a doorway or storefront.

TREAD   The flat horizontal surface of a step.

TREAD BRACKET   See BRACKET.

TRIGLYPH   A block with vertical grooves (usually three) used in series to ornament a Greek or Greek Revival cornice. In academic architecture used only with the Doric order.

TRIPARTITE   Three-part.

TUDOR ARCH   See ARCH.

TUDOR REVIVAL STYLE   A style derived from the architecture of Medieval and Early Modern England popular in Rockbridge County in the second quarter of the twentieth century. A late phase of the Gothic Revival style occasionally built to the present.

TURNED   Fashioned on a lathe to have a round section.

TURRET   A small tower or tower-like roof element.

TYMPANUM   See PEDIMENT.

V-NOTCHING See LOG CONSTRUCTION.

VAULT An arched ceiling typically structural and of masonry construction.

VERGEBOARD See BARGEBOARD

VERNACULAR Traditional and often ethnically based common architecture that reflects local conditions and may develop partly or wholly separately from academic or "correct" systems of design and ornament. An academic style may be expressed in a vernacular way, meaning it reflects a local or idiosyncratic interpretation. Vernacular architecture is generally transmitted by example or orally. See also ACADEMIC, POPULAR, TRADITIONAL.

VICTORIAN See QUEEN ANNE STYLE.

VOLUTE See ORDER.

VOUSSOIR See ARCH.

WAINSCOT/WAINSCOTING A wood lining along the lower part of a wall.

WEATHERBOARD SIDING Overlapping horizontal sheathing boards that are sawn rather than split.

WEATHERING The sloping portion of a chimney stack or buttress.

Orchard Side Log Cabins,
Fairfield vicinity.
Courtesy SC, WLU

WINDER   A wedge-shaped step in the turn of a stair.

WINDOW   An opening in a wall for light and ventilation. Windows are typically glazed (provided with glass). Most historic buildings have double-hung sash windows, and the number of panes of glass in each sash is referred to numerically. For example, a window with nine panes in the upper sash and six panes in the lower sash is referred to as a nine-over-six-sash window. A bay window projects from an elevation, typically in canted polygonal form, and may have several individual windows. Bay windows of one or more stories in height are associated with Queen Anne style domestic architecture. An oriel window is a cantilevered bay window. A dormer is a window that projects from a roof. A casement window has hinged rather than sliding sashes. A Palladian window, named for the Italian architect Andrea Palladio (1508–1580), has a central arched opening flanked by lower square-headed openings. A lunette is a semicircular window, usually in a gable or pediment. A muntin is the narrow dividing piece (usually of wood) between panes of glass. Tracery is a decorative pattern of wood or stone muntins and is characteristic of lancet-arched stained glass windows.

WRAPAROUND PORCH   A porch that extends to two or more sides of a building, characteristic of Queen Anne houses.

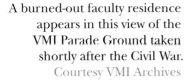

A burned-out faculty residence appears in this view of the VMI Parade Ground taken shortly after the Civil War.
Courtesy VMI Archives

Notes

Early 19th-century Rockbridge homebuilders often treated stairs decoratively, as demonstrated by a scrolled handrail terminus in the James McChesney House.
Photo by J. Manuel, courtesy DHR

Preface

1. Bodie, *Remarkable Rockbridge*, 55.

2. McCleskey, *Road to Black Ned's Forge*; Bodie, *Remarkable Rockbridge*, 17.

3. Lyle and Simpson, *Architecture of Historic Lexington*, 10.

4. Simpson, *Cheap, Quick & Easy*, 4.

1   Approaching Buildings

1. Simpson, "Architecture of Rockbridge County," 77–78.

2. Simpson, "Architecture of Rockbridge County," 79–81.

3. Simpson, "Architecture of Rockbridge County," 82–83.

4. Simpson, "Architecture of Rockbridge County," 83–84; Tompkins and Davis, *Natural Bridge and its Historical Surroundings*, 57–58, after 116.

5. Rockbridge Historical Society Collection; *Lexington Gazette*, July 3, 1874.

6. Simpson, "Architecture of Rockbridge County," 81; Herman, "18th Century Quaker Houses," 210; McCleary, "Forging a Regional Identity," 94; Kastner, Loth, and McRae, "Vineyard Hill"; Rockbridge County Will Book 1, p. 254.

7. *Weaver v. Jordan, Davis & Company*, 224.

8. Jordan and Kaups, *American Backwoods Frontier*, 135–136; McClung, *Rockbridge County Log Structures*, 8–10, 16, 20.

9. Lyle and Simpson, *Architecture of Historic Lexington*, 10, 12.

10. Loth, "Mackey, William, House," 1–3, 5; Simpson, "Elder House."

11. Lyle and Simpson, *Architecture of Historic Lexington*, 10–17, 50; Mutual Assurance Society index.

Portico detail,
Buena Vista Post Office.
Photo by Dan Pezzoni

12. McDaniel, Russ, and Potter, *Archaeological and Historical Assessment of the Liberty Hall Academy Complex*, 93–95; Pulice, *Nineteenth-Century Brick Architecture*, 39–40

13. Pulice, *Nineteenth-Century Brick Architecture*, 46–50.

14. Simpson, "Molded Brick Cornice," 30, 32, 33.

15. *Weaver v. Jordan, Davis & Company*, 417.

16. Pulice and Kern, "Buffalo Forge," 2, 7–8; Lipscomb, "Mulberry Grove," 1.

17. *Lexington Gazette*, July 20, 1854.

18. Mutual Assurance Society records; Mutual Assurance Society index.

19. Mutual Assurance Society records.

20. Mutual Assurance Society records.

21. Dew, *Bond of Iron*, 4, 54, 66, 71–72, 93–94; *Weaver v. Jordan, Davis & Company*.

22. *Weaver v. Jordan, Davis & Company*, 208–209; Dew, *Bond of Iron*, 75.

23. *Weaver v. Jordan, Davis & Company*, 210–211.

24. *Weaver v. Jordan, Davis & Company*, 210–211.

25. Lyle and Simpson, Architecture of Historic Lexington, 9; Shepherd, *Statutes at Large of Virginia*, Vol. 1, p. 266, and Vol. 2, p. 262.

26. Stewart Bennington personal communication with the author, 2015; *Weaver v. Jordan, Davis & Company*, 43, 210–211; Jordan and Kaups, *American Backwoods Frontier*, 166–175; McClung, *Rockbridge County Log Structures*, 11.

27. *Weaver v. Jordan, Davis & Company*, 211, 213.

28. *Weaver v. Jordan, Davis & Company*, 22–23, 218.

29. Pulice and Kern, "Buffalo Forge," 4, 8–9; Dew, *Bond of Iron*, 229–231, 243, 245.

30. Kurt Russ personal communication with the author, June 2014.

2 Styles

1. Lipscomb, "Mulberry Grove," 5; Crawford and Lyle, *Rockbridge County Artists & Artisans*, 156–157.

2. Crawford and Lyle, *Rockbridge County Artists & Artisans*, 156–157; Rauser, *Caricature Unmasked*, 86; Pezzoni, "Cartooning in Stone."

3. Brownell et al.., *Making of Virginia Architecture*, 54–55.

4. McAlester and McAlester, *Field Guide to American Houses*, 158.

5. Giles, "Marlbrook," 4, 8–9; Upton and Peters, "Thorn Hill"; Lyle and Simpson, *Architecture of Historic Lexington*, 13, 122–125.

6. Lyle and Simpson, *Architecture of Historic Lexington*, 13, 15, 122–125; Upton and Peters, "Thorn Hill."

7. Upton and Peters, "Thorn Hill."

8. Cote and Scarlett, "Zachariah Johnston House"; Simpson, "Mulberry Hill"; Lyle and Simpson, *Architecture of Historic Lexington*, 123, 126, 128, 148; Simpson, "Architecture of Rockbridge County," 84–85.

9. Simpson, "Fruit Hill"; Dudka, "Seven Hills"; McCormick, *Genealogies and Reminiscences*, 13–14, 51; Raynal, "Family of 'Soldier John' Grigsby," 3; Watkins, "Seven Hills of Rockbridge," 120.

10. Loth, "Level Loop," 3, 6–7.

11. Loth, "Level Loop," 6–7; Upton, "Pattern Books and Professionalism," 109.

12. Lyle and Simpson, *Architecture of Historic Lexington*, 10–11, 18–19, 23, 128–129; Upton, "Stono"; Mutual Assurance Society records; Pulice, "Springdale," 1, 3.

13. Martin and Giles, "John Moore House," 3.

14. Calder Loth personal communication with the author; Pezzoni, "Chapel Hill," 5.

15. Coffey, "Maple Hall."

16. Coffey, "Maple Hall"; Lee et al., *Buildings of Virginia*, 138.

17. Hasfurther, "Hickory Hill," 7.

18. Hasfurther, "Hickory Hill," 7–8.

19. Pezzoni, "Margaret E. Poague House," 3; Upton and Peters, "Church Hill."

20. Hasfurther, "Hickory Hill"; Lyle and Simpson, *Architecture of Historic Lexington*, 27, 29, 106–107, 126.

21. Westebbe, "Bryant House"; Lyle and Simpson, *Architecture of Historic Lexington*, 141.

22. Cote and Scarlett, "Glen Maury."

23. Lyle and Simpson, *Architecture of Historic Lexington*, 29, 31, 96–97.

24. Lyle and Simpson, *Architecture of Historic Lexington*, 96–97; Fauber, "Research report relating to the Lexington Presbyterian Manse," 9–10.

25. Lyle and Simpson, *Architecture of Historic Lexington*, 97; Fauber, "Research report relating to the Lexington Presbyterian Manse," 3.

26. Lyle and Simpson, *Architecture of Historic Lexington*, 97, 278–284.

27. Lyle and Simpson, *Architecture of Historic Lexington*, 31, 96–99, 135–137.

28. Kain, "Falling Spring Presbyterian Church Manse," 1, 4–5; Bodie, *Remarkable Rockbridge*, 127.

29. Thurman, "Red House," 8–9.

30. McCleary, "Forging a Regional Identity," 99; McCleary, "Ethnic Influences on Vernacular Architecture," 269–270.

31. Phillips, "Grand Illusions," 156–157; Moss and Winkler, *Victorian Interior Decoration*, 22–23.

32. Lyle and Simpson, *Architecture of Historic Lexington*, 109; Pezzoni, "Blandome," 2, 19.

33. Lyle and Simpson, *Architecture of Historic Lexington*, 28, 184; Stevens and Williams, *Lexington*, 107–109.

34. Pezzoni, "Margaret E. Poague House," 4; Upton and Peters, "Church Hill."

35. Martin and Giles, "John Moore House," 3.

36. Lyle and Simpson, *Architecture of Historic Lexington*, 12, 126; Cote and Scarlett, "Zachariah Johnston House"; Herring Hall website.

37. Pezzoni, "Willson House," 3; Beth and Art Cusick personal communication with the author, June 2014.

3 Town and Country

1. Reps, *Tidewater Towns*, 7–9, 65–66.

2. Lyle and Simpson, *Architecture of Historic Lexington*, 7–9, 34–35; Bodie, *Remarkable Rockbridge*, 66–67.

3. Nelson, "Lexington Motor Sales Building"; Rockbridge County Deed Book N, p. 373.

4. Lyle and Simpson, *Architecture of Historic Lexington*, 10.

5. Shepherd, *Statues at Large of Virginia* volume 1, 266, and volume 2, 262; Lyle and Simpson, *Architecture of Historic Lexington*, 9.

6. Brady, "From Springfield to Zack"; Rockbridge County Deed Book V, p. 144; Rockbridge County tax records; "County of Rockbridge."

7. Lyle and Simpson, *Architecture of Historic Lexington*, 78–87; Pezzoni, "Reid-White-Philbin House."

8. Mutual Assurance Society records.

9. Lipscomb, "Mulberry Grove," 2.

10. Pezzoni, "Willson House," 12; Mutual Assurance Society records.

11. Upton, "Stono"; Fishwick, "John Jordan, Man of Iron"; Lyle and Simpson, *Architecture of Historic Lexington*, 131.

12. Mutual Assurance Society records; *Lexington Gazette*, November 8, 1860.

13. Mutual Assurance Society Records; Rockbridge Historical Society photos.

14. Hasfurther, "Hickory Hill," 4, 6.

15. Pezzoni, "Mountain View Farm," 5–6; Lipscomb, "Mulberry Grove," 3. McClung and Martin, *Rockbridge County Log Structures* 106, 122; *Lexington News-Gazette*, December (5?), 2008.

16. Mutual Assurance Society records; *Lexington Gazette*, November 8, 1860.

17. Simpson, "Col Alto," 249–252; Loth and Salmon, "Col Alto," 2.

18. "Clifton," 8.7–8.9; Bodie, *Remarkable Rockbridge*, 1; Rockbridge Lime Works file, Special Collections and Archives, James G. Leyburn Library, Washington and Lee University, Lexington, Va.

19. Turner, "Agricultural Expositions and Fairs," 388, 392, 394–395.

20. *Lexington Gazette*, December 1, 1859, and October 11 and 18, 1860.

21. Coffey, "Reconstruction and Redemption," 275, 277; *Lexington Gazette*, September 28, 1921, September 26, 1923, and September 3 and 10, 1924.

A stage coach approaches the
Forest Inn at Natural Bridge.
Miley Collection, courtesy SC, WLU

22. Turner, "Agricultural Expositions and Fairs," 397, 402; Horton, "Hidden Gardens," 115–119; Lynn, "Stonewall in the Garden," 62–63.

23. Pezzoni, "Mountain View Farm," 10–11.

24. Pezzoni, "Mountain View Farm," 12–14.

25. Pezzoni, "Mountain View Farm," 6, 12–14.

26. Frazier and Tucker, "Kennedy-Lunsford Farm," 4, 6–7; *Lexington News-Gazette*, April 21, 2002; *Rockbridge Weekly*, March 28, 1990.

27. Dooley, "Dairies of Rockbridge County," 30, 39, 42; Lancaster, "Sunnyside," 8.2; *Lexington Gazette Bi-centennial Issue*, Section 4 page 6.

28. Dooley, "Dairies of Rockbridge County," 30.

4   Churches

1.   Pezzoni, "Cedar Hill Church and Cemeteries."

2.   Pezzoni, "Cedar Hill Church and Cemeteries"; Tucker, *House on Fuller Street*, 11.

3.   Pezzoni, "Cedar Hill Church and Cemeteries."

4.   Bodie, *Remarkable Rockbridge*, 17, 43–46; Meade, *Old Churches*, 64.

5.   Morton, *History of Rockbridge County*, 173; Hileman, *Historical Sketch*, 5–6, 31; *Timber Ridge Presbyterian Church*, 6; Upton, *Holy Things and Profane*, 56.

6.   Hileman, *Historical Sketch*, 9–10, 20; "Timber Ridge Presbyterian Church" (National Register nomination); Loth, *Virginia Landmarks Register*, 469; Sanders, *Journey of Faith*, 39, 119.

7.   Boley, *Lexington in Old Virginia*, 27; Hunter, *Lexington Presbyterian Church*, 20; Lyle and Simpson, *Architecture of Historic Lexington*, 30, 97.

8.   Reed and Matheson, *Narrative of the Visit*, 151; Fauber, "Research report relating to the Lexington Presbyterian Manse," 2.

9.   Reed and Matheson, *Narrative of the Visit*, 151–152.

10. Reed and Matheson, *Narrative of the Visit*, 151–154.

11. Sessional Records of Lexington Church vol. 1, historical preface (written in 1856), 71, 95, 174, 175; Hunter, *Lexington Presbyterian Church*, 20.

12. *Rockbridge County, Virginia, Heritage Book*, 58, 68; Hanson, church tour notes.

13. Taylor Sanders, personal communication with the author; Pezzoni, "Cedar Hill Church and Cemeteries," 6; Bodie, *Remarkable Rockbridge*, 45; Sessional Records of Lexington Church vol. 1, historical preface (written in 1856); Boley, *Lexington in Old Virginia*, 27.

14. Lyle and Simpson, *Architecture of Historic Lexington*, 26–28; Hunter, *Lexington Presbyterian Church*, 32, after 33; Brooke, *General Lee's Church*, 8–9.

15. Sanders, *Journey of Faith*, plates; Upton, "New Providence Presbyterian Church"; Langdon, "Collierstown Presbyterian Church."

16. Upton, "New Providence Presbyterian Church"; Heffelfinger, "Tinkling Spring Presbyterian Church"; *Architectural Drawing in Lexington*, 19–20; Loth, *Virginia Landmarks Register*, 467.

17. Lyle and Simpson, *Architecture of Historic Lexington*, 62–64.

18. Hanson, church tour notes; Brooke, *General Lee's Church*, 9; Sessional Records of Lexington Church vol. 1, 175; Boley, *Lexington in Old Virginia*, 27; Reed, *Narrative of the Visit*, 151.

19. Kain, "Falling Spring Presbyterian Church Manse," 3, 5; *Rockbridge County, Virginia, Heritage Book*, 59; *Proceedings of the Rockbridge Historical Society*, vol. 1, 56–57.

20. Michael Pulice personal communication with the author, May 2014.

21. Brooke, *General Lee's Church*, 26–27; *Lexington Gazette*, June 13, 1873.

22. Cheshire, *Stained Glass*, 33–34.

23. Brooke, *General Lee's Church*, 28–29; Bethany Lutheran Church records.

24. Pezzoni, "Glasgow Historic District," 9, 22.

25. Pezzoni, "First Baptist Church," 7.

26. Bangley, *Historical Sketch of Bethesda Presbyterian Church*, 10, 19.

27. "Timber Ridge Presbyterian Church"; Lyle and Simpson, *Architecture of Historic Lexington*, 159–161, 182–183; Pezzoni, "First Baptist Church," 10–11.

28. Don Hasfurther personal communication with the author, May 16, 2014.

29. Wells and Dalton, *Virginia Architects*, 61; Lyle and Simpson, *Architecture of Historic Lexington*, 47; *Rockbridge County, Virginia, Heritage Book*, 54.

30. St. Patrick Catholic Church records.

31. Strickler, "News Articles"; *Lynchburg News*, April 19, 1953.

32. Good Shepherd Evangelical Lutheran Church.

5   Schools

1. Morton, *History of Rockbridge County*, 184; *Christian Nation*, November 9, 1898; Gillespie, "Reverend William Graham," 14; McDaniel, Russ, and Potter, *Archaeological and Historical Assessment of the Liberty Hall Academy Complex*, 38–39; Simpson, "Reflections on White Columns," 3; Lyle and Simpson, *Architecture of Historic Lexington*, 145; "Predecessors of Liberty Hall."

2. McDaniel, Russ, and Potter, *Archaeological and Historical Assessment of the Liberty Hall Academy Complex*, 39–40; Gillespie, "Reverend William Graham," 20–21.

3. Lyle and Simpson, *Architecture of Historic Lexington*, 146–147, 298.

VMI Parade Ground.
Courtesy RHS/SC, WLU

4. Lyle and Simpson, *Architecture of Historic Lexington*, 147; Sanders, "Churches, Congregations and Community in Antebellum Lexington"; Wakeley, *Bold Frontier Preacher*, 15–16, 28.

5. McDaniel, Russ, and Potter, *Archaeological and Historical Assessment of the Liberty Hall Academy Complex*, 41, 120–121; Lyle and Simpson, *Architecture of Historic Lexington*, 149; Baxter, "Reminiscences of Dr. [George] A. Baxter," 18.

6. McDaniel, Russ, and Potter, *Archaeological and Historical Assessment of the Liberty Hall Academy Complex*, 41, 59, 69, 95, 100, 114, 131–134; Baxter, "Reminiscences of Dr. [George] A. Baxter," 18; Alison Bell personal communication with the author, May 2014.

7. Morton, *History of Rockbridge County*, 149–150; Mutual Assurance Society records; Coffey, "Reconstruction and Redemption in Lexington," 281.

8. Pulice, "Hamilton Schoolhouse," 1–3; Diehl, "Saga of Hamilton's School House," 14–15; McCleary, "Walker's Creek Schoolhouse"; Hasfurther, "Educational Legacy of the Southern Shenandoah Valley."

9. "Washington and Lee University Historic District"; Lyle and Simpson, *Architecture of Historic Lexington*, 149–153, 156; Lee et al., *Buildings of Virginia*, 127.

10. Lyle and Simpson, *Architecture of Historic Lexington*, 211–222; *Lexington Gazette*, June 20, 1873; Virginia Military Institute Board of Visitors Minutes Volume 1, 5; Levy, "Virginia Military Institute Historic District"; Melvin, "Barracks, Virginia Military Institute."

11. Lyle and Simpson, *Architecture of Historic Lexington*, 212–217.

12. Lyle and Simpson, *Architecture of Historic Lexington*, 217–222; Lee et al., *Buildings of Virginia*, 129.

13. Lyle and Simpson, *Architecture of Historic Lexington*, 220–223, 246, 255–257.

14. Lyle and Simpson, *Architecture of Historic Lexington*, 226–227, 249, 259, 265–269.

15. Pusey, "Lexington's Female Academy," 41–42; William Caruthers to Thomas Jefferson, July 25, 1809, Jefferson papers; Lyle and Simpson, *Architecture of Historic Lexington*, 87–88.

16. Brownsburg Museum exhibits; Perry-Miller, "Brief Study of Brownsburg"; *Rockbridge County News*, September 22, 1938; Hasfurther, "Educational Legacy of the Southern Shenandoah Valley"; Lynn, *"Fesser" McCluer*, A5; Anderson, *Palmer*, 10; Douty, *Rockbridge, Virginia*, 227; Russell, "Fancy Hill," 8; "Our Heritage—Mountain View."

17. Gilliam, "Jordan's Point," 129–130; Lyle and Simpson, *Architecture of Historic Lexington*, 259–260.

18. Pezzoni, "Newcomb Hall."

19. Leander McCormick Observatory Museum website; *Lexington Gazette*, June 13, 1873.

20. Lyle and Simpson, *Architecture of Historic Lexington*, 193; *Southern Collegian*, July 3, 1876; Brooks Museum collection.

21. Brooks Museum collection.

22. Brooks Museum collection; Turner, *Mrs. McCulloch's Stories*, 14–16, after 36; Lee Chapel exhibits.

23. Pezzoni, "Cedar Hill Church," 10; Hasfurther, "Educational Legacy of the Southern Shenandoah Valley"; Ben Peart email to Arthur Bartenstein, July 15, 2014.

24. Lynn, "Buena Vista Colored School," 5–10; Bodie, *Remarkable Rockbridge*, 316.

25. *Maid of the Mountains.*

26. Lynn, "History of Hotel Buena Vista," 16; *Maid of the Mountains.*

27. Lynn, "History of Hotel Buena Vista," 16.

28. *Lexington News-Gazette*, October 15, 2003; Anderson, *Palmer*, 17, 21, 33; Effinger Ruritan Club website.

29. Clark, *"Thy Faithfulness is Unto All Generations,"* 86; Henry, "Goshen Memories"; Kinnear, "History of Old Mt. View School"; Hasfurther, "Educational Legacy of the Southern Shenandoah Valley."

30. McCleary, "Public Schools in Augusta County," 8.3–8.4; Friends of Waddell and Woods Creek Park, "Save Waddell School and Woods Creek Park," 24.

31. Link, *Hard Country and a Lonely Place*, 139.

32. Pezzoni and Kern, "Lylburn Downing School"; Rainville, "Rosenwald Schools of Virginia."

33. *Rockbridge County, Virginia, Heritage Book*, 85; Friends of Waddell and Woods Creek Park, "Save Waddell School and Woods Creek Park," 24–25; Hasfurther, "Educational Legacy of the Southern Shenandoah Valley."

34. Hasfurther, "Educational Legacy of the Southern Shenandoah Valley"; Lyle and Simpson, *Architecture of Historic Lexington*, 87–88.

35. Lynn, *"Fesser" McCluer*, 31, 41; Brown and Chambers, "History of Natural Bridge High School."

6   Resorts

1. Dabney, *Virginia: The New Dominion*, 260; McPhillips, "Yellow Fever Epidemic of 1855."

2. McCulloch, "Blue Hotel," 18–20; *Weaver v. Jordan, Davis & Company*, 417; Lyle and Simpson, *Architecture of Historic Lexington*, 134–135; Boley, *Lexington in Old Virginia*, 17.

3. Boley, *Lexington in Old Virginia*, 17; "Self-Guided Walking Tour of Historic Brownsburg"; Heffelfinger, "Well-Preserved Village," 110.

4. Russell, "Fancy Hill," 3, 7.

5. "Our Heritage—Mountain View."

6. Bausum and Bausum, "Tankersley Tavern"; *Lexington Gazette*, July 17, 1946; Donald Gaylord, personal communication with the author, July 15, 2014.

7. Campbell, "Rockbridge Alum Springs."

8. "Rockbridge Alum Springs/Jordan Alum Springs"; Paxton, "Rockbridge Alum Springs," 7; Campbell, "Rockbridge Alum Springs"; Rockbridge County tax records and Deed Book Z, p. 418, and Deed Book CC, p. 164.

Guests gather by a gazebo at Cold Sulphur Springs near Goshen. Photo (ca. 1900) courtesy of RHS/SC, WLU

Camp Okahahwis
swimming pool
Courtesy RHS/SC, WLU

9.   "Rockbridge Alum Springs/Jordan Alum Springs."

10. "Rockbridge Alum Springs/Jordan Alum Springs"; Cohen, *Historic Springs of the Virginias*, 95–97.

11. "Rockbridge Alum Springs/Jordan Alum Springs"; Beyer, *Album of Virginia* (booklet pages vi and 8).

12. "Rockbridge Alum Springs/Jordan Alum Springs."

13. Paxton, "Rockbridge Alum Springs," 14; Letcher, *Only Yesterday in Lexington, Virginia*, 102; *Lexington Gazette*, May 22, 1952; Cai, "Rockbridge Alum Springs."

14. Cai, "Rockbridge Alum Springs"; Paxton, "Rockbridge Alum Springs," 14; *Jordan Rockbridge Alum Springs*; Letcher, *Only Yesterday in Lexington, Virginia*, 101.

15. "Rockbridge Alum Springs/Jordan Alum Springs"; Cohen, *Historic Springs of the Virginias*, 95–99; Cai, "Rockbridge Alum Springs"; *Jordan Rockbridge Alum Springs*; Paxton, "Rockbridge Alum Springs," 1.

16. Cai, "Rockbridge Alum Springs."

17. Paxton, "Rockbridge Alum Springs," 17–19; Cai, "Rockbridge Alum Springs"; "Rockbridge Alum Springs/Jordan Alum Springs"; Letcher, *Only Yesterday in Lexington, Virginia*, 103.

18. Bodie, *Remarkable Rockbridge*, 123; Cohen, *Historic Springs of the Virginias*, 102–103; *Lexington Gazette*, June 6, 1873.

19. Turner, *Mrs. McCulloch's Stories*, 43.

20. Cohen, *Historic Springs of the Virginias*, 102–103, 121–122; McClung, *Wilson Springs*; Letcher, *Only Yesterday in Lexington, Virginia*, 96–98.

21. Cohen, *Historic Springs of the Virginias*, 102–103, 121–122; Boley, *Lexington in Old Virginia*, 152–153; McClung, *Wilson Springs*; Letcher, *Only Yesterday in Lexington, Virginia*, 96–98.

22. Hollberg, "Natural Bridge" (National Historic Landmark nomination), 9; Jefferson, *Notes on the State of Virginia*, 25.

23. "Natural Bridge" (Thomas Jefferson's Monticello website); Coffey, "Thomas Jefferson, Patrick Henry, and the Natural Bridge," 144–145; David Coffey personal communication with the author, May 8, 2014; Tompkins and Davis, *Natural Bridge and its Historical Surroundings*, 12.

24. Hollberg, "Natural Bridge" (National Historic Landmark nomination), 15–16; Pezzoni, "Natural Bridge Historic District"; Rockbridge County tax records and Deed Book T, p. 476; Davis, *Bits of History and Legends*, 134–135; Beyer, *Album of Virginia*; *Richmond Times-Dispatch*, November 30, 1952.

25. Hollberg, "Natural Bridge" (National Historic Landmark nomination), 15–16; Hollberg, "Natural Bridge" (National Register nomination), 7–8; Yeates, "Map of Natural Bridge"; Rockbridge County Mechanics Lien Book 2, pp. 74–75; Wells and Dalton, *Virginia Architects*, 390; Hoyt, *Valley Views*, photo 77; Davis, *Bits of History and Legends*, 28, 49, 62, 134–135.

26. "Southern Seminary Main Building"; Lynn, "History of Hotel Buena Vista," 1–2; Wells and Dalton, *Virginia Architects*, 151–152; Pezzoni, "Buena Vista Historic District," 31.

27. Lynn, "History of Hotel Buena Vista," 7, 18; "Southern Seminary Main Building"; Lynn, *"Fesser" McCluer*, 19.

28. Wells and Dalton, *Virginia Architects*, 494; Allen, *Lost Landmarks of Goshen*, 10.

29. *Rockbridge County, Virginia, Heritage Book*, 29; *Proceedings of the Rockbridge Historical Society*, volume 5, 26; Rife Ram website; Cornwall prospectus.

30. Pezzoni, "Glasgow Historic District," 2; *Glasgow Herald*, May 21 and July 5, 1890; Davis, *Bits of History and Legends*, 88, 90.

31. Lyle and Simpson, *Architecture of Historic Lexington*, 39–42, 53, 55–56; Pezzoni, "McCampbell Inn."

32. Pezzoni, "Buena Vista Historic District," 4, 8, 15; Lynn, *Buena Vista: The Bud Not Yet Blossomed*, 89.

7   Industries

1. Donald Gaylord personal communication with the author, June 2014; Morton, *History of Rockbridge County*, 40, 169; Ball, "Notes on the Use of Tubmills in Southern Appalachia," 1–2; Clark, *Manual of Rules*, 939.

2. Mutual Assurance Society records.

3. "Grist Milling Process."

4. Mutual Assurance Society records.

5. Figgers, "Hays Creek Mill," 1, 3, 6, 7.

6. Upton and Peters, "Kennedy-Wade Mill"; Frazier, McCleary, and Tucker, "Kennedy-Wade's Mill Historic District," 7.3–4, 8.1–2; Lee et al., *Buildings of Virginia*, 136.

7. Upton and Peters, "Kennedy-Wade Mill"; "Our Heritage—Mountain View."

8. Morton, *History of Rockbridge County*, 169; Crawford and Lyle, *Rockbridge County Artists & Artisans*, 60; Bodie, *Remarkable Rockbridge*, 47; Kosisky, "Searight's Fulling Mill"; Rockbridge County Will Book 1, p. 254.

9. Mutual Assurance Society records.

10. Morton, *History of Rockbridge County*, 169; Douglas E. Brady Jr. papers; "Old Woolen Mill in Rockbridge"; 1850 census.

11. Bodie, *Remarkable Rockbridge*, 156, 285, 381; Crawford and Lyle, *Rockbridge County Artists & Artisans*, 60–61; "Old Woolen Mill in Rockbridge."

12. Davis, *Bits of History and Legends*, 80–81; Watson, *Mineral Resources of Virginia*, 163; *Staunton Spectator*, January 28, 1873; Simpson, *Cheap, Quick & Easy*, 10–11; Locher, *Family Divided*, 7–9; "History of Glasgow"; Miller, *One Hundred Years of Dreams*, 17–18.

13. Davis, *Bits of History and Legends*, 80–81; Watson, *Mineral Resources of Virginia*, 163; Locher, *Family Divided*, 7–9; "History of Glasgow"; Trout, *Upper James River Atlas*, 56, 60; Miller, *One Hundred Years of Dreams*, 17–18; 1880 census.

14. Morton, *History of Rockbridge County*, 262–263; Locher, *Family Divided*, 7–9.

15. Giles, "Marlbrook," 9; Mutual Assurance Society Records.

16. Bodie, *Remarkable Rockbridge*, 85; Bodie, "Down the Paper Trail," 160; Accounts, 1802, Robinson with George Edgar, John Robinson Papers, courtesy of Charles Bodie; Boley, *Lexington in Old Virginia*, 68–69; Koons, "'The Staple of Our Country,'" 511.

17. *Lexington Gazette*, November 24, 1859; Dew, *Bond of Iron*, 67; Dabney, "Moonshine"; Regan and Regan, *Book of Bourbon*, 59–60.

18. 1880 census; "Our Heritage—Mountain View."

19. Simpson, "Tuckaway"; Hoyt, *Valley Views*, photos 97 and 122; Pezzoni, "Willson House," 8.

20. "Self-Guided Walking Tour of Historic Brownsburg"; Heffelfinger, "Brownsburg Historic District"; Heffelfinger, "Well-Preserved Village," 108–111; "Mutual Assurance Society index; Brownsburg Museum exhibits.

21. Mutual Assurance Society records.

Isaac Weinberg's Store, Lexington.
Photo (ca. 1900) courtesy
RHS/SC, WLU

22. Russ, "Pottery," 170–176.

23. Thomas Jefferson to William Caruthers, December 3, 1814, Jefferson papers; Looney, *Papers of Thomas Jefferson, Retirement Series*, volume 8, 96; *Lexington Gazette*, March 15, 1872; Hollberg, "Natural Bridge," 9.

24. *Lexington Gazette*, March 15, 1872.

25. William Caruthers to Thomas Jefferson, February 22 and March 4, 1815, and Thomas Jefferson to William Caruthers, March 15, 1815, Jefferson papers; *Lexington Gazette*, March 15, 1872; Hollberg, "Natural Bridge," 9.

26. William Caruthers to Thomas Jefferson, July 25, 1809, Jefferson papers; Hubbard, "Geology and Related Information," 7.

27. Reeds, *Natural Bridge*, 31–33; Hubbard, "Geology and Related Information," 7; *Journal of Spelean History* 3:3 (Summer 1970): 43–44; Hauer, "Saltpetre Cave at Natural Bridge," 55–57.

28. Hubbard, "Geology and Related Information," 7; Brady, "Manufacture of Iron by William Weaver," 6; *Journal of Spelean History* 3:3 (Summer 1970): 43–44; Hauer, "Saltpetre Cave at Natural Bridge," 55–57; *Southern Planter*, 14:3 (March 1854), 86; Organ Cave website.

29. Gilliam, "Jordan's Point," 110–117, 122; Thompson, "Compass Book No. 1," 67, 69.

30. Donald Gaylord personal communication with the author, June 2014; Gilliam, "Jordan's Point," 118–122.

31. Donald Gaylord personal communication, June 2014; Gilliam, "Jordan's Point," 124–126, 133–134; Thompson, "Compass Book No. 1," 67, 69.

32. Crowl and Moffson, "Glenwood Furnace," 7–8.

33. Crowl and Moffson, "Glenwood Furnace," 7–8.

34. Morton, *History of Rockbridge County*, 170; Brady, "Iron Valley Revisited," 9; Bodie, *Remarkable Rockbridge*, 86; *Lexington Gazette*, July 20, 1854.

35. Brady, "From Springfield to Zack"; Brady, "Iron Valley Revisited," 1–2; Fishwick, "John Jordan, Man of Iron"; Capron, "Virginia Iron Furnaces of the Confederacy," 15; *Proceedings of the Eleventh Annual Meeting of the Fire Underwriters' Association of the Northwest*, 96.

36. Fishwick, "John Jordan, Man of Iron"; Capron, "Virginia Iron Furnaces of the Confederacy," 15.

37. Bodie, *Remarkable Rockbridge*, 93–94; Melvin, "McCormick (Cyrus) Farm and Workshop."

38. Dew, *Bond of Iron*, 19–22; Bodie, *Remarkable Rockbridge*, 94–95.

39. Dew, *Bond of Iron*, 19–22; Lee et al., *Buildings of Virginia*, 133.

40. Dew, *Bond of Iron*, 10–11, 224–225, 245; Pulice and Kern, "Buffalo Forge."

41. Dew, *Bond of Iron*, 66–67.

42. Dew, *Bond of Iron*, 75; *Weaver v. Jordan, Davis & Company*, 41–45, 249.

43. *Weaver v. Jordan, Davis & Company*, 42, 227, 235, 416; *Proceedings of the Eleventh Annual Meeting of the Fire Underwriters' Association of the Northwest*, 97; Russ, McDaniel, and Wood, "Archaeology of Nineteenth-Century Iron Manufacturing," 139.

44. *Lexington Gazette*, February 9, 1838.

45. Pezzoni, "Chapel Hill," 8–9; D. E. Brady Jr. papers.

46. Brady, "From Springfield to Zack"; Blanton, "Echols Farm," 4, 7–8.

47. Bodie, *Remarkable Rockbridge*, 223–224; Lynn, *Buena Vista*, 4; Pezzoni, "Buena Vista Downtown Historic District," 25–26.

48. Pezzoni, "Buena Vista Downtown Historic District," 25–26; Bodie, *Remarkable Rockbridge*, 224.

8 Cities

1. Thomas P. Grasty to Frank Glasgow, January 8, 1890, Glasgow Family Papers; *Staunton Spectator and Vindicator*, February 19, 1909; Bodie, *Remarkable Rockbridge*, 225.

2. Bodie, *Remarkable Rockbridge*, 225; Pezzoni, "Buena Vista Downtown Historic District," 27.

3. *Lexington Gazette*, March 13, 1890.

4. *Lexington Gazette*, March 13, 1890; Bodie, *Remarkable Rockbridge*, 228; Pezzoni, "Glasgow Historic District," 20.

5. *Lexington Gazette*, March 13, 1890; Bodie, *Remarkable Rockbridge*, 228, 238–240.

VMI aerial view.
Photo (1938) courtesy
RHS/SC, WLU

6.   Miller, *One Hundred Years of Dreams*, 152.

7.   Miller, *One Hundred Years of Dreams*, 152–153.

8.   Pezzoni, "Glasgow Historic District," 22.

9.   Miller, *One Hundred Years of Dreams*, 41–49; Pezzoni, "Glasgow Historic District," 8–9, 13.

10. Pezzoni, "Buena Vista Downtown Historic District," 28.

11. Chesapeake and Ohio Historical Society online photographs.

12. Pezzoni, "Buena Vista Downtown Historic District," 15–16, 28; Cote and Peters, "Buena Vista Land Company."

13. Pezzoni, "Buena Vista Downtown Historic District," 29–30.

14. Kostelni, Leslie, and Hatcher, "Two County Industries," 345–347; Lynn, *Buena Vista: The Bud Not Yet Blossomed*, 37.

15. Lynn, *Buena Vista: The Bud Not Yet Blossomed*, 31, 33.

16. Davis, *Bits of History*, 114–116; Miller, *One Hundred Years*, 65–68; Couper, *History of the Shenandoah Valley*, 1152; Withrow Scrapbook vol. 5, p. 28; Kostelni, Leslie, and Hatcher, "Two County Industries," 348–352; Lynn, *Buena Vista: The Bud Not Yet Blossomed*, 37.

17. Coleman, "Southern Inn"; Pezzoni, "Southern Inn."

18. Lyle and Simpson, *Architecture of Historic Lexington*, 9, 45, 49.

19. Pezzoni, "Buena Vista Downtown Historic District," 6–7.

20. McAlester and McAlester, *Field Guide to American Houses*, 268.

21. Lyle and Simpson, *Architecture of Historic Lexington*, 92.

22. Lyle and Simpson, *Architecture of Historic Lexington*, 92–93, 127–128; Wells and Dalton, Virginia Architects, 284; Simpson, "Mulberry Hill."

23. Lyle and Simpson, *Architecture of Historic Lexington*, 39, 72, 90–91; Cote and Peters, "Buena Vista Land Company"; Pezzoni, "Buena Vista Downtown Historic District," 15.

24. Lynn, "Twenty Historic Buena Vista Boom Houses."

25. Lynn, "Twenty Historic Buena Vista Boom Houses"; Pulice and Kern, "W. N. Seay House," 1–4.

26. Keith Gibson, personal communication with the author, June 2014; Lynn, "Twenty Historic Buena Vista Boom Houses."

27. Lynn, "Twenty Historic Buena Vista Boom Houses."

28. Lynn, "Twenty Historic Buena Vista Boom Houses"; Lynn, "More Boom Houses."

29. Pezzoni, "Glasgow Historic District," 6; Miller, *One Hundred Years of Dreams*, 52–60.

30. Pezzoni, "Glasgow Historic District," 3; Hall, "Our Goshen Heritage," 11.

31. Rockbridge County Deed Book 78, p. 12, 1893 Land Book, and Mechanics Lien Book 2, pp. 57–72; "Robert Love and Sarah Matilda Alexander — Descendants"; Spencer, "Stonewall lost"; *Virginia-Pilot*, June 29, 1899; *News-Gazette*, April 18, 2012.

32. Bodie, *Remarkable Rockbridge*, 207–208; Lyle and Simpson, *Architecture of Historic Lexington*, 94–96.

33. Wells and Dalton, *Virginia Architects*, 494.

34. "The Alleghany"; Letcher, *Only Yesterday in Lexington, Virginia*, 101.

35. Boley, *Lexington in Old Virginia*, 203, 208–d; Rockbridge County tax records and Deed Book PP, p. 529.

36. Boley, *Lexington in Old Virginia*, 203, 208–d.

37. McAlester and McAlester, *Field Guide to American Houses*, 344, 346.

9 Automobile Age

1. Jackson, "Prosperity, Tourism, and the Hotels of Marcellus E. Wright," 1, 3; "Robert E. Lee Hotel Corporation"; Robert E. Lee Hotel file.

2. Robert E. Lee Hotel file.

3. "Robert E. Lee Hotel Corporation."

4. Pezzoni, "Lexington & Covington Turnpike Toll House," 1, 13, 15.

5. Pezzoni, "Lexington and Covington Turnpike Toll House," 18–19, 24.

6. Emerson, "116 North Main Street"; Stevenson and Jandl, *Houses by Mail*, 20–22, 286; Hadsel, *Streets of Lexington*, 59.

7. *Lexington Gazette*, September 3, 1937; Saul et al., "Historic Structure Report: Pure Oil Station, Hartwell, GA," 3–5; Pezzoni, "Buena Vista Downtown Historic District," 32.

8. Pezzoni, "Buena Vista Downtown Historic District," 7–8.

9. *Lexington Gazette Bi-centennial Issue*, 14–15; Stevens and Williams, *Lexington*, 33; Cocke, "Woody Chevrolet Building," 1, 2, 4, 6.

10. Heffelfinger, "Well-Preserved Village," 109; Bodie, *Remarkable Rockbridge*, 135; "Self-Guided Walking Tour of Historic Brownsburg"; Simpson, *Cheap, Quick & Easy*, 18.

11. Pezzoni, "Buena Vista Downtown Historic District," 3–4; Stevens and Williams, *Lexington*, 3–4; 24–25.

12. Lyle and Simpson, *Architecture of Historic Lexington*, 88–89, 202; Wells and Dalton, *Virginia Architects*, 150; Pezzoni, "Buena Vista Downtown Historic District," 8–9.

13. *Lexington Gazette*, February 4, July 29, and August 19, 1937; Cross, "Survey of the State and Lyric Theaters"; Wallick, "State Theater"; Pezzoni, "State Theatre"; Wells and Dalton, *Virginia Architects*, 129; Cinema Treasures website; Bodie, *Remarkable Rockbridge*, 283, 288.

14. Blue Ridge Garden Club, "Hidden Gems of Lexington"; *Lexington News-Gazette*, April 23, 2014.

15. Simpson, "Col Alto," 253–254; Loth and Salmon, "Col Alto."

16. Pierce, "Vine Forest," 8.1–8.2; Pezzoni, Forest Oaks notes.

Goshen Pass.
Photo (ca. 1940s)
courtesy RHS/SC, WLU

17. Pierce, "Vine Forest," 7.5, 8.2; Weaver, *Around Lexington*, 24.

18. Ted Delaney, personal communication with the author, July 2014; Longobardo, "Nine Tucker Street"; Tucker, *House on Fuller Street*, 40; Pezzoni, "Blandome," 15–17.

19. Reeds, *Natural Bridge*, 54–55; Davis, *Bits of History and Legends*, 64, 84, 105; Rockbridge County, "Rockbridge County Proposal for a Survey and Planning Cost Share Program at the Natural Bridge Property."

20. *News-Gazette*, April 24, May 1, and September 11, 1963, and August 26, 1964; Davis, *Bits of History*, 135.

21. Camp Mont Shenandoah website; Camp Okahahwis Collection.

22. Tompkins and Davis, *Natural Bridge*, 69; Withrow Scrapbook vol. 5, pp. 89–90; *Roanoke Times*, July 16, 1939.

23. Coffey, "The 'New Deal' Comes to Rockbridge," 486–487.

24. Coffey, "The 'New Deal' Comes to Rockbridge," 486–487; Otis, *Forest Service and The Civilian Conservation Corps*, Chapter 13 "George Washington National Forest"; Spradley-Kurowski and Pulice, "Natural Bridge Juvenile Correctional Center."

25. Visit Natural Bridge website; *Lexington Gazette*, September 11, 1936; Tompkins and Davis, *Natural Bridge*, 69; Withrow Scrapbook vol. 5, p. 92.

26. *News-Gazette*, December 4, 1963, and August 26, 1964.

27. McAlester and McAlester, *Field Guide to American Houses*, 454.

28. Andy Wolfe, personal communication with the author, July 2014; Lyle and Simpson, *Architecture of Historic Lexington*, 298; McAlester and McAlester, *Field Guide to American Houses*, 454; Pezzoni, "Glasgow Historic District," 7–8.

29. Lyle and Simpson, *Architecture of Historic Lexington*, 47–48.

30. Giles, "Boxerwood"; Pezzoni and Giles, "Boxerwood"; Arthur Bartenstein personal communication with the author, February 2015; *Better Homes and Gardens* (September 1955), 51.

31. *Lexington Gazette*, May 31, 1940.

32. Bodie, *Remarkable Rockbridge*, 254; "Caring for the Community"; *Lexington Gazette*, July 13, 1949, and August 16, 1950.

33. Kopp, "Virginia Drive-In Movie Era," 393–395; Hulls Drive-in Movie Theatre website.

34. Michalove, "Coffee Pot," 2–3; Lee et al., *Buildings of Virginia*, 130–131.

10   Preservation

1. McCulloch, "How the Rockb. His. So. was Started"; McCulloch, "Beginnings of the Rockbridge Historical Society"; McClung, "Home of Dr. James R. Jordan."

2. McCulloch, "How the Rockb. His. So. was Started"; McCulloch, "Beginnings of the Rockbridge Historical Society."

3. Pezzoni, "Willson House," 11; Lyle and Simpson, *Architecture of Historic Lexington*, 62–63.

4. Bodie, *Remarkable Rockbridge*, 288–289.

5. Michael Pulice, personal communication with the author, November 2014; Russell, "Fancy Hill," 3, 6, 9.

6. Tompkins and Davis, *Natural Bridge and its Historical Surroundings*, 125; Lee et al., *Buildings of Virginia*, 134.

7. Brownsburg website; *Lexington News-Gazette*, September 2, 2009.

8. Ray Alexander, personal communication with the author, October 2014; Frog Hollow, Herring Hall, Hummingbird Inn, and Steeles Tavern Manor websites; Stoneridge brochure.

9. Novelli, Lexington tax credit rehabilitation spreadsheet; "Lexington Historic District"; Lyle and Simpson, *Architecture of Historic Lexington*, 287–288; The Georges website.

10. Novelli, Rockbridge County/Buena Vista tax credit rehabilitation spreadsheet; Wade's Mill website.

11. Spencer, "Short History of the Rockbridge Area Conservation Council"; Rockbridge Area Conservation Council and Friends of Natural Bridge websites.

12. *Rockbridge Report*, April 7, 2011.

13. Lyle and Simpson, *Architecture of Historic Lexington*, 286–290.

14. Historic Lexington Foundation website.

The Greek Revival house known as Northwoods.
Courtesy RHS/SC, WLU

A mantel at Mulberry Hill.
Courtesy RHS/SC, WLU

Bibliography

Accounts, 1802, Robinson with George Edgar, John Robinson Papers, 1810–1837, McCormick Mss BD, Wisconsin Historical Society, Madison.

"Alexander-Withrow House." National Register of Historic Places Inventory-Nomination Form, 1970.

"The Alleghany, Goshen, Va." Brochure, 1893.

Allen, John T., III. *Lost Landmarks of Goshen.* Staunton, Va.: McClure Printing, n.d.

Anderson, Clinton L., ed. *Palmer: The First Hundred Years in the Buffalo Community.* Lexington, Va.: Palmer Community Center, 2003.

Architectural Drawing in Lexington. Lexington: Washington and Lee University, 1978.

Ball, Donald B. "Notes on the Use of Tubmills in Southern Appalachia." *Material Culture* 40:2 (Fall 2008): 1–20.

Bangley, Bernard K. *Historical Sketch of Bethesda Presbyterian Church.* 1971.

Bausum, Henry, and Dolores Bausum. "Tankersley Tavern." National Register of Historic Places Inventory-Registration Form, 1987.

Baxter, Louisa. "Reminiscences of Dr. [George] A. Baxter and his Times." Manuscript (ca. 1880), George A. Baxter Papers, Special Collections and Archives, James G. Leyburn Library, Washington and Lee University, Lexington, Va.

Benjamin, Asher. *The Builder's Guide.* 1839.

Bethany Lutheran Church records. Bethany Lutheran Church, Lexington, Va.

Better Homes and Gardens.

Beyer, Edward. *Album of Virginia.* Richmond: Virginia State Library, 1980 (reprint).

Blanton, Alison S. "Echols Farm." National Register of Historic Places Registration Form, 1998.

Blue Ridge Garden Club. "Hidden Gems of Lexington: Gillette Gardens, Monroe Park and Woods Creek." Brochure (2014).

Bodie, Charles A., "Down the Paper Trail: Manuscript Collections of Rockbridge County." *Proceedings of the Rockbridge Historical Society* 12 (1995–2002): 147–162.

_____. *Remarkable Rockbridge: The Story of Rockbridge County, Virginia*. Lexington, Va.: Rockbridge Historical Society, 2011.

Boley, Henry. *Lexington in Old Virginia*. Richmond: Garret and Massie, 1936.

Brady, Douglas E., Jr. "From Springfield to Zack." Typescript (1988), Rockbridge Regional Library, Lexington, Va.

_____. "Iron Valley Revisited: South River Valley, Rockbridge County." Typescript (1989), Rockbridge Regional Library, Lexington, Va.

_____. "Manufacture of Iron by William Weaver." Typescript (1970), Special Collections and Archives, James G. Leyburn Library, Washington and Lee University, Lexington, Va.

_____. Papers. Special Collections and Archives, James G. Leyburn Library, Washington and Lee University, Lexington, Va.

Britton, W. S. G., III. "Goshen Land Company Bridge." National Register of Historic Places Inventory-Registration Form, ca. 1977.

Brooke, George M., Jr. *General Lee's Church: The History of the Protestant Episcopal Church in Lexington, Virginia, 1840–1975*. Lexington, Va.: News-Gazette, 1984.

Brooks Museum collection. Special Collections and Archives, James G. Leyburn Library, Washington and Lee University, Lexington, Va.

Brown, Jo Anne, and Timmy Chambers. "A History of Natural Bridge High School." Report, n.d.

Brown, Katharine L. *New Providence Church, 1746–1996: A History*. Raphine, Va.: New Providence Presbyterian Church, 1996.

Brownell, Charles E., et al. *The Making of Virginia Architecture*. Richmond: Virginia Museum of Fine Arts, 1992.

Brownsburg website (http://www.brownsburgva.wordpress.com/), accessed August 27, 2014.

Brownsburg Museum exhibits. Brownsburg, Va.

Cai, Xiao Peng. "Rockbridge Alum Springs." Report (ca. 1995), Special Collections and Archives, James G. Leyburn Library, Washington and Lee University, Lexington, Va.

Camp Mont Shenandoah website (http:www.campmontshenandoah.com), accessed July 23, 2014.

Camp Okahahwis Collection. Special Collections and Archives, James G. Leyburn Library, Washington and Lee University, Lexington, Va.

Campbell, Leslie Lyle. "Rockbridge Alum Springs." Undated handwritten account at Special Collections and Archives, James G. Leyburn Library, Washington and Lee University, Lexington, Va.

Capron, John D. "Virginia Iron Furnaces of the Confederacy." *Virginia Cavalcade* (Autumn 1967).

"Caring for the Community." Supplement to the *Lexington News-Gazette* and the *Buena Vista News*, March 29, 1979.

Carmichael, John. "The County of Rockbridge, Virginia." Map, 1883.

Chesapeake and Ohio Historical Society online photographs (http://www.cohs.org).

Cheshire, Jim. *Stained Glass and the Victorian Gothic Revival*. Manchester, U.K.: Manchester University Press, 2004.

Cinema Treasures website (http://cinematreasures.org/architects/34), accessed July 22, 2014.

Clark, Carmen E. *"Thy Faithfulness is Unto All Generations:" Collierstown Presbyterian Church, 1842–1992*. Lexington, Va.: Collierstown Presbyterian Church, 1991.

Clark, Daniel Kinnear. *A Manual of Rules, Tables, and Data for Mechanical Engineers*. London: Blackie and Son, 1878.

Cocke, Thomas. "Woody Chevrolet Building." Report (1982) at Special Collections and Archives, James G. Leyburn Library, Washington and Lee University, Lexington, Va.

Coffey, David W. "Maple Hall." National Register of Historic Places Registration Form, 1985.

————. "The 'New Deal' Comes to Rockbridge." *Proceedings of the Rockbridge Historical Society* 12 (1995–2002): 481–504.

————. "Reconstruction and Redemption in Lexington." *Proceedings of the Rockbridge Historical Society* 12 (1995–2002): 273–300.

————. "Thomas Jefferson, Patrick Henry, and the Natural Bridge of Virginia." *Proceedings of the Rockbridge Historical Society* 12 (1995–2002): 135–146.

Cohen, Stan. *Historic Springs of the Virginias*. Charleston, W.V.: Pictorial Histories Publishing Company, 1981.

Coleman, Chisholm. "The Southern Inn: Exemplifying the Ideals of the Southern Shrine." Paper (1990), Special Collections and Archives, James G. Leyburn Library, Washington and Lee University, Lexington, Va.

Cornwall prospectus (ca. 1890), Special Collections and Archives, James G. Leyburn Library, Washington and Lee University, Lexington, Va.

Cote, Richard C., and Margaret T. Peters. "Buena Vista Land Company (Old Court House)." National Register of Historic Places Inventory-Nomination Form, 1978.

Cote, Richard C., and Vicenta D. Scarlett. "Glen Maury." National Register of Historic Places Inventory-Registration Form, 1978.

————. "Zachariah Johnston House." National Register of Historic Places Inventory-Registration Form, 1978.

Couper, William. *History of the Shenandoah Valley*. Volumes 1 through 3. New York: Lewis Historical Publishing Company, ca. 1952.

Crawford, Barbara, and Royster Lyle Jr. *Rockbridge County Artists & Artisans*. Charlottesville: University Press of Virginia, 1995.

Cross, Allen R. III. "Survey of the State and Lyric Theaters." Report (1982), Special Collections and Archives, James G. Leyburn Library, Washington and Lee University, Lexington, Va.

Crowl, Heather, and Steven H. Moffson. "Glenwood Furnace." Draft National Register of Historic Places Registration Form, 1996.

Dabney, Joseph E. "Moonshine." In Rudy Abramson and Jean Haskell, eds. *Encyclopedia of Appalachia*. Knoxville: University of Tennessee Press, 2006.

Dabney, Virginius. *Virginia: The New Dominion*. Charlottesville: University Press of Virginia, 1971.

Davis, J. Lee. *Bits of History and Legends Around and About the Natural Bridge of Virginia from 1730 to 1950*. Natural Bridge, Va.: Natural Bridge of Va., Inc., 1950.

Dew, Charles B. *Bond of Iron: Master and Slave at Buffalo Forge*. New York: W. W. Norton, 1994.

Diehl, George West. "The Saga of Hamilton's School House." Report, 1956.

Dooley, Louise K. "The Dairies of Rockbridge County." *Proceedings of the Rockbridge Historical Society* 12 (1995–2002): 29–44.

Dorsey, Douglas C. "Black and White Log Cabins, Lee-Way Motel, Buffalo Creek Motel, Stevesville Drive-In." Report (1980) at Special Collections and Archives, James G. Leyburn Library, Washington and Lee University, Lexington, Va.

Douty, Horace. *Rockbridge, Virginia: History lessons from a Country Church.* Author: 2008.

Dudka, David M. "The Seven Hills: The Mansions of Rockbridge County." Thesis (1981), Washington and Lee University.

Effinger Ruritan Club website (http://www.effingerruritan.org/palmer-community-center.html), accessed May 19, 2004.

Emerson, Kendra. "116 North Main Street." Report (2006), Special Collections and Archives, James G. Leyburn Library, Washington and Lee University, Lexington, Va.

Fauber, J. Everette, Jr. "Research report relating to the Lexington Presbyterian Manse." Report (1966), Special Collections and Archives, James G. Leyburn Library, Washington and Lee University, Lexington, Va.

Figgers, Mary Elizabeth. "Hays Creek Mill." National Register of Historic Places Registration Form, 1991.

Fishwick, Marshall W. "John Jordan, Man of Iron." *Ironworker* (Autumn 1957): 1–9.

Foreman James C. "Fairfield, Virginia, An Architectural Survey of an Eighteenth Century Village." Report (1978) at Special Collections and Archives, James G. Leyburn Library, Washington and Lee University, Lexington, Va.

Frazier, William; Ann E. McCleary; and Lisa Tucker. "Kennedy-Wade's Mill Historic District." National Register of Historic Places Registration Form, 1993.

Fredericks, Suzanne J. "The Bank of Brownsburg." Report (2000) at Special Collections and Archives, James G. Leyburn Library, Washington and Lee University, Lexington, Va.

Friends of the Natural Bridge website (http://www.friendsofthenaturalbridge.org/), accessed October 8, 2014.

Friends of Waddell and Woods Creek Park. "Save Waddell School and Woods Creek Park." Report, 2007.

Frog Hollow Bed and Breakfast website (http://www.froghollowbnb.com/), accessed October 8, 2014.

The Georges website (http://www.thegeorges.com/), accessed October 8, 2014.

Giles, Leslie A. "Boxerwood." Virginia Department of Historic Resources Preliminary Information Form, 2014.

————. "Marlbrook." National Register of Historic Places Registration Form, 2002.

Gilham, William. "Map of the county of Rockbridge." 1860.

Gillespie, Robert Goggin. "Reverend William Graham, Presbyterian minister and rector of Liberty Hall Academy." Thesis (1970), University of Richmond.

Gilliam, Catharine M. "Jordan's Point—Lexington, Virginia: A Site History." *Proceedings of the Rockbridge Historical Society* 9 (1975–1979): 109–138.

Glasgow Family Papers, Special Collections and Archives, James G. Leyburn Library, Washington and Lee University, Lexington, Va.

Glasgow Herald.

Good Shepherd Evangelical Lutheran Church dedication service brochure, 1963.

Gray, O. W., and Son. "Gray's New Map of Lexington in Rockingham [sic] County, Virginia." 1877.

"Grist Milling Process." Article online at the Building Community: Medieval Technology and American History website (http://www.engr.psu.edu/mtah/articles/grist_milling_process.html), accessed May 10, 2014.

Hadsel, Winifred. *The Streets of Lexington.* Lexington, Va.: Rockbridge Historical Society, 1985.

Hall, Teresa, et al. "Our Goshen Heritage." Report (1985) by students of Rockbridge High School on file at the Rockbridge Regional Library, Lexington, Va.

Hanson, Maury. Church tour notes prepared for Historic Lexington Foundation tour of area churches, 2014.

Harralson, Elizabeth. "Clifton." National Register of Historic Places Registration Form, 1994.

Hasfurther, Donald J. "The Educational Legacy of the Southern Shenandoah Valley: Rockbridge County's Historic Schools." Presentation script and images, 2011.

_____. "Hickory Hill." National Register of Historic Places Registration Form, 2006.

Hauer, Peter M. "The Saltpetre Cave at Natural Bridge, Va." *Journal of Spelean History* 3:3 (Summer 1970): 55–57.

Heffelfinger, Grace P. "Brownsburg Historic District." National Register of Historic Places Inventory-Nomination Form, 1972.

_____. "Tinkling Spring Presbyterian Church." National Register of Historic Places Inventory-Nomination Form, 1972.

Henry, Bobby Sue Barnette. "Goshen Memories." Report, 1991.

Herman, Bernard. "18th Century Quaker Houses in the Delaware Valley and the Aesthetics of Practice." In Emma Jones Lapsansky and Anne A. Verplank, eds. *Quaker Aesthetics: Reflections on a Quaker Ethic in American Design and Consumption.* Philadelphia: University of Pennsylvania Press, 2003.

Herring Hall website (http://www.herringhall.com/), accessed July 19, 2014.

Hileman, Charles S. *Historical Sketch and Year Book of Timber Ridge Presbyterian Church.* 1931.

"The History of Glasgow." Article online at the Town of Glasgow website (http://www.glasgowvirginia.org/History_Article_s_Page.html) accessed June 1, 2014.

Hollberg, Sara S. "Natural Bridge." National Historic Landmark Nomination, 1997.

_____. "Natural Bridge." National Register of Historic Places Registration Form, 1997.

Horton, Tonia Woods. "Hidden Gardens: The Town Gardens of T. J. 'Stonewall' Jackson and His Lexington Contemporaries." In Kenneth E. Koons and Warren R. Hofstra, *After the Back Country: Rural Life in the Great Valley of Virginia, 1800–1900.* Knoxville: University of Tennessee Press, 2000.

Hoyt, William D. *Valley Views: Lexington and Rockbridge County, Virginia, 1924–1940.* Ca. 1990.

Hubbard, David. "Geology and Related Information about Natural Bridge and the Caves in the Vicinity." *Virginia Cellars* 3:2 (ca. 1990): 3–7.

Hull's Drive-in Movie Theatre website (http://www.hullsdrivein.com), accessed July 23, 2014.

Hummingbird Inn website (http://www.hummingbirdinn.com), accessed August 27, 2014.

Hunter, Robert. *Lexington Presbyterian Church, 1789–1989*. Lexington, Va.: Lexington Presbyterian Church, 1991.

Jackson, Will. "Prosperity, Tourism, and the Hotels of Marcellus E. Wright." Paper (1983) at Special Collections and Archives, James G. Leyburn Library, Washington and Lee University, Lexington, Va.

Jefferson, Thomas. *Notes on the State of Virginia*. New York: W. W. Norton, 1982 (reprint of book first published in 1787).

_____. Papers, Library of Congress.

Jordan Rockbridge Alum Springs. Charlottesville: Chronicle Steam Printing House, 1873.

Jordan, Terry G., and Matti Kaups. *The American Backwoods Frontier: An Ethnic and Ecological Interpretation*. Baltimore: Johns Hopkins University Press, 1989.

Journal of Spelean History.

Kain, Kathleen M. "Falling Spring Presbyterian Church Manse." National Register of Historic Places Registration Form, 2005.

Kastner, Thomas M.; Calder Loth; and Jean McRae. "Vineyard Hill." Draft National Register of Historic Places Registration Form, 2006.

Kinnear, Lyle. "History of Old Mt. View School." In "Our Heritage — Mountain View." Report (1978) by Mountain View Elementary School, Buena Vista, Va.

Koons, Kenneth E. "'The Staple of Our Country': Wheat in the Regional Farm Economy of the Nineteenth-Century Valley of Virginia." *Proceedings of the Rockbridge Historical Society* 12 (1995–2002): 505–538.

Kopp, James R. "The Virginia Drive-In Movie Era." *Proceedings of the Rockbridge Historical Society* 12 (1995–2002): 383–396.

Kosisky, Helen L. "Searight's Fulling Mill." National Register of Historic Places Inventory-Registration Form, 1972.

Kostelni, Charles, Buck Leslie, and Henry Hatcher. "Two County Industries: Bontex and Lees Carpets." *Proceedings of the Rockbridge Historical Society* 12 (1995–2002): 345–352.

Lancaster, Susan V. "Sunnyside." National Register of Historic Places Registration Form, 2001.

Langdon, J. Bradford. "Collierstown Presbyterian Church." Virginia Department of Historic Resources Preliminary Information Form, ca. 2000.

Leander McCormick Observatory Museum website (http://www.astro.virginia.edu/research/observatories/26inch/history/debate.php), accessed May 16, 2014.

Lee Chapel exhibits, information on Traveller displayed outside the building. Washington and Lee University, Lexington, Va.

Lee, Anne Carter, et al. *Buildings of Virginia: Valley, Piedmont, Southside, and Southwest*. Charlottesville: University of Virginia Press, 2015.

Letcher, John Seymour. *Only Yesterday in Lexington, Virginia*. Verona, Va.: McClure, 1974.

Levy, Benjamin. "Virginia Military Institute Historic District." National Register of Historic Places Inventory-Registration Form, 1974.

Lexington Gazette (also at different times the *Gazette* and the *Lexington News-Gazette*).

Lexington Gazette Bi-centennial Issue. 1938.

"Lexington Historic District." National Register of Historic Places Inventory-Registration Form, 1971.

Library of Virginia website (http://www.lva.virginia.gov/).

Link, William A. *A Hard Country and a Lonely Place: Schooling, Society, and Reform in Rural Virginia, 1870–1920*. Chapel Hill: University of North Carolina Press, 1986.

Lipscomb, Mary Sterrett. "Mulberry Grove." National Register of Historic Places Registration Form, 1994.

Locher, George. *A Family Divided*. Pittsburgh: Dorrance Publishing, 2010.

Longobardo, Alice. "Nine Tucker Street." Report (2011) at Special Collections and Archives, James G. Leyburn Library, Washington and Lee University, Lexington, Va.

Looney, J. Jefferson. *The Papers of Thomas Jefferson, Retirement Series*. Volume 8 (October 1814 to August 1815). Princeton: Princeton University Press, 2011.

Loth, Calder. "Level Loop." National Register of Historic Places Registration Form, 1993.

————. "Mackey, William, House." National Register of Historic Places Registration Form, 1993.

————, ed. *Virginia Landmarks Register*. Charlottesville: University Press of Virginia, 1999.

Loth, Calder, and John Salmon. "Col Alto." National Register of Historic Places Registration Form, 1988.

Lyle, Royster, Jr. "Rockbridge County's Boom Hotels." *Virginia Cavalcade* (Winter 1971): 4–13.

Lyle, Royster, Jr., and Pamela Hemenway Simpson. *The Architecture of Historic Lexington*. Charlottesville: University Press of Virginia, 1977.

Lynchburg News (also known as the *Lynchburg Daily News*).

Lynn, Francis W. "Buena Vista — After the Boom." Buena Vista, Va.: Paxton House Historical Society, 2013.

————. "Buena Vista Colored School." National Register of Historic Places Registration Form, 2002.

————, ed. *Buena Vista: The Bud Not Yet Blossomed*. Buena Vista, Va. Buena Vista Centennial Celebration, 1992.

————. *"Fesser" McCluer: The Life and Times of J. Parry McCluer*. Buena Vista, Va.: Paxton House Historical Society, 2001.

————. "More Boom Houses — Still Standing, Workers' Houses — Mostly Gone and Forgotten!" Buena Vista, Va.: Paxton House Historical Society, 2011.

————. "The Paxton House: Two Crucial Years (1828 & 1968)." Buena Vista, Va.: Paxton House Historical Society, 2011.

————. "Twenty Historic Buena Vista Boom Houses, Still Standing, Still Inhabited." Buena Vista, Va.: Paxton House Historical Society, 2011.

Lynn, Michael. "Stonewall in the Garden." *Virginia Country* (undated clipping).

Maid of the Mountains. Yearbooks (1920s to 1950s) of Southern Seminary, Buena Vista, Va., at Special Collections and Archives, James G. Leyburn Library, Washington and Lee University, Lexington, Va.

Martin, Everett A., Jr., and Leslie A. Giles. "John Moore House." National Register of Historic Places Registration Form, 1998.

Martin, Joseph. *A new and comprehensive gazetteer of Virginia, and the District of Columbia*. Charlottesville: J. Martin, 1835.

McAlester, Virginia, and Lee McAlester. *A Field Guide to American Houses*. New York: Alfred A. Knopf, 1988.

McCleary, Ann E. "Ethnic Influences on Vernacular Architecture." In Michael J. Puglisi, *Diversity and Accommodation: Essays on the Cultural Composition of the Virginia Frontier*. Knoxville: University of Tennessee Press, 1997.

_____. "Forging a Regional Identity: Development of Rural Vernacular Architecture in the Central Shenandoah Valley, 1790–1850." In Kenneth E. Koons and Warren R. Hofstra, *After the Back Country: Rural Life in the Great Valley of Virginia, 1800–1900*. Knoxville: University of Tennessee Press, 2000.

_____. "Public Schools in Augusta County, Virginia, 1870–1940." National Register of Historic Places Registration Form Thematic Nomination, 1984.

_____. "Walker's Creek Schoolhouse." Thematic National Register Nomination Inventory Form, 1984.

McCleskey, Turk. *The Road to Black Ned's Forge: A Story of Race, Sex, and Trade on the Colonial American Frontier*. Charlottesville: University of Virginia Press, 2014.

McClung, Anne D. *Rockbridge County Log Structures*. Lexington, Va.: Alone Mill Media, 2008.

_____. *Wilson Springs*. Lexington, Va.: 2007 (DVD presentation).

McClung, James W. *Historical Significance of Rockbridge County, Virginia*. Staunton, Va.: McClure Company, 1939.

_____. "Home of Dr. James R. Jordan." Works Progress Administration of Virginia Historical Inventory report (1936) at the Library of Virginia, Richmond.

McCormick, Henrietta Hamilton. *Genealogies and Reminiscences*. Chicago: 1897.

McCulloch, Ruth Anderson. "Beginnings of the Rockbridge Historical Society." *Proceedings of the Rockbridge Historical Society* 3 (1949): front matter.

_____. "How the Rockb. His. So. was Started." Manuscript (ca. 1949) at Special Collections and Archives, James G. Leyburn Library, Washington and Lee University, Lexington, Va.

McDaniel, John M., Kurt C. Russ, and Parker B. Potter. *An Archaeological and Historical Assessment of the Liberty Hall Academy Complex, 1782–1803*. Lexington, Va.: Liberty Hall Press, 1994.

McPhillips, Peggy Haile. "Yellow Fever Epidemic of 1855." Online article at the Norfolk Public Library website (http://www.npl-va.org), accessed May 6, 2014.

Meade, William. *Old Churches, Ministers, and Families of Virginia*. Baltimore: Genealogical Publishing Company, 1966.

Melvin, Frank S. "Barracks, Virginia Military Institute." National Register of Historic Places Inventory-Registration Form, 1972.

_____. "McCormick (Cyrus) Farm and Workshop." National Register of Historic Places Inventory-Registration Form, 1972.

Michalove, Aaron. "The Coffee Pot: Rockbridge County's Slice of Americana." Report (1998) at Special Collections and Archives, James G. Leyburn Library, Washington and Lee University, Lexington, Va.

Miller, Lynda Mundy-Norris. *Glasgow, Virginia: One Hundred Years of Dreams*. Natural Bridge Station, Va.: Rockbridge Publishing Company, 1992.

Morton, Oren F. *A History of Rockbridge County, Virginia*. Bowie, Md.: Heritage Books, 1998 (reprint of 1920 edition).

Moss, Roger W., and Gail Caskey Winkler. *Victorian Interior Decoration: American Interiors, 1830–1900*. New York: Henry Holt, 1986.

Mutual Assurance Society index and records. Online at the University of Mary Washington website (http://fbgresearchindxes.umw.edu/MASIdxSch.asp). Accessed May 10, 2014.

"Mutual Assurance Society Records." Article online at the Library of Virginia website (http://www.lva.virginia.gov/public/guides/rn_24mutassur.pdf), accessed May 10, 2014.

Nash, Carole, et al. "The Middlebrook-Brownsburg Corridor: A Survey of Cultural and Natural Resources." Valley Conservation Council, 1997. "Natural Bridge." Article on Thomas Jefferson's Monticello website (http://www.monticello.org). Accessed May 8, 2014.

Nelson, Elizabeth Shields. "Lexington Motor Sales Building." Paper (1982) at Special Collections and Archives, James G. Leyburn Library, Washington and Lee University, Lexington, Va.

Novelli, Chris. Lexington tax credit rehabilitation spreadsheet generated from Virginia Department of Historic Resources database, August 2014.

_____. Rockbridge County/Buena Vista tax credit rehabilitation spreadsheet generated from Virginia Department of Historic Resources database, August 2014.

"An Old Woolen Mill in Rockbridge." Undated newspaper clipping at Special Collections and Archives, James G. Leyburn Library, Washington and Lee University, Lexington, Va.

Organ Cave website (http://www.organcave.com/civil-war/), accessed July 21, 2014.

Otis, Alison T. *The Forest Service and The Civilian Conservation Corps: 1933–42*. Report (1986) online at the National Park Service website (http://www.nps.gov/history/history/online_books/ccc/ccc/preface.htm), accessed June 3, 2014.

Paxton, Matthew W. "The Rockbridge Alum Springs." Report (1963) at Special Collections and Archives, James G. Leyburn Library, Washington and Lee University, Lexington, Va.

Perry-Miller, Davidson A. "A Brief Study of Brownsburg." Report (1977) at Special Collections and Archives, James G. Leyburn Library, Washington and Lee University, Lexington, Va.

Pezzoni, J. Daniel. "Blandome." National Register of Historic Places Registration Form, 2001.

_____ "Buena Vista Downtown Historic District." National Register of Historic Places Registration Form, 2009.

_____. "Cartooning in Stone: Political and Religious Satire in Phelps Workshop Memorials of Revolutionary War-era Massachusetts." Article in preparation.

_____. "Cedar Hill Church and Cemeteries." National Register of Historic Places Registration Form, 2001.

_____. "Chapel Hill." National Register of Historic Places Registration Form, 2011.

_____. "First Baptist Church." National Register of Historic Places Registration Form, 2005.

_____. Forest Oaks, presentation notes for tour, 2013.

_____. "Glasgow Historic District." National Register of Historic Places Registration Form, 1995.

_____. "Lexington & Covington Turnpike Toll House." National Register of Historic Places Registration Form, 2004.

_____. "Margaret E. Poague House." National Register of Historic Places Registration Form, 2006.

_____. "McCampbell Inn." Text for part 1 rehabilitation tax credit applications (2013) on file at the Virginia Department of Historic Resources, Richmond.

_____. "Natural Bridge Historic District." Virginia Department of Historic Resources Preliminary Information Form, 2014.

_____. "Newcomb Hall." Text for part 1 and part 2 rehabilitation tax credit applications (2007) on file at the Virginia Department of Historic Resources, Richmond.

_____. "Southern Inn." Text for part 1 rehabilitation tax credit application (2010) on file at the Virginia Department of Historic Resources, Richmond.

_____. "State Theatre." Text for part 1 rehabilitation tax credit application (2004) on file at the Virginia Department of Historic Resources, Richmond.

_____. "Willson House." National Register of Historic Places Registration Form, 2009.

Pezzoni, J. Daniel, and Leslie A. Giles. "Boxerwood." National Register of Historic Places Registration Fom, 2014.

Pezzoni, J. Daniel, and John Kern. "Lylburn Downing School." National Register of Historic Places Registration Form, 2003.

Phillips, Laura A. W. "Grand Illusions: Decorative Interior Painting in North Carolina." In Thomas Carter and Bernard L. Herman, eds. *Perspectives in Vernacular Architecture, IV*. Columbia: University of Missouri Press, 1991.

Pierce, Dianne. "Vine Forest." National Register of Historic Places Registration Form, ca. 1991.

"Predecessors of Liberty Hall." Article at the Washington and Lee University website (http://www.wlu.edu/sociology-and-anthropology/), accessed December 11, 2014.

Proceedings of the Eleventh Annual Meeting of the Fire Underwriters' Association of the Northwest. Milwaukee: Cramer, Aikens and Cramer, 1880.

Proceedings of the Rockbridge Historical Society.

Pulice, Michael J. "Hamilton Schoolhouse." National Register of Historic Places Registration Form, 2002.

_____. *Nineteenth-Century Brick Architecture in the Roanoke Valley and Beyond: Discovering the True Legacies of the Deyerle Builders*. Roanoke: Historical Society of Western Virginia, 2011.

_____. "Springdale." National Register of Historic Places Registration Form, 2005.

Pulice, Michael J., and John R. Kern. "Buffalo Forge." National Register of Historic Places Registration Form, 2003.

_____. "W. N. Seay House." National Register of Historic Places Registration Form, 2007.

Pusey, William Webb, III. "Lexington's Female Academy." *Virginia Cavalcade* 32:1 (Summer 1982): 40–47.

Rainville, Lynn, website manager. "Rosenwald Schools of Virginia." Website maintained by the Virginia Department of Historic Resources, http://www2.vcdh. virginia.edu/schools/about.html, accessed June 21, 2014.

Rauser, Amelia Faye. *Caricature Unmasked: Irony, Authenticity, and Individualism in Eighteenth-Century English Prints*. Cranbury, N.J.: Associated University Presses, 2008.

Raynal, Henry Middleton, comp. "The Family of 'Soldier John' Grigsby." Report (1979) at the Rockbridge Regional Library, Lexington, Va.

Reed, Andrew, and James Matheson. *Narrative of the Visit to the American Churches*. New York: Harper and Brothers, 1835.

Reeds, Chester A. *The Natural Bridge of Virginia and its Environs*. Richmond, Va.: Standard Printing, 1931.

Regan, Gary, and Mardee Haidin Regan. *The Book of Bourbon*. Shelburne, Vt.: Chapters Publishing, 1995.

Report of the Exploration of the Hayes' Creek Mound, Rockbridge County, Va. Richmond, Va.: Valentine Museum, 1903.

Reps, John W. *Tidewater Towns: City Planning in Colonial Virginia and Maryland*. Williamsburg, Va.: Colonial Williamsburg Foundation, 1972.

Richmond Times-Dispatch.

Rife Ram website (http://www.riferam.com/index.html), accessed July 16, 2014.

Roanoke Times.

"Robert E. Lee Hotel Corporation." Circular (ca. 1925), Special Collections and Archives, James G. Leyburn Library, Washington and Lee University, Lexington, Va.

"Robert Love and Sarah Matilda Alexander — Descendants." Online at http:// www.accessgenealogy.com/genealogy/robert-love-and-sarah-matilda-alexander -descendants.htm, accessed June 20, 2014. The information is from Franklin D. Love's Love Family genealogy.

"Rockbridge Alum Springs/Jordan Alum Springs." National Register of Historic Places Registration Form, 1987.

Rockbridge Area Conservation Council website (http://www.rockbridgeconservation.org/), accessed October 8, 2014.

Rockbridge County. "Rockbridge County Proposal for a Survey and Planning Cost Share Program at the Natural Bridge Property." Application to the Virginia Department of Historic Resources, 2014.

Rockbridge County deed, Mechanics Lien Book 2, tax (land book), and will records. Rockbridge County Courthouse, Lexington, Va.

Rockbridge County News.

Rockbridge County, Virginia, Heritage Book. Rockbridge Area Genealogical Society, 1997.

Rockbridge Historical Society Collection. Special Collections and Archives, James G. Leyburn Library, Washington and Lee University, Lexington, Va.

Rockbridge Report.

Rockbridge Weekly.

Russ, Kurt C. "Pottery." In Barbara Crawford and Royster Lyle Jr., *Rockbridge County Artists & Artisans*. Charlottesville: University Press of Virginia, 1995.

Russ, Kurt C., John M. McDaniel, and Katherine T. Wood. "Archaeology of Nine-teenth-Century Iron Manufacturing in Southwestern Virginia: Longdale Iron Mining Complex." In Kenneth E. Koons and Warren R. Hofstra, *After the Back Country: Rural Life in the Great Valley of Virginia, 1800–1900.* Knoxville: University of Tennessee Press, 2000.

Russell, Margaret M. "Fancy Hill." National Register of Historic Places Registration Form, 1997.

St. Patrick Catholic Church records, Lexington, Va.

Sanders, Taylor. "Churches, Congregations and Community in Antebellum Lexington." Presentation in Historic Lexington Foundation's Sacred Places lecture series, May 2014.

————. *Journey of Faith: The History of Timber Ridge Presbyterian Church.* Lexington, Va.: Timber Ridge Presbyterian Church, 1999.

Saul, Alana, et al. "Historic Structure Report: Pure Oil Station, Hartwell, GA." Report (2013).

"A Self-Guided Walking Tour of Historic Brownsburg, Virginia." Brochure, ca. 2010.

Shepherd, Samuel. *The Statutes at Large of Virginia.* Vols. 1 and 2. Richmond: Samuel Shepherd, 1835.

Simpson, Pamela H. "The Architecture of Rockbridge County, Chapter 1; Or, How Does a House Mean?" *Proceedings of the Rockbridge Historical Society* 10 (1980–1989): 77–86.

————. *Cheap, Quick & Easy: Imitative Architectural Materials, 1870–1930.* Knoxville: University of Tennessee Press, 1999.

————. "Col Alto, Some Comments on the Architecture." *Proceedings of the Rockbridge Historical Society* 12 (1995–2002): 249–256.

————. "Elder House." Virginia Historic Landmarks Commission Survey Form, 1978.

————. "The Molded Brick Cornice in the Valley of Virginia." *APT* 12:4 (1980): 29–33.

————. "Mulberry Hill." National Register of Historic Places Inventory-Registration Form, 1982.

————. "Reflections on White Columns." In Mame Warren, ed. *Come Cheer for Washington and Lee: The University at 250 Years.* Lexington, Va.: Washington and Lee University, 1998.

————. "Tuckaway." Virginia Historic Landmarks Commission Survey Form, 1978.

Southern Planter.

"Southern Seminary Main Building." National Register of Historic Places Inventory-Registration Form, 1971.

Spencer, Ed. "A Short History of the Rockbridge Area Conservation Council (RACC)." Article online at the Rockbridge Area Conservation Council website (http://www.rockbridgeconservation.org/), accessed December 11, 2014.

Spencer, Hawes. "Stonewall lost: Pictures recall burned Natural Bridge mansion." *The Hook*, May 31, 2012.

Spradley-Kurowski, Kelly, and Michael Pulice. "Natural Bridge Juvenile Correctional Center." Presentation (2010) to the Virginia Department of Historic Resources Evaluation Team and Evaluation Team findings and other associated material in the survey file, Virginia Department of Historic Resources, Richmond.

Staunton Spectator (also *Staunton Spectator and Vindicator*).

Steeles Tavern Manor Bed and Breakfast website (http://www.steelestavern.com/the-inn-about-the-inn), accessed October 12, 2014.

Stevens, Sharon Ritenour, and Alice Trump Williams. *Lexington*. Charleston, S.C.: Arcadia, 2009.

Stevenson, Katherine Cole, and H. Ward Jandl. *Houses by Mail: A Guide to Houses from Sears, Roebuck and Company*. Washington, D.C.: Preservation Press, 1986.

Stoneridge Bed and Breakfast brochure.

Strickler, Elsie Cox. "News Articles and Human Interest Stories, 1950–1960." Scrapbook at the Buena Vista Branch of the Rockbridge Regional Library, Buena Vista, Virginia.

Thompson, W. B. "Compass Book No. 1 of the Survey of the North Fork of James River." James River and Kanawha Canal Papers, Board of Public Works Records, Library of Virginia, Richmond.

Thurman, Francis Lee. "Red House." *Proceedings of the Rockbridge Historical Society*. Vol. 1 (1939–41): 8–11.

Timber Ridge Presbyterian Church. 1906.

"Timber Ridge Presbyterian Church." National Register of Historic Places Inventory-Nomination Form, 1969.

Tompkins, E. P., and J. Lee Davis. *The Natural Bridge and its Historical Surroundings*. Natural Bridge, Va.: Natural Bridge of Va., Inc., 1939.

Trout, William E., III. *The Upper James River Atlas*. Richmond: Virginia Canals and Navigations Society, 2001.

Tucker, Beverly. *The House on Fuller Street: African American Memories in Lexington, VA*. Buena Vista, Va.: Mariner Publishing, 2013.

Turner, Charles W. "Agricultural Expositions and Fairs, 1828–1891." *Proceedings of the Rockbridge Historical Society* 10 (1980–1989): 387–409.

_____. *Mrs. McCulloch's Stories of Ole Lexington*. Verona, Va.: McClure Press, 1972.

Upton, Dell. *Holy Things and Profane: Anglican Parish Churches in Colonial Virginia*. Cambridge: MIT Press, 1986.

_____. "New Providence Presbyterian Church." National Register of Historic Places Inventory-Nomination Form, 1978.

_____. "Pattern Books and Professionalism: Aspects of the Transformation of Domestic Architecture in America, 1800–1860." *Winterthur Portfolio* 19 (Summer/Autumn 1984):107–150.

_____. "Stono." National Register of Historic Places Inventory-Registration Form, 1974.

Upton, Dell T., and Margaret T. Peters. "Church Hill." National Register of Historic Places Inventory-Registration Form, 1977.

_____. "Kennedy-Wade Mill." National Register of Historic Places Inventory-Registration Form, 1978.

_____. "Thorn Hill." National Register of Historic Places Inventory-Registration Form, 1974.

Virginia Department of Historic Resources website (http://www.dhr.virginia.gov/).

Virginia Military Institute Board of Visitors Minutes Volume 1 (1839 May-1844 July). Archives, Virginia Military Institute, Lexington, Virginia.

Virginian-Pilot.

Visit Natural Bridge website (http://www.visitnaturalbridge.com/natural-bridge -campground.php), accessed June 3, 2014.

Wade's Mill website (http://www.wadesmill.com), accessed August 27, 2014.

Wakeley, J. B. *The Bold Frontier Preacher, a Portraiture of Rev. William Cravens, of Virginia*. Cincinnati: Hitchcock and Walden, 1869.

Wallick, Rachel. "The State Theater." Report (2004) at Special Collections and Archives, James G. Leyburn Library, Washington and Lee University, Lexington, Va.

"Washington and Lee University Historic District." National Register of Historic Places Inventory-Registration Form, 1970.

Watkins, Martha Reynolds. "The Seven Hills of Rockbridge." In *Rockbridge County, Virginia, Heritage Book*. Rockbridge Area Genealogical Society, 1997.

Watson, Thomas Leonard. *Mineral Resources of Virginia*. Lynchburg, Va.: J. P. Bell, 1907.

Weaver v. Jordan, Davis & Company (1843). Special Collections and Archives, James G. Leyburn Library, Washington and Lee University, Lexington, Va.

Weaver, Richard. *Around Lexington, Virginia*. Charleston, S.C.: Arcadia Publishing, 1999.

Wells, John E., and Robert E. Dalton. *The Virginia Architects, 1835–1955: A Bibliographical Dictionary*. Richmond: New South Architectural Press, 1997.

Westebbe, Mark. "Bryant House." Virginia Department of Historic Resources Preliminary Information Form, 2012.

Withrow Scrapbooks. At Special Collections and Archives, James G. Leyburn Library, Washington and Lee University, Lexington, Va.

Yeates, Charles M. "Map of Natural Bridge." 1882.

A misty day at Natural Bridge.
Courtesy of the Library of Virginia

Index

Wayne, John, 218
WDBJ radio station, 222
Weatherman, Clara Belle, xvii
Weaver, William, xxvii, 16, 17, 20, 160, 161, 167–169
Weaver v. Jordan, Davis & Company, xxvii, 6, 11, 16, 169–170
Wee Dornoch (see Tuckaway)
Weinberg, Isaac, Store, 265
Weir, Hugh, 63
Weir barn, 64
Weiss, John H., Sr., 192–193
Weiss, Mrs., 193
Welch, Benjamin, 127
Welch, Eliza Grigsby, 37
Welch, Thomas, III, 37, 50
Welch family, 36, 224
Wells and Meagher, 215
Welsh Farm, 74
West Point Cadet Chapel, 109
Wetmore, James A., 202
Western Virginia, 54
Wheat fan factory, 172
Whipple, Mollie Sue, 226
White, Hugh, 195–196
White Sulphur Springs, 128
Whiteside, 39
Whitewash, 44–45
Whiting Oil Company Service Station, 198
Whitmore, J. H., family, 112
Wilburn Saddle, 158
William and Mary, College of, 117
Williams, John, 177
Williams, R. W., 201
Williams sash and blind factory, 177
Williams House, 215–216
Williamson, Thomas, 95
Willis, R. H., 201
Wills, Kenneth, 218
Wills, M., 218
Wills, Thomas, 218
Willson, James, 157
Willson, John, 157
Willson, Robert, 157
Willson, Samuel, 157
Willson distillery, 157
Willson Farm (Tuckaway), 157
Wilson, Eric, xvii
Wilson, Hugh, 104
Wilson, Hugh, schoolhouse, 104
Wilson, William, 168
Wilson, William A., 136
Wilson family, 66
Wilson Springs, 136–137, 209
Wilson-Walker House, 221

Withrow, James, 111
Withrow, John, 111
Wolfe, Mrs. W. H., 145
Wolfe, Mrs. W. H., boarding house, 145
Womeldorf, W. T., 156
Womeldorf, W. T., fruit distillery, 156
Women, 70, 109–110, 182
Wooden chimneys, 18, 57
Woods Creek, 109, 112, 122, 162
Woods Creek Park trail, vi
Woodson, H. P., 190
Woody, D. D., 201
Woody Chevrolet Dealership, 200–201
Worker housing, 17, 19–20, 69, 172, 183
World War II, 183, 211, 214, 216, 222
World's Columbian Exposition, 116, 193
Wright, Frank Lloyd, xxvi, 214, 215
Wright, Marcellus E., Sr., 195
Wythe County lead mines, 159

Y

Yarnell, Albert, 143, 191
York and Sawyer, 217
Yorktown, 102
Young Carpenter's Assistant, The, 29
Young Men's Christian Association (YMCA), 209

Z

Zollman, Adam, 157
Zollman, Adam, distillery, 157
Zollman Farm, 209

About the Author

J. Daniel Pezzoni is an architectural historian and preservation consultant who has written or edited over ten county architectural histories since 1995. Dan served as an architectural historian with the Virginia Department of Historic Resources from 1989 to 1991 and has since provided clients nationwide with National Register nominations and other forms of architectural historical research and preservation and rehabilitation assistance. Dan lives in Lexington with his wife, Leslie A. Giles, a former executive director of Historic Lexington Foundation, and their two children.